The Power of Non-Violence

The Enduring Legacy of Richard Gregg

For Susan —

In Peace & Love

John Wood

The Power of Non-Violence

The
Enduring Legacy
of Richard Gregg

A Biography by John Wooding

LOOM PRESS
LOWELL & AMESBURY, MASSACHUSETTS
2020

Published in the United States of America
First Edition

Loom Press
P.O. Box 1394, Lowell, MA 01853
& 15 Atlantic View, Amesbury, MA 01913
www.loompress.com
info@loompress.com

Design: Higgins & Ross
Author photo: Joan Parker
Photograph credits: Page 266
Map, p. 86: 1909 Imperial Gazetteer of India, Wikimedia Commons
Typefaces: Josefin Slab, Adobe Garamond
Printing: King Printing Co., Inc. Lowell, MA

FOR JOAN PARKER

Contents

I'm Nobody! Who are you?
Are you—Nobody—too?
Then there's a pair of us!
Don't tell! they'd advertise—you know!

How dreary—to be—Somebody!
How public—like a Frog—
To tell one's name—the livelong June—
To an admiring Bog!

Emily Dickinson
(Richard Gregg's favorite poem)

CHAPTER ONE

Finding Gandhi

Anyone who pretends to be neutral writes himself down here as a fool and a sham.

—William James

DURING THE FIRST DECADES of the twentieth century, America seethed with invention and promise. The cities churned out steel, autos, food, and all manner of consumer goods. The ports moved stuff in and moved stuff out, dockside cranes swinging for the fences. Workers toiled on assembly lines, in giant factories, workshops, and stores, their days measured by the clock-in, their nights by needed sleep. They went home to crowded streets and homes. Factory owners, bankers, and entrepreneurs ate in fancy restaurants and found comfort in opulent suburban homes. The captains of industry knew how to set the course. But big capital had too much, the workers too little. Conflict was everywhere. And Richard Gregg was in the thick of it in Chicago, Illinois, in 1922. There was perhaps no place else that quite so vividly captured the contradiction of American capitalism.

The city's sweatshops and slaughterhouses ripened the air in the stifling summer months, and the high tide of immigrant labor flooded streets and filled the tenements. Capitalism steamed through the city like the freight trains that endlessly fed the warehouses and stockyards. Railroads and shipping lanes connected east and west, the Great Lakes, and the Mississippi. Trolleys and early autos jockeyed with horse-pulled buggies and the human throngs at intersections. Men in top hats and fancy suits bought their newspapers from half-starved street urchins. Money and poverty tusseled with each other through the neighborhoods. Tenements overflowed with multi-generational families, the mothers with kids on their hips stringing laundry on the third-floor rope line. And then there was the smell. The Union Stockyards dominated the city's killing fields where 40,000 souls pounded and cut and hauled in the death pits of millions of cows, sheep, pigs, and god knows what else on four feet. The reek spread like oil on sand.

Chicago was growing and fighting. Immigrant groups and labor unions organized movements for social change and fighting injustice. The Irish and Germans, the Swedes, and the Dutch, poured in after the Civil War, joined by Jews fleeing European pogroms, Italians, Czechs, and Poles looking for a new life as the twentieth century got rolling. With them came cheap labor and socialist ideas. Unions and organizers spread everywhere. Workers and capitalists circled each other, fighters in the ring of the Gilded Cage. The heritage of the Haymarket and the Pullman strikes, and a litany of other labor struggles built a rich web of conflict and progress, innovation, and degradation. That web extended beyond Chicago, but it is there that the strands were most tightly woven. Only twenty or so years after the Great Chicago Fire when more than two thousand acres of downtown were destroyed, came the stunning success of the iconic 1893 World's Fair, fueling the city's return to prominence. By the 1920s, the rapid growth of manufacturing, transport, and trade sealed Chicago's status as an urban powerhouse. Electrification became commonplace as roads and homes glowed brightly. Electric trolleys ran with full loads, automobiles began to replace horses, and rail lines had already etched an intricate pattern through the city, linking west and east, south and north. Chicago blossomed as the old century closed: by 1900, there were 1.7 million calling the city home.[1] This was, indeed, Carl Sandburg's "City of the Big Shoulders."

The International Workers of the World (IWW), the Wobblies, founded in Chicago in 1905, were vital again after the hiatus of World War I. Jane Addams' well-established Hull House experimented with new forms of social activism by bringing the poor and the middle class together in "settlement houses" so that they could share experiences. The experiment also provided medical and social services to the poor. The city embraced technological and social innovation and bled from both. Later, vast numbers of African Americans would come, giving birth to the Chicago Black Renaissance, whose artists and musicians would drive much of the cultural innovation of the U.S. during the mid-twentieth century, and lead to much racial conflict. The whole dizzying mess of an expanding city brought excess and want. By the 1920s, another million people made it their home, and Chicago took its place as one of the great American cities, with a population of more than three million. It would soon become notorious as the city of gangsters Al Capone and Bugs Moran.[2]

The Comfort of Books

Living in Chicago with no permanent job, and shocked by the violence of the strikes and conflicts between capital and labor, young lawyer Richard Gregg was at a critical moment in his life and thinking. The core of the city was a shopping metropolis where people could buy everything that the new consumer capitalism could offer. The department store was already commonplace—and Marshall Field's opulent retail cathedral anchored much of the downtown. Around it, the city center was host to many bookstores, serving an increasingly literate and curious population. On a humid day in the summer of 1922, Gregg walked listlessly toward his favorite, McClurg's down on South Wabash. A fixture in the Loop, McClurg's was a treasure trove of progressive works: socialist tracts, radical magazines, and innovative literature. The company published W. E. B. Du Bois' *The Souls of Black Folk* and a spin-off of the original *Dial* magazine associated with Ralph Waldo Emerson and the Transcendentalists. The summer 1922 issue features work by John Dos Passos, T.S. Eliot, D.H. Lawrence, and a host of influential new writers.

Inside Gregg wandered the aisles of books, his narrow shoulders slightly hunched, an air of sadness about him as he moved quietly between the shelves. A lot was going on in the world that troubled him, and not just the labor conflict in America. Stalin had just come to power in the Soviet Union, and Mussolini had taken control of Italy, adding fascism and black shirts to the vocabulary of misery that would come to haunt the next thirty years. His father had died that May, and, despite their sometimes fraught relationship, the sense of loss was real and immediate. Gregg had worked for several years in labor relations and arbitration. Mostly his efforts to reconcile those conflicts failed. The failures lay on him like a wet and ugly cape.[3] He was a little bit lost and a little bit lonely.

Gregg was a reader. Books and bookstores were lifeblood. He had read widely, not novels and fiction so much, but politics, social theory, and the new work in psychology that was innovative and sometimes a little strange. He enjoyed history and current affairs, ideas that could explain and challenge, and religion and philosophy. He understood complex economics well by this time, too. Gregg, at thirty-seven, was an erudite man, and this bookstore was a sanctuary, one he had wandered into often over the past few years. On one shelf, he spotted a small magazine and opened it carefully, for he was precise, not one to damage a book or to hurry. The work was under the Huebsch imprint, a small new progressive publisher in the U.S. Gregg started to read. The pages in front of him told the compelling story of the struggle for social justice for Indians in South Africa and the activism of a young Indian lawyer. Turning the pages, he started to think, not only about this story of the fight for the rights and dignity of the Indian population in that far-off place, but also of his life. The last few years had been tough, with lots of conflict between management and labor throughout the country, and he'd been in the thick of it.

Even as he stood reading, the great Railroad Strike of 1922 was at its height: 400,000 workers staying home, and the transport veins of the country choked and narrowed. Although his work in labor relations had engrossed him, and he had learned much, recent events left him exhausted and cynical. The strike was not going well. He had been deeply involved in negotiations that ultimately collapsed, and that failure hung in the Chicago air with the smell, the dust, and the humidity.[4]

The magazine in his hands told of Mohandas Gandhi's fight against racism in South Africa: *Young India* was the weekly journal where Gandhi reported his thinking and ideas, and, for Gregg, it was a revelation. Although he had heard of Gandhi, he didn't know much about him as he was only then beginning to gain a reputation in the U.S.[5] Gregg could not help but compare his life as a labor negotiator, and his struggle to make the world a better place for those with little power or resources, with that of the slight and energetic Indian (also a lawyer) whose words and ideals were on every page. Here was a man who had been beaten and jailed, vilified and abused, yet who called for peace and tolerance and never gave up. The work of Gandhi stunned him.

Gregg had seen some of the world and a lot of the United States, but these reports and the details of Gandhi's struggle moved him. As he read, he began thinking about his life: what he might do to bring meaning and relevance to his work, and what the future held. Perhaps, more than anything, he needed to be in a place where his ideas and values could be more in harmony with the culture in which he lived. In mid-life, Gregg felt deeply alienated from America and the tumultuous and seemingly unstoppable industrial capitalism maturing throughout the country.

By the time he found himself in that Chicago bookstore, Gregg had spent seven years working as a labor mediator for employers, unions, and government. He had served as counsel, investigator, reporter, and advocate. He had defended workers in textiles and railroads, tanning and transportation, coal mining and shipping. All told he had participated in trying to resolve capital and labor conflicts in more than twenty different industries, great and small, and in every corner of the United States.[6] But the events in India and South Africa and the actions of this brave and resolute Indian lawyer seemed to offer a different way, a chance to rethink how conflict could be resolved and how injustice might be fought. Gregg was determined to find out more about this man, and so he dug deeper and found more information about Gandhi under the Huebsch imprint.

The Huebsch publications appeared at a critical moment: radicalism and progressive ideas and politics resonated across the country, and Benjamin Huebsch, a daring and innovative thinker, had just started his own publishing house, bringing out work by then-controversial figures such as James Joyce and D.H. Lawrence. No surprise, then, that Huebsch would be among the first to provide a voice for what was going on in South Africa and India. He had joined the board of the recently created American Civil Liberties Union and became a founder of the progressive and independent Viking Press. In the early twenties, Huebsch was publishing collections of writings from Gandhi's weekly paper, *Young India*. After finding his first copy, Gregg devoured them.[7]

On that July day, Gregg made a decision that would change his life, and would echo down a violent and troubled century: he would move to India to study with Gandhi. From that moment on, he made plans for his trip. He was determined to live with and learn from Gandhi, and leave behind his family and work, friends, and the life he knew. It was wrenching. Gregg loved his siblings, and they had just gone through the trauma of losing their father, the gentle patriarch; his mother was getting on in years. He was close to his brothers and sisters and they formed a tight-knit and supportive network. But he no longer wanted to live in America, and he could not tolerate the contradictions. India was in the throes of an often-violent struggle against British rule, soon to be led by his new hero. It was possible, even then, that he would be exchanging one conflict-ridden country for another.

The trip would not be easy even though international travel was relatively commonplace; it would mean a voyage to an unfamiliar country a long, long way from home. He had made the journey before with his brother-in-law, and India had won his heart, even though that was a visit under circumstances not of his choosing. This time he would go to live there for the rest of his life. He wanted to experience that culture, to work and learn from Gandhi, and to leave behind America's strife and inequality. Big capital looked all-powerful, industrialization had polluted the earth and the minds of Americans, littering the land with abandoned spiritual and moral values.

Gregg tended toward introspection and carefulness, so a decision like this he did not take lightly. But what could he lose? His family and friends, yes, but there was so much to gain and so much to learn from India, its culture, and its history. Little did he know at the time that his decision would set him on a course to become a key figure in bringing Gandhi's ideas to a Western audience and to be the author of one of the most important works on pacifism of the twentieth century. Nor did he know, as he stood reading in that bookstore, that he would become a personal friend, of not only Gandhi (a friendship that would continue until Gandhi's assassination), but also a colleague, friend, and correspondent of such leaders of the pacifist and civil rights movements as Aldous Huxley, A.J. Muste, Reinhold Niebuhr, Bayard Rustin, and Martin Luther King, Jr. These thinkers and doers who would stride across the mid-twentieth century with god and right on their side. For now, all ahead, all unknown.

CHAPTER TWO

Finding Richard Gregg, Finding My Father

WHEN RICHARD GREGG DISCOVERED the work of Gandhi in Chicago, little did he know that it would set him on a remarkable adventure and transform his life. We all experience such moments, ones that set wheels turning and belts rolling. These events are catalysts, waiting for things to be in place (a conversation, a location, a friendship, a crisis), and for history to be awakened and remembered. Gregg finding Gandhi was such a moment. Another was my discovery of Richard Gregg and his work. And that story starts long ago, with my father, a war, and a cup of coffee.

My dad was sent to prison in August 1941. Not for some heinous crime or minor burglary but because he thought killing people was wrong. He was a "conchie," one of many thousands who were conscientious objectors (COs) in the United Kingdom during World War II. He spent nine months in Cardiff Prison through a winter when the Luftwaffe was bent on flattening the city, a curiously German urban redevelopment strategy. I don't know much about what happened to him there; he died when I was sixteen, and I never got the chance to talk to him about it. At the time, I didn't know he was a pacifist, let alone a conscientious objector. We all lived in Northampton, a midlands post-industrial town, now much faded and the glory of its one-time vibrant boot and shoe factories long gone. There's even less there of interest than when I roamed its streets as a kid.

Men my age now often write about their dads, usually not in flattering ways. But I have no tales of abuse or neglect, of coldness or distance. The Dad I remember was sweet and affectionate, smelling of coal dust and Brylcreem, the hair product he used to hold down what little he had left on the top. I don't remember any serious conversations. We didn't talk about politics. I didn't know he had been to jail, or what for, until I was in my late teens. My guess is that he thought it would be hard for me to explain this at school—after all, there were plenty of kids in my class who had lost their dads or other family members in the war. And that had been a war against fascism. Hard to be against it. But Dad was one of some sixty-thousand COs who refused to fight in WWII, and only about three thousand did time in jail for their beliefs, so he was one of the few who had the honor. From what I can gather, the price was pretty high.

He wrote weekly letters to my mum from his cell, and I have all of them, rescued from the old biscuit tin where mum kept the family treasures. There are pages and pages of slanty writing, mostly asking about the family's health, the weather, and how friends were doing. There are complaints about the food and some of the warders, but these are stunningly unremarkable and unrevealing letters of a man who loved his wife and who was prepared to suffer prison time because he believed it was wrong to kill people. The only actual comment I remember mum making about all this was she knew that they didn't give COs toothbrushes, claiming that's why Dad had lost most of his teeth. That may be true. I can't say. I do remember her telling us that in jail he suffered much "conchie" baiting. Clearly, my parents paid the price—excluded from jobs, shunned by friends, victims of dark comments, and pointing fingers. My older brother and sister tell me that a couple of their schoolteachers in the '50s made remarks about them being the kids of a conchie.

There is not much left of my dad. No books or articles, no movies, or academic studies. All I have is his old watch that doesn't work and hasn't since the end of time—which it announced, apparently—and the letters he wrote from prison. I also have the little wooden toolbox he bought even though he didn't have a clue about tools or fixing things, and the mantelpiece clock he got after twenty-five years of working at the Northampton Cooperative Society, universally and affectionately known as the "Co-Op." There are some photos, of course: holidays, weddings, funerals, and the like. Most of the pictures I have of him were from when he was probably in his forties, when the little Brownie box cameras were cheap. My brother had one. I look at those pictures now and think mostly about how I look more and more like him. My dad was a pretty ordinary bloke, or so I thought.

For most of the last several decades I never really thought about Dad as a pacifist or what he had gone through or why it might be essential to understand. But a few years ago, working with a colleague at the University of Massachusetts, Boston (UMB), John Saltmarsh, on another project, we got to talking over coffee about our fathers, the way you do. John wrote a biography of Scott Nearing—whom I had vaguely heard of—and John happened to have been friends over the years with Bill Coperthwaite, whom I had never heard of. Coperthwaite was an internationally known yurt designer and builder who had been friends with Nearing back in the 1950s and '60s. Nearing was a communist in the 1920s and a radical all his life. He was also a guiding light for ecologists and back-to-the-landers in the '60s and '70s. The book he wrote with his wife, Helen, *Living the Good Life*, was published in 1954 and had a huge impact when it was rediscovered in the '70s as a bible for the counterculture. Bill Coperthwaite, himself a polymath, was a teacher, pacifist, and builder whose farm and homestead in northern Maine attracted people who were seeking both a simpler life and instruction on how to build his remarkable yurts. I never met Coperthwaite, so I didn't hear it myself, but apparently, he once said, "I want to live in a society where people are intoxicated with the joy of making things."[8] A pretty nice thing to say.

I mentioned to John Saltmarsh that my dad had been a conscientious objector in WWII, and he started to tell me the tale of Richard Gregg, another remarkable man—an American pacifist whose book *The Power of Non-Violence* was highly influential in the mid-twentieth century. I had not heard of him. Coperthwaite, who had been a CO during the Korean War, had been close to the Nearings and Gregg. John told me that Gregg kept notebooks most of his life, and that they were moldering in the back of one of Bill Coperthwaite's yurts in northern Maine. More than fifty of them. Coperthwaite thought they would be useful someday. My interest was piqued.

John and I rescued the notebooks. I started to get more curious about Gregg. Like the highly trained academic that I am—I Googled him. Gregg was a prolific writer and far more influential than I had expected. Born in 1885, the son of a Congregational minister, he grew up in Colorado Springs, went to Harvard College and Harvard Law School, became a lawyer and labor advocate, and a philosopher, not the typical career track. A pacifist and organic farmer, an intellectual, an activist, Gregg was one of the first Americans to study with Mohandas Gandhi, the great independence leader, social philosopher, and founder of the Indian nonviolence movement. Gregg lived at Gandhi's ashram in the 1920s and became his friend and confidant. The author of numerous books and articles, Gregg is best known for *The Power of Non-Violence*, the pathbreaking work on nonviolent resistance that transformed the structure of American pacifism in the 1930s. He was vital in transmitting Gandhi's ideas about social, economic, and political change into a western context. Throughout, Gregg developed a powerful critique of industrialization and technology. He believed a peaceful world could only come about as humans developed inner peace and recognized their harmony with nature. *The Power of Non-Violence* turned out to be one of the most important works on pacifism of the twentieth century. Martin Luther King, Jr., wrote the foreword to the reprinted and revised 1959 edition. King's commitment to nonviolent resistance in the civil rights struggle came, in no small part, from his reading and contact with Gregg.

This was the man whose fifty-odd notebooks we rescued. They are simple ruled composition books, the kind you can still buy at any office supply store. The ones with faux marbled covers. They are filled with notes, reflections, and extensive quotes from hundreds of authors. I remember picking up one of them at random and out fell several typed pages, headlined "My Memories of Gandhi." As I began to read the notebooks and his published writing, I realized that here was a man saying some pretty innovative things about pacifism, living simply, and how to reorder the world in a way that would restore meaning and harmony. He lived his beliefs and did so with humility and kindness. He spent his life trying to figure out how to be in the world.

The notebooks are the record of a thoughtful and good man. In one of his earliest (from 1925), Gregg wrote of his first experience with Gandhi: "Gandhi's kindliness and reserve power calling on rich and humble at the Ashram, when he took me to work. His humor and beautiful smile. The joy of little girls at his feet and by his side at evening prayers. The wonder and surprise of these people when I thank them for their kindness. Their embarrassment at my thanks. It is their communal spirit, an ingrained sense of unity?"[9] The notebooks are full of little gems like this, comments on daily experiences, extensive notes on a wide range of literature, and innumerable to-do lists. The basis for the many works Gregg would go on to write.

In 1936, when *The Power of Non-Violence* was published in England, charismatic British pacifist Dick Sheppherd was creating the fledgling Peace Pledge Union (PPU). The PPU folks invited Gregg to England to talk about his ideas. My dad was a member of this organization, and the connection to the PPU was one of many links that emerged between Richard Gregg and me. Dad knew people in the PPU, many of them Quakers, and, while reading one of

Gregg's notebooks (he wrote one or more every year for the better part of three decades), I noticed a familiar name that turned out to be a colleague of my father's who had visited our house when I was ten or so. How likely was that?

As I dug deeper into Gregg's life and work, more connections came up: Gregg's father was born in Medford, Massachusetts (where I now live). Gregg's older brother, James, spent three years as the minister at the Kirk Street Church in Lowell, where I have taught for thirty years at the University of Massachusetts. The first book that Gregg wrote (with Gandhi's nephew and then heir apparent, Maganlal Gandhi), is a how-to about home-spinning. It is hard to find these days, but one of the few copies in existence was held by the American Textile History Museum in Lowell. I went there one day, and a kindly librarian rushed off to locate the book and appeared minutes later with the slim volume, holding it the way one might a rare Fabergé Egg.

Gandhi greatly admired the British atheist MP Charles Bradlaugh, who represented my hometown, Northampton, in the 1880s. Bradlaugh advocated for birth control and home-rule for Ireland, and supported trade unions as a member of the then Liberal Party.[10] Not popular positions at the time. A very young Gandhi went to his funeral in 1891. There's a statue of Bradlaugh in the town center. I used to sit on the base when I was a kid, eating fish and chips. My dad admired Bradlaugh, and I do remember Dad telling me about him. It seemed boring at the time.

This progression of discoveries set me on a course to write a biography of Richard Gregg. As I have gotten to know Gregg through his writing and his letters and the comments and reflections of surviving family, I became deeply impressed that this reticent and kind man had such an impact on the history of the twentieth century. Perhaps Gregg was too quiet. He never made any significant speeches, there are no grainy newsreels featuring him haranguing an audience, there are no memorial libraries or statues of him in squares, no grave exists, so no acolytes are genuflecting over his remains. Undergraduates don't read his books. There are none of these things for my father, either. Yet Gregg's work left an enormous legacy that helped make the world a better place. His writing on nonviolent resistance helped shape the civil rights movement in the United States, as that, in turn, shaped such movements from Ireland to South Africa and across many countries in the following decades. His experiments and commitment to organic farming and the arguments in *The Value of Voluntary Simplicity* could have been written today as a manifesto on sustainability. His dedicated belief in the value of manual labor and his concern with nutrition and good, unadulterated food rise in popularity today. In Lowell, young people organize maker spaces, support community gardens, grow local food, build parks, and the like—most of them also fighting for social justice as they try to carve out spaces free of commodification and alienating work. Gregg would have liked them and would have been happy to stand at their side, with a shovel in hand and a warm smile.

There is no full-length biography of this remarkable man who brought Gandhi's ideas to the West. There is no biography of my dad, either. My dad never wrote anything but grocery lists and letters to my mum. He never went to college and, as far as I know, he knew no famous people, made no lasting public impression, and never left England. And he wasn't terribly physical and was utterly hopeless at household projects. He would not have had the foggiest idea of what a yurt was. But he went to jail because he believed, like Gregg and Gandhi, that killing people was wrong. I like that about him. It makes me proud. Now I have written a book about a quiet and serious pacifist and farmer who was into Gandhi and peace and organic farming and manual labor. My dad would have liked him too.

My father was born some thirty years later than Gregg but died before him. After he passed away, I expected to leave school and get a job to help support the family. But, partly as a result of my older brother's intervention, I stayed on until I was of the age to take the exams that, at the time, were the ticket to *maybe* going to university. Not that I did immediately. Like many of my social class, becoming a college student was not something I had imagined. But after a couple of years working at low-paying jobs in my hometown, one of my former teachers got in touch with me, pushing me to consider university because my exam results would let that happen. Tired of manual labor and the grimness of my hometown, I applied to the London School of Economics to study international relations and was accepted. I moved to London in the fall of 1972 with my girlfriend, finding a pretty awful bed-sit in Sheppherd's Bush to begin life as an undergraduate. My girlfriend left after a few weeks.

Years later, I came to America to pursue a doctoral degree in politics, and, when I finished it, I was lucky enough to get a job at the University of Massachusetts, Lowell. I taught there for thirty years, trying to help kids who were just like me. I threw some energy into being a scholar, but more into trying to re-imagine the university, promoting progressive teaching techniques and the critical importance of civic engagement for our students, and articulating what I believe was the proper mission of a public university. One of the leading activists and scholars of civic engagement and in defining the purpose of public higher education is John Saltmarsh. That's how we became friends and why we were drinking coffee together that day in the café. I also began to teach in the university's peace and conflict graduate program, although I had but little background in the field. At the same time, I helped found and direct the Greeley Peace Scholar program at the school. We brought noted international peace activists and scholars to the campus and the local community (including two Nobel Peace prize winners) for short residencies, giving them the opportunity to meet and talk with students and citizens of Lowell.

Looking back on this, it is clear that mine has been an unplanned and accidental life. I didn't think about a career as an academic until much later

(I was forty when I finished my doctorate). Nor did I really know what life I should lead. And yet, there were these traces of my father: the progressive politics and the rejection of violence in all forms. And a little bit of my grandfather who was also a working man and Labour Party. My grandmother was a working-class Tory—they canceled out each other's vote for the best part of sixty years. Still, Grandad taught me woodworking and practical stuff, and he had a very well-defined sense of morality and integrity (not religious, he thought of himself as a secular humanist). Grandad was always writing letters to the local paper about some perceived outrage that negatively affected the working man (a streetlight out, local councilor spending the taxpayer's money on fancy dinners, etc.). He once told me the story of how he signed up during the Great War, to be in the Royal Medical Corps, but when the government ran out of cannon fodder, he was reassigned to the infantry. Outraged at this move, my grandad wrote a letter to the King saying that he signed a contract to be in the Medical Corps and he had kept his side and the King should keep his. He stayed in the Medical Corps. There's a little bit of my father and grandfather in me and, in many ways, a great deal of both in Richard Gregg.

This background, and the profound ambivalence I felt about being an academic, was brought into focus by my finding Richard Gregg. First, thinking about my father and how his death left some unconnected strands in my life and, second, by contemplating the contrasts between this American pacifist and Dad. Yes, there are the coincidences I mentioned, but after knowing more, I can clearly see both the parallels and the puzzle: why did my dad believe what he did? Why did Richard Gregg? In Gregg's case, why would a man who had many successful and largely politically and socially active progressive siblings, who had a law degree from Harvard and a job at a prestigious law firm, decide to abandon all that and go to India? Why would he have then lived an often-marginal existence, written more than most academics, and dedicated himself to organic farming and a vision of the world that was in complete opposition to the industrial, technologically driven, consumer society that America, and most of the West, had become during his lifetime?

Why would my Dad, without any formal education past the age of fourteen, but who had educated himself sufficiently to have a not-bad-job, first in a grocery and then in a coal depot, become such a committed advocate of the cooperative movement? Why did he embrace pacifism to the point where he was willing to go to jail and expose his new wife and himself to the insult thrown at "conchies"? Why did he not talk about that? I think part of the answer is that both men were principled in a way that was beyond their control. It was what they had to do by making the most of what they had. Can a thorough examination of the life of Richard Gregg, who had a very strong sense of what it meant to live life with commitment and purpose, yet entertain the doubts and fears that plague us all, answer some of these questions? What can he tell us about how to live in the world?

So, this is the story of Richard Bartlett Gregg. But it contains within it another story, one about a working man who grew up in England, who went to prison because he believed in something, and was willing to stand up for that belief. My father, like Gregg, lived his life by those beliefs; he knew that, even if you didn't preach, you had to practice what you said and claimed. Like Gregg, my dad was a quiet and gentle man. I now know much more about Gregg than I will ever know about my dad. But Gregg's story has given me a map to the hazy contours of my memories and a way to look at the route I took. When a parent dies when you are young, there is no chance to have all those conversations, no way of knowing what was expected or how you measured up, no place to check-in. What follows is not only the life of Richard Gregg, but it is also the story of my father and his youngest son. It is the conversation we never had.

On Gregg's Trail

Way up near the border of Canada, on the east coast of Maine, there's a path marked as Dickinson's Reach Trail. The path leads west for about a mile-and-a-half from Bucksport and is only passable on foot. It is a bit of a trek (and rough in winter), but if you keep going, you will find yourself at a five hundred-acre homestead created by writer and social critic Bill Coperthwaite.[11] It is a beautiful spot looking over a large pond and dotted with many of Bill's creations, the incomparable hand-built wood-framed yurts for which he became internationally and rightly famous. Dickinson's Reach sits close to Mill Pond, but there is no running water or electricity—by design, for this is the place that Coperthwaite created as an alternative living center. The land slopes down to the pond and to the wonderfully named Yoho Creek that feeds into Moose Snare Cove. Keep going by boat, and you can make it out to Englishman's Bay and into the Atlantic Ocean. It's a remote piece of land, Dickinson's Reach, named as such because Emily Dickinson was Coperthwaite's favorite poet, and he lived there for the best part of fifty years, building yurts, and tending the land. My friend and colleague John Saltmarsh knew Coperthwaite well and brought his family to Maine to stay at the homestead. Most summers, they lived in one of the yurts, giving the kids the chance to explore the land, climb the trees, and learn from the avuncular Coperthwaite.

I knew nothing of the place or Bill Coperthwaite until that one spring day when John and I were drinking coffee in a café in Wellesley, Massachusetts, when John told me about Coperthwaite and Richard Gregg and the story of the pile of notebooks that Gregg, just before he moved to a retirement home in Oregon, had given to Coperthwaite for safekeeping. Bill had tucked them away on the bottom corner of a bookshelf in one of his yurts. They had been sitting there for close to forty years. John said, "Let's get them!" I agreed. All of this would have been of passing interest—a conversation—over coffee, except that John told me Gregg was the leading pacifist of his generation, and that this might interest me since my father had also been a pacifist. I now realize that this chat, like so many conversations we all have, had consequences I could not imagine.

Saltmarsh had known Scott Nearing, the radical and organic farmer, and had written a biography of him, meeting Coperthwaite through that connection. The work started as his doctoral dissertation and emerged out of many conversations John had with Nearing and his wife, Helen.[12] Coperthwaite was a close friend of the Nearings and Richard Gregg. John was planning a visit to his old friend in Maine and said he would try to bring the notebooks back to Boston. John knew where they were and had looked at a few of them a while back but had not seen them recently. Some fifty notebooks in remarkably good condition. After a few days staying with Coperthwaite, John collected them and, with Bill's help, dragged the load on a cart down the trail from Dickinson's Reach to the main road, packed them into boxes in the back of his Toyota, and brought them to his home. Rather than risk further damage, we decided to place them in an archive at the Thoreau Institute in Concord, Massachusetts, where John had a contact and where there was already some archival material on the Nearings. It seemed like the right home.

We got the boxes to the Institute where they were scanned and digitized, and then I started to read. At first, this was tough going as Gregg's handwriting was not much better than my own, and many of the pages had faded, not surprisingly, as the first notebook was dated 1925. Pretty soon, I gave up reading them, but I did pursue research on Gregg and his writings. And I also started to think about my dad, the conscientious objector.[13] I would come back to the notebooks eventually when I decided that somebody should probably write a book about Gregg. I would come back to Dad, too.

I went looking for Richard Gregg. Over the years, I have finally read the notebooks and most everything he wrote. I met and talked with some of his surviving family, who gave me a treasure trove of his personal and business letters, as well as access to many pictures of him, his family, and his travels. They were kind and immensely proud of their remarkable relative. They wondered, as did I, why no biography had been written about him. I was shown photo albums with the family history of grandfathers and grandmothers, aunts, and uncles, and given the many letters that he wrote to his family during his extensive travels. I explored his connections and correspondence with thinkers, writers, and activists of the twentieth century, and I followed his travels around the world. I went to Eugene, Oregon, where there is a small archive of his papers that were left there when he died. Through all of this, I was trying to figure out this man and get a sense of what he was saying and why. I also realized that I was trying to figure out my father.

CHAPTER THREE

Son of a Preacher Man

If you understood me as well as Richard Gregg does, I would die happy.
—Mohandas Gandhi, to a group of Indian leaders[14]

RICHARD BARTLETT GREGG CARRIED a reliable family name, full of the history of New England, redolent of the traditions of Massachusetts and the thinkers of Boston and Concord. He carried it proudly. He wasn't born there, but his parents grew up in the state. All his family have links to Massachusetts, and Gregg, as did his father and brothers, went to Harvard College. He worked for a while as a lawyer in Boston before becoming a labor negotiator and government inspector. Later in life, Gregg would live and work in New York, Vermont, and New Hampshire, but Massachusetts was always the place he would circle back to. He was very fond of his oldest sister, Faith, who lived in Boston most of her life, and he would find shelter with her during periods when he was without a permanent home or when money was tight. Faith and her family owned a house and land in South Tamworth, New Hampshire, and the family frequently gathered there in the summers. His sister, Marjorie, lived nearby and was part of the Tamworth circle. Richard's father and mother moved back to Massachusetts in their last few years, and his father died in Brookline, at Faith's home. His

brother Don spent his life working at a psychiatric hospital in Wellesley.[15]
Richard was no stranger, therefore, to Cambridge or Boston or the Harvard
alumni and their powerful social circle. He was no stranger either to the
intellectual and philosophical traditions of the Transcendentalists and the
works of Hawthorne, Thoreau, and Emerson, those jewels of Massachusetts
philosophical and literary life.

Gregg's connections to New England and its milieu helped develop
his ideas about pacifism and simple living, but they germinated a long way
away, in the new and bustling town of Colorado Springs, Colorado. His
early years in the town shaped his values, beliefs, and ideas, and it was there
that he grew up, surrounded by his remarkable family. It was there, too, that
he was exposed to a sophisticated and intellectual elite, a unique science experiment, and a glorious landscape. There he would come to witness some
of the most critical conflicts between capital and labor in the early history
of American capitalism.

Colorado Springs

Colorado Springs was one of many new and vibrant towns growing
quickly in the southwest. The city, founded by General William Jackson
Palmer just twelve years before Gregg was born, quickly became a boom-
town. Palmer, a significant figure at the time, an engineer and industrialist,
had served the Union well in the Civil War (he was awarded the Medal of
Honor) and, after only four years, rose to the rank of general. After the war,
he helped build the Kansas-Pacific Railroad and, with his business partner,
William Abraham Bell, forged the Denver and Rio Grande Western rail link.
The railroad Palmer founded with Bell would eventually become the Union
Pacific. He is remembered today for promoting the narrow gauge and the use
of coal in the fireboxes of the magnificent steam locomotives that ruled the
rails in those days, ideas he absorbed from observing the new British railroads.

Palmer came to Colorado to explore the possibility of building a north-south railroad, joining Denver to Mexico, and tapping into the traffic already running across the country as the great railroads began to slice up the West. Intent on living under western skies and seeking a home for his prospective bride—and lured no doubt by the money to be made from a new railroad route—he bought ten thousand acres of land and planned a railroad.[16] The land he bought would make him very rich and help create a vibrant western town soon to be the place that the Greggs would raise their family.

When Palmer stepped off a stagecoach near Fountain Creek in Colorado and looked up to see the white cap of Pikes Peak, visible although the sun had not yet risen, he felt the pull of the West's magnificence. Seeing the beauty of the place got his heart beating and his engineer's mind working. He thought this place should be something different from yet another western town, hacked out of the scrub and dotted by farms and cattle ranches, with ramshackle collections of saloons and brothels and tack stores. Palmer's vision was for something grander, a place of sophistication and elegance, a resort filled with art and learning that would be in stark contrast to the mining and ranching towns then littering the West. Palmer was not one to let a vision rot like the idle gossip of imagination. He was a doer. He helped transform the small huddle of buildings nestled in the desert in the 1870s into more than just a beautiful view, and the town prospered over the next decade.[17] The pace of growth was swift. Colorado College, where nearly all the Gregg children studied, was founded in 1872. Churches, schools, and homes filled the desert land. Of those new churches, the First Congregational Church, linked to the recently built Colorado College, was established in 1874. Membership in the church multiplied fast, and more space was desperately needed. Pushed to create a new building, the church community worked hard to raise the $40,000 for construction, and, by 1889, an elegant Romanesque house of worship graced the new town. The first service, held in July of that year, was presented by the Reverend James Gregg, Richard's father.[18]

By the time the Greggs had moved to Colorado Springs in 1882, it was already a busy and vibrant place, fed by the railroads. A few years later, in 1891, gold was struck in the foothills of Pikes Peak, and, overnight, Colorado Springs was a gold rush town. And rush it did: money flowed into the city, and the population (just over 4,000 in 1880) more than doubled only ten years later and doubled again by 1900. As Palmer had envisioned, the city flourished as the hub of several new railroad lines and the gold in its hills. Palmer was also right about his vision for this beautiful place as a potential resort town but, perhaps, not quite as he had imagined. As the city grew, it became a destination of choice for people suffering from tuberculosis (TB). Alan Gregg, Richard's older brother, recalled that this meant a constant stream of wealthy (although sick) visitors who brought money and sophistication to the community. Indeed, Colorado Springs became a magnet for TB patients, causing something of a property boom in hospitals (at one point, there were seventeen of them). Due to the high altitude and clean, dry air, it was the town of choice for those seeking relief from the disease. Some estimates claim that by the 1890s, over one-third of the population of Colorado Springs had the disease.[19]

Colorado Springs was also a significant destination for many English visitors (the connection of Palmer's partner, the Englishman William Bell, drew many from Britain), and it quickly became known as "Little London." The combination of excellent transportation, the city as a railroad hub, the gold rush, and the superb climate and scenic splendor of the place ensured the city's vitality at the end of the nineteenth century. The lack of rain and mild temperatures made it particularly attractive to those fleeing a damp England or a freezing American Northeast. The cultured class that made the town their home provided the Greggs, used to New England's educated elite, with a sophisticated social circle and access to world-class educational institutions for all their children.[20]

Going West, Raising a Family

Gregg's mother and father moved to Colorado Springs after eight years in Connecticut at James Gregg's first pastorate, Windsor Avenue Congregational Church in Hartford. The opportunity for a new job and his own church, to be in cleaner air, and to have a place to raise a family was a big incentive for James. Mary Gregg, Richard's mother, was also happy about the move. She worried that the malaria then rampant in the east would expose them to the horrors of the disease (soldiers returning from the South at the end of the Civil War brought all manner of illnesses to New England, malaria among them). The epidemic that spread across the Connecticut River Valley after the war would not burn itself out until the 1890s.[21] For James and Mary Gregg, this would be as good a reason as any to go West.

Colorado Springs was quite a change for a family used to the sophistication and hubbub of Connecticut and Massachusetts. They went there with their first three children: James, Faith, and Donald. The family lived in the parsonage on East Dale Street. It is still there: a substantial house, with a low-hipped roof and overhanging eaves shading tall and narrow arched windows and a welcoming porch leading to a big double panel door that, in turn, invited entry. And invite it did. The house became a social gathering place for many in the town seeking the companionship and advice of the Reverend, his practical and gifted wife, and many children. Later, Mary Gregg, with the financial skills she brought to bear, sold part of their original land and built a new house at the other end of the lot. This transaction enabled her to rent out the property, providing an income that later helped pay for her children to go to college. This house was home to the whole Gregg family, their maid Fanny Smith, and their cook Lizzie Castle, both of whom were with them for many years.[22]

For Gregg's father, this was a real opportunity: a new church, a new home, and a bustling and growing town. The church building was completed a few years after the family arrived, and James Bartlett Gregg was its third minister.

There is a Gregg Library in the church, still functioning, and partly maintained by a $10,000 endowment provided by the Gregg family. James stayed as pastor of the church for twenty-seven years, giving his weekly sermons in a building designed by the architect Henry Rutgers Marshall (one of only two churches designed by him) in the Romanesque style. The many pillars and the ornate and robust portico announced this house of God with little subtlety. It is a beautiful building and the oldest church in Colorado that has continuously served the same congregation. Over a century later it was placed on the National Register of Historic Buildings.[23] This church with its parsonage was a focal point for the entire Gregg family and where Richard would grow up.

The Reverend James Bartlett Gregg was born in Medford, Massachusetts, in 1846, the only child of James Bartlett Gregg and Mary Bartlett Bailey, first cousins, who were married in Medford in 1844. The Bartlett name derives from the second marriage of Samuel Gregg, Richard Gregg's great-great-grandfather, to Lydia Bartlett. Many in the family today carry the Bartlett name, as did Richard. His grandparents had a small family business in Medford at the time, a "West India Goods Store," that had done well, selling products imported from what was then called the West Indies. Medford was commercially linked to the Caribbean through slavery and was already established as a shipbuilding town and the source of "Medford Rum." The city, which straddles the Mystic River that flows into Boston Harbor, gaining access to the Atlantic Ocean, thrived on the profits made in rum and shipbuilding in the mid-nineteenth century. It was home to one of the wealthiest families in the colonies, the Royalls. Isaac Royall made a fortune from his sugar plantation in Antigua and by trading in slaves. He purchased five hundred acres in Medford on which he built a magnificent Georgian-style mansion (using slave labor) and established the deep connection between Medford, slavery, shipbuilding, and rum that would become the economic engine of the city. Several Medford families made fortunes producing rum, using molasses imported from the Caribbean plantations and then shipped out to other parts of the U.S. and Europe. It was, at the time of Gregg's father's birth, already a prosperous and bustling town.[24]

Tragically, Gregg's grandfather was killed by a train in Medford in April 1848.[25] He had lain down between the rails and was run over. The Second Congregational Church of Medford recorded the death as "instantly by the cars, induced by intemperance," in other words, he was drunk and fell asleep on the tracks. History does not record, however, whether the drink of choice was rum. The widowed Mary successfully ran the store she had founded with her husband for a couple of years after her husband's death until, sadly, it was destroyed by fire. Despite these losses, she was determined that her only son James (Gregg's father), would get a good education. After he graduated from Medford High School, she prepared him for college by making sure he was accepted at the prestigious Phillips Academy in Andover, increasing his chances of being accepted at Harvard. To help pay for her son's education, she opened a profitable boarding house in Medford. Income from the boarding house and store yielded enough funds for her to move, with her son, to Cambridge—the better to prepare him for Harvard. After rigorous training at Phillips, the young James went on to Harvard College, graduating in 1866.[26]

There's little doubt that Medford at that time provided a solid base for the development of the religious beliefs of both Gregg's grandfather and father. With only four thousand inhabitants, Medford boasted seven houses of worship, including two congregational churches, one of which (the most conservative) counted the Greggs among their flock.[27] The combination of an excellent education, a devoted mother, and solid religious training were more than enough to guide Richard's father into the church. After college, he spent five years as sub-master at the Eliot High School in Jamaica Plain before going on to the Theological Seminary in Andover in 1871. He graduated from the Academy in 1874 and was ordained that year. In that same year, he married Mary Needham in Cambridge, Massachusetts. Mary was twenty-two. After the wedding, the Reverend Gregg immediately took his bride to Hartford, Connecticut, where he served as pastor at the Windsor Avenue Church for eight years, during which time Richard's older siblings: James, Faith, and Donald were born.[28]

Mary Needham (Richard Gregg's mother) was born and raised in Louisville, Kentucky, one of seven children. She was a talented and exceptional musician: good enough that she gained entrance to the New England Conservatory of Music in Boston. While she was there, she met the young James, who, at the time, was teaching at Eliot High School in Jamaica Plain. The musical Mary and the serious and newly ordained minister were a good match. Mary was small by today's standards, a compact woman both demure and strong-willed. Her compact frame belied someone who was very much the manager and very much the ruler of her family. Her good health and her intelligence were a resource for, and a great foil to, her somewhat otherworldly husband.[29]

In addition to her intelligence and practical skills, Mary had a deep love for music and art, and she would ensure that all her children had an appreciation for both. She was tactful and gentle, very much a daughter of the South, and a little prim (she thought that Mark Twain was rather vulgar). Her father, Edgar Needham, of whom she was very proud, was one of only two representatives in the state assembly in Kentucky who voted the "Free-Soil" ticket (the short-lived party that opposed bringing slavery to the newly created western states) before the Civil War. This made him so unpopular that he had to move his family to Ohio.[30] Mary, therefore, was a product of a strange combination: the antebellum South and an anti-slavery father. She was educated and sophisticated and could hold her own with the minister from Medford. As Gregg later recalled: "She was also a good financial manager. She and father wanted to send us four boys to college, and as many of the girls as possible. On merely a minister's salary in those days such a plan was impossible."[31] Without Mary's financial acumen, it is doubtful the family would have had the resources to send their children to college. Indeed, Mary managed her household with a gentle yet firm manner. She was not one to lose her temper and never yelled at her children in anger. She was devoted to her husband and protective of her brood. She was a skilled needlewoman and, sitting in the window at their home on Dale Street in Colorado Springs, was endlessly darning socks and sewing, keeping a close eye on the children playing outside. Often, she would rap on the window to call them in from the hot Colorado air for lunch or dinner.

The Reverend, with his stout frame and already balding head, looked very much the part of a preacher. He was short-sighted and wore pince-nez glasses most of his life. They gave him a studious air. He was no athlete and, by all accounts, very uncoordinated, but his bushy eyebrows and beard framed a face whose eyes glowed with warmth. The eyes he would bequeath to his son Richard, along with the eyebrows. His sermons always had depth and intellectual rigor, for he was a philosophical man, well-read and thoughtful. Although the Reverend Gregg lacked practical abilities and could barely drive a nail or repair anything in his home, his great strength lay in his intellect: he loved literature and languages and spent much time and, to his wife Mary's dismay, much money, on books, a habit and love he would pass on to Richard.

James Gregg was a man of God who placed great stock in integrity and honesty. He had little interest in money or wealth, but he cared deeply about ideas and people, and had a gentleness that drew friends and colleagues to him and his family. These traits, too, James would pass on to Richard, although he remained a Republican and, unlike Richard, had little time for unions or radicals. He was very much of the party of Lincoln: internationalist in outlook and progressive on issues of justice and equality. James Gregg was kind and decent and believed that reading and discussions were civilizing influences on all. Perhaps his only weakness (apart from spending too much money on books) was his tendency to be, as his son Alan remembers, rather clannish, favoring other Congregationalists, Harvard alums, and anyone of Scots-Irish ancestry.

For any of these, he had a particular sympathy and would willingly give of his time or lend them money.[32] Such was the connection to his *alma mater* that Alan Gregg once described their home as a temporary outpost of Harvard.[33]

The family was not wealthy, but they were comfortable, although money was always a concern—James's highest salary at the First Congregational Church was around one thousand dollars a year. With Mary's excellent management of the family finances, this provided enough to support an extensive and remarkable brood, but not without struggle. Much later, when James's health was failing and they were contemplating a move back to Massachusetts to live with their daughter Faith, Elinor Gregg wrote to her brother Don: "Father and Mother feel that they can't come away till they sell at least two of the three pieces of property they own out here thereby relieving themselves of several hundred dollars interest on mortgage." Mary Gregg had complained to her children about the strain of hosting constant dinners "(You) don't realize how it is to sit down to the same table full of people seventy-five times a month. If there were any money to spend I could be quite happy. But as every penny counts, I can't feel at liberty to ask people to meals often."[34]

Some of the financial pressure stemmed from this constant need and desire to entertain. The Gregg family was at the center of much of Colorado Springs' growing intellectual and business life, and James Gregg served on many boards of local organizations, including being president of the Rocky Mountain Harvard Club. As pastor, it was only natural that he would be at the core of the town's social life and, indeed, his home was always welcoming and full. Clearly, this was a strain for Mary as she worked the family finances to make sure that she could keep a good table and maintain appearances. But they managed, and Richard's father had a successful and rewarding life: he was given an honorary degree by Colorado College in 1893, where he served as a Trustee from 1885-1909, and by Harvard in 1907. The Harvard degree was presented by President Charles Eliot who described him "as a man who has stood stoutly for freedom of thought, personal righteousness, and public justice."[35] After their children grew up and left for college and careers, Mary and James remained in Colorado, only finally returning to Massachusetts in 1909 to live with Faith and to be with their children and grandchildren. The couple spent a dozen happy years in retirement at Faith's Brookline, Massachusetts, home, savoring their grandchildren and their family and friends.

James Bartlett Gregg died at the age of seventy-six at Faith's home in May 1922 and is buried (with his wife) at Mount Auburn Cemetery in Cambridge. Mary lived for another four active years, although failing in health in the years after she lost her husband. In May 1926, at Elinor's prompting, she planned a trip to Paris (with Elinor) to visit her son Alan who was working with the Rockefeller Foundation in Paris. Mother and daughter went to Europe to spend time together and to heal some old wounds that still festered between them. One day, while shopping at the magnificent Galeries Lafayette in Paris with Elinor, she felt dizzy and collapsed. The following day she was dead.[36]

These were Richard's parents. An intellectual and profoundly religious father who was kind and of impeccable integrity, and a strong and artistic mother who was as practical as her husband was unworldly. They gave all their children early schooling at home, gathering them in the evenings to study and ask questions, starting them out to learn French or Greek or Latin when they were eight or ten years old.[37] The house was full of books and exciting visitors and very much part of the sophisticated elite of the town.

The Early Years

Richard Gregg's early childhood in Colorado Springs seems to have been a happy one. His was a close family. He grew up in the imposing two-story parsonage on Dale Street with a view of the mountain ranges and Pikes Peak.[38] Despite its appearance, the cozy house was popular among the neighborhood children. Known as the "Gregg orphanage," many neighborhood children played in the large yard every day. As the family of one of the city's pastors, the Greggs occupied a central place in the community. The family often found themselves in the position of mingling with the very well-off of Colorado Springs while being in a distinctly lower income bracket. Richard's brother Alan recalled, "We were poor as the devil behind the scenes, but we got asked to the parties just the same."[39] Despite the constant money worries, all in all, Gregg's childhood was without trauma. Stable, loving, and respected by the community, the family today would seem to embody the classic American middle-class life. It was a home of books and conversation, religion, and love, a solid foundation for Gregg's life. Later letters to his mother and father reveal few significant rifts in their relationships. Disputes and disagreements, yes, but no schisms. Family gatherings kept the siblings close, and a constant stream of letters among them reinforced these ties.

Richard remembered Colorado Springs as a beautiful and bucolic place. But he did have one experience there as a teenager that would engage him in a way he perhaps did not fully appreciate at the time, for this was also the home, for a brief period, to some startling and unique construction. It was at Knob Hill, a small rise just out of town and about a mile from the Gregg house that, in 1899, Nikola Tesla refined his experiments on electricity and built a laboratory, making use of the free land and the electrical power available in the town.

Tesla had been working on a means to transmit electricity wirelessly through the earth and use it to send messages. His laboratory in New York was too small to house the giant oscillator he needed to test his idea. Tesla believed that a large coil placed at high altitude and in a location with little humidity would be the best combination to ensure the success of his transmission experiments, and Knob Hill fit the bill. He aimed to send messages through the earth "from Pikes Peak to Paris." Tesla's work was encouraged and supported by his friend Leonard E. Curtis, a patent lawyer who had moved to Colorado Springs for health reasons, and who helped bring Tesla and his laboratory to Colorado.[40]

The wealthy Curtis had worked with Tesla and Thomas Edison. Tesla had also worked with Edison and, after he had invented and perfected the alternating current motor, he had become wealthy, although not rich enough to support his complex experiments. Curtis promised Tesla he would find the land, money, and power for Tesla's operations. In Colorado Springs, he found all three: the land at Knob Hill, the power from the Colorado Springs Electric Company, and money from a wealthy investor: John Jacob Astor. So, Tesla headed to Colorado Springs in May of 1899, encamping at the Alta Vista hotel for the next nine months.

Tesla's experimental station created much local fascination and some fear. It was indeed a bizarre construction. The central laboratory was fifty by sixty feet and approximately eighteen feet high. The roof could be opened, and, above it, an eighty-foot tower clawed the air, topped by a large copper ball. The elite of "Little London" were thrilled to have the great scientist in their midst (for he was already well-known) and, of course, were fascinated by this exotic building and its mysterious sparking tower. But significant work was done here. The building contained the largest Tesla coil ever constructed, topped by a massive orb some fifty feet in diameter. With this apparatus, Tesla made lightning and generated huge voltages as he tried to establish if electricity could pass through the earth and thereby be transmitted anywhere. It was quite a show as giant bolts and the smell of sulfur filled the summer evening air. But such an enterprise needed complex equipment—wires, batteries, a huge Westinghouse transformer—most of which came from New York. It also needed labor to build the complex structure and assistance in outfitting the lab. The Tesla laboratory brought intense local and national interest. It also consumed a lot of power from the local utility. More than once, Tesla blew the entire power supply of Pikes Peak.[41]

Once the lab was established, Tesla hired a skinny local teenager as an errand boy and general helper: Richard Gregg. At the age of fifteen, Gregg, like many teenagers, was looking for a summer job, and his father had asked Curtis, Tesla's backer, to put in a word with Tesla about hiring Richard. Curtis lived not far from Gregg's family home and knew his father. Richard had no experience to offer, but Curtis's recommendation and Richard's interest in science got him the job. It was menial work (sweeping, winding wire for the huge coils Tesla was building, running errands) and tough on hot days. Tesla could be a demanding and intimidating boss with little time for people and things unrelated to his work. Despite Tesla's reputation for being difficult and obsessively focused, when Gregg met with him after his first week at the lab to ask for pay, he generously offered him eight dollars a week, much more than a teenager at that time would have expected. Richard was all set to use the summer's wages to get himself a bicycle, but the experiments and Tesla's ideas changed his mind. Enamored of the science, he told his mother that he would now use his wages to buy "electrical books."

Motivated by the strange electrical laboratory, Gregg made up his mind to study engineering in college. Gregg later recalled Tesla's experiments and his time working at the lab, saying that when Tesla threw the switch, "enormous sparks appeared," which "made a big crash that echoed inside the lab and could be heard from some distance away."[42] These dramatic experiments impressed the young Gregg, giving him a life-long appreciation for science, an interest he would later call on when he taught physics and math to young children in India. While Tesla remained in Colorado Springs for only a year, Gregg took the knowledge he gained in Tesla's lab to high school, where he completed a science curriculum, and to Harvard College, where he studied at first to become an electrical engineer.

The Labor Struggles in Colorado

Another critical feature of Gregg's early life was his exposure to violent labor unrest.[43] In 1894 the miners at Cripple Creek went on strike for the first time, under the Western Federation of Miners (WFM). During the strike, mine owners hired armed strikebreakers to intimidate the workers. In a rare moment, the U.S. government sided with the workers against this intimidation by the employers. With the support of the state, the strike lasted for only five months, at the end of which workers were victorious. With this success, mine workers extended their efforts at unionization of workers across industries in Colorado, including other miners, waiters, laundry workers, and newsboys. This unprecedented labor activity, however, culminated in the violent Colorado Labor Wars in 1903. Unlike the 1894 strike, violence quickly came to characterize the unrest. During the strike, explosions killed strikebreakers. Mine owners destroyed union halls, shot union miners, and, along with the military, rounded up union strikers to be "deported" to Kansas and New Mexico.[44] It was a brutal conflict and eventually led the miners' union to move away from the craft unionism of the American Federation of Labor and to the WFM, being instrumental in helping establish the Industrial Workers of the World (IWW) in 1905 in Chicago.[45] At eighteen, Gregg witnessed these violent conflicts just as he was about to pack his belongings to move across the country to attend Harvard College.

In this exposure to labor struggles at a young age, Gregg witnessed both the enormous potential and profound limitations of the labor movement at the end of the nineteenth century. The labor strife of the Gilded Age, the strengthening of the American labor movement at the turn of the century, and the monopolization of American industry in the hands of the likes of J.P. Morgan, John D. Rockefeller, and the Scots titans Andrew Carnegie and Andrew Mellon, all led to enormous turmoil and struggle throughout the U.S. His reaction to these experiences was reinforced by the work he would take up later in life before he left for India, and that would add fire to his alienation from American capitalism.

Gregg grew up caught between the conservatism of his father and the radicalism of the labor movement that took root nearby. Gregg's youngest brother Alan recalled that Gregg's father, as the local pastor, kept an eye on the labor unrest, and he was not always sympathetic. Alan Gregg thought of their father as a man of "corporate" loyalties: trusting of anyone of Scottish descent, or who had graduated from Harvard. He tended to be suspicious of all others. His father was skeptical of unions and the miners' cause. While the children likely encountered conservatism at home, Alan Gregg recalled how he gained some exposure to the labor side of the conflict: "When the IWW [Industrial Workers of the World] struggles were at their liveliest in Colorado…I slipped out of the house one evening and I went to a labor meeting downtown. I heard both the local people [business owners] and John D. Rockefeller maligned to a point that one couldn't believe…The result was that I was completely puzzled by this formidable difference of interpretation of human behavior."[46] No doubt, it had the same effect on Richard.

Richard Gregg never quite shook off the tensions between conservatism and radicalism or the religious values that were at the heart of his family experience. In part, these formative experiences provide an understanding of why Richard stayed in the background of the events about which he provided so trenchant an analysis. He was always careful to pose both sides of an argument but remained aggressive in his commitment to the downtrodden, the exploited, and the disenfranchised. Gregg's values, and the way he presented them, were formed in this family background and early experience. They were the soil in which would later grow his admiration for Gandhi, his pacifism, and his advocacy of voluntary simplicity as the turbulent twentieth century rolled out. He would take this upbringing and all that it taught him to India, where enormous changes were taking place, changes that Gregg would engage in, document, analyze, and bring back to the West.

Brothers and Sisters

Richard Gregg's siblings are essential to his story and his life. The close-knit Gregg family was the nest from which all the Gregg children went into the world as young, highly educated professionals. Throughout his life he wrote to them regularly and visited them frequently; they often served as a sounding board for his ideas and sometimes provided shelter and financial support. He shared his interest in science, art, and philosophy with his brothers and sisters: his older brother Don became a psychiatrist, his sister Elinore a nurse, and his youngest brother, Alan, became a renowned medical doctor after graduating from Harvard Medical School. Alan was a constant science advisor and commentator for Richard's ideas.

Alan Gregg: Physician (1890-1957)

The youngest of Gregg's brothers and sisters, erudite and serious, Alan Gregg became a leading figure in medical education and public health and published extensively in the fields of medicine and medical education, ending up as a Vice President of the Rockefeller Foundation. Alan received many honors, including the French National Order of the Legion of Honor and Honorary Fellow of the Royal Society of Medicine in Great Britain. As a teenager in Colorado Springs, it was a family physician who had ignited his interest in medicine but, initially, he wanted to be a writer. He had been President of the Harvard Lampoon in his senior year and worked on the Harvard *Advocate* with a young T. S. Eliot. He was a friend and classmate of Jack Reed, the American journalist, author, and communist activist. Alan visited his tomb the first time he went to the Soviet Union.

In the end, writing was not to be his career. He was much influenced by the respect his mother showed to a family doctor who came to the Gregg house to look after Alan when he was ill. Alan realized that doctors have a special place in the world and turned away from writing. He graduated from Harvard in 1911 with a BA, and from the medical school in 1916. Alan interned at Massachusetts General Hospital and, on completion, went to France to serve in the Harvard Medical Unit of the British Army Medical Corp until 1919. It was an experience that would move him deeply, as he served as a surgeon on the front lines of WWI, witnessing carnage on an epic scale.

Deeply interested in preventive medicine and public health, on returning from France, Alan joined the Rockefeller Foundation's International Health Board and spent three years in Brazil working on public health initiatives. Back in the States, he continued with the Foundation, eventually becoming the head of the Medical Sciences Division. That same year he married Eleanor Barrows, a mental health social worker, whom he had known in Colorado. The couple moved to Europe immediately after their wedding when the Rockefeller Foundation's Medical Division asked him to study European medical education. The Greggs lived in Paris until 1930. Alan Gregg's work over the next decade is credited with funding and encouraging much innovative research and training in the U.S., Europe, and South America. When he became VP of the newly created Division of Medical and Public Health at Rockefeller, he was able to broaden the vision of public health as a social issue, including a focus on mental health, pushing the Foundation to expand funding for the teaching of psychiatry at many major American universities, including Harvard, Yale, Johns Hopkins, and George Washington. He was one of the leaders in changing the face of medical education across the globe. He once wrote, while still working in hospitals behind the trenches in France, "You are an artist if you pay homage through one medium to all that you feel from another. The scientific training permits of reliability and accuracy, not of adequacy. Thus from these it follows that medicine may be both a science and an art." He died in 1957.[47]

Donald Edgar Gregg: Physician and Psychiatrist (1880-1939)

Richard's older brother, Don, also pursued science and medicine. Six-foot-and-half tall, he impressed as a strong, muscular, and athletic young man. He took more after his mother's side of the family in temperament and personality. Don liked to sing (this, too, from his mother), and his brown eyes would sparkle when he hit his stride. Don was studious but, according to Alan, not an intellectual. He loved animals and wanted to know how things worked. After completing his undergraduate studies, Don spent a year teaching at Milton Academy in Massachusetts and then studied medicine at Harvard Medical School, graduating in 1907. Interested in psychiatry (an area that also fascinated Alan and Richard) he interned at Massachusetts General Hospital and did a couple of years of medical work in the Philippines' capital city, Manila, before joining the psychiatric institute founded by Walter Channing in Wellesley, Massachusetts. Working there, he met and married Walter's daughter, Barbara, in 1912. Her father died in 1922, and Don took over as Director of the Channing Sanitarium and remained there until his death.[48]

For most of the 1930s, Don was president of the Massachusetts Society for Mental Hygiene. He played a role in promoting greater respectability for the mentally ill in some of the same ways his younger brother Alan would at the Rockefeller Foundation in the 1940s. Don was a bit of a snob and enjoyed the company of the social circle of Wellesley and the professional community of Boston. He dedicated his life to the Channing Sanitarium and built on its founder's progressive ideas for the treatment of mental illness, ones that encompassed psychotherapy, hydrotherapy, and the determined advocacy of a supportive and individualized environment for those considered mentally ill. Patients weren't confined to cell-like rooms but rather encouraged to walk among the surrounding woods. Unusually for the time, each also had his or her private suite with a living room, bathroom, and open-air sleeping porch. The vast majority of patients were middle-aged or older, often wealthy, women, mostly widowed or single, and their average length of stay was at least five years.[49] For the most part, the Sanitarium served wealthy patients. Don Gregg died from cancer of the esophagus in 1939, leaving no children.[50]

Elinor Delight Gregg: Nurse and Advocate (1886-1970)

Richard's younger sister (by just over a year), Elinor, also went into the medical profession. Born in May 1886, like Richard, she grew up in the dry, clean air of Colorado Springs, and like her brothers and sisters, attended the Cutler Academy and Colorado College, graduating in 1905. As was the case in many families of the period, it was expected that Elinor would follow her mother as a housewife and family caretaker. But that was not the course she chose. Elinor attended the unconventional Waltham Training School for Nurses in Massachusetts, the first in the country to develop professional training for nurses and the first to provide instruction on Home Nursing and District Visiting Nursing.[51] After graduation, she took a job as an industrial nurse at the Boston Manufacturing Company in Waltham, work she found exciting and a far cry from the life she had led in Colorado. She stayed with the company until 1913, and, after a short stint as a private duty nurse and a summer course on nursing administration, she moved to Cleveland, Ohio, to be Assistant Superintendent of Nurses at Cleveland City Hospital. Elinor learned much about administering a nursing body in Cleveland, and the experience was a good foundation for the position of Superintendent of Nurses at the Infants Hospital in Boston, the job she was offered in 1915 that precipitated her move back to Boston. After the U.S. joined the war effort, Elinor went to Europe as a Red Cross Army Nurse. Her image, in full uniform, was used on a famous WWI recruitment poster. She was there at roughly the same time as her brother Alan and they were based not far apart. On returning from Europe, she took courses in public health nursing at Simmons College in Boston and in 1922 became a Red Cross nurse at the Federal Bureau of Indian Affairs in Washington, D.C.

Nursing was one of the most acceptable professions for a woman of Elinor's social standing at the time. But she went much further than most in the nursing profession. She became the first-ever Public Health Nurse with the Bureau of Indian Affairs and went on to be a significant force in the development of nursing for Native Americans. Eventually, she was the supervisor of public health nursing for the Bureau from 1924 until 1939.[52]

In retirement, she wrote a book about her life, *The Indians and the Nurse*, which documented her many experiences and travels.[53] After her successful career, she moved to Santa Fe in 1938, where she lived on the property of the noted architect John Gaw Meem, who was married to Faith Bemis Gregg, the daughter of Elinor and Richard's sister, Faith. His daughter, Nancy Wirth, recalls her fondly as a great cook who was "very warm, very funny." Nancy said that Elinor was Richard's favorite sister and that they were very close. Indeed, Richard visited Elinor there frequently in the '40s and '50s, often bringing homeopathic medicines. Nancy remembers her as a charismatic figure: "earthy and large." Elinor never married. She died in Santa Fe in 1970 at the age of eighty-four.[54]

James Edgar Gregg: Clergyman and Educator (1875-1946)

The Gregg family was deeply religious. Religion would guide Richard's life and that of his oldest brother, James Edgar, although their beliefs would diverge widely: James retained allegiance to conventional religious institutions, while Richard developed an unconventional and eclectic spirituality. James came into the world when the family was still in Hartford. The first child for the newlyweds, he was, perhaps, the son most like his father and grew up to be physically similar. His dark hair made his blue grey eyes stand out from his chiseled face, giving him a serious and intense look. But that fitted his personality—like so many first-borns, he was quiet and precise. Again, like his father, James Edgar was never much of a handyman and not one for sports of any kind.

James went to Harvard Divinity School to get his master's degree. Wanting to continue and deepen his studies, he spent two years at Yale University studying theology, graduating in 1903. That same year he married Pauline Pumpelly, the twenty-five-year-old daughter of a Harvard geology professor, Raphael Pumpelly, in Newport, Rhode Island. Immediately after the wedding, James moved with his new wife to take a position as minister at the Pilgrim Memorial Church in Pittsfield, Massachusetts, where they stayed for six years.[55] When the opportunity came up, they moved back to eastern Massachusetts, and James became the minister at the Kirk Street Church in Lowell, where he remained for about three years, tending to his flock in the mill town. His marriage to Pauline ended with her death in 1911 at the age of thirty-three. He remarried in 1914 and returned to Pittsfield until 1918, when he left the ministry to serve as the principal at the Hampton Institute in Virginia, where he did much to enhance the institution. The Institute, originally founded as a school for freed slaves, became the Hampton and Agricultural Institute and, during James' presidency, it became accredited as a college. In the Principal's Report of 1929, James stated, "Every one of its collegiate divisions or schools—Agriculture, Home Economics, Education, Business, Building, Librarianship, Music—is fitting its students for their life-work as teachers or as practitioners in their chosen calling."[56]

He raised the number of African Americans in teaching positions and promoted many to chair of their department. As a published scholar, James developed progressive ideas on race in several articles, including an article challenging how races were compared on intelligence tests (that were then widely used by the U.S. military).[57] He continued as principal at Hampton until 1929.

Richard does not mention his brother often in correspondence or his notebooks. The gap in age, and the fact that James was, perhaps, too much like their father, or too much an advocate for the traditional established religion, may have kept them a little bit at a distance from each other. James Edgar died of a heart attack in 1946.

Marjorie True Gregg: Teacher and Inventor (1883-1968)

Richard was close to his older sister Marjorie. Only two years separated them, and they grew up together in Colorado Springs, sharing the yard and house as children do. Marjorie True Gregg was a religious woman, an Episcopalian, and deeply spiritual. She was an avid reader and wrote numerous poems and commentary on all matters. She was generous and self-sacrificing.[58] A Radcliffe graduate, she taught at the Buckingham School in Cambridge, Massachusetts, and other private schools, and served in the Red Cross in Europe during WWI providing cultural entertainment (she loved Shakespeare), and, after coming back from France, moved permanently to South Tamworth, New Hampshire. Marjorie was never much interested in business or money. Popular in Tamworth as a teacher and friend to children, she pursued her many ideas for crafts and projects. Marjorie with her horse and buggy were a familiar sight to the local children, as she went to teach Sunday School, put on yearly Nativity Pageants, or visit the families of children, bringing books, mittens, fun and kindness. She was long remembered for hosting children's sledding and cocoa parties at her house.

Based, perhaps, on her experience in France and frustrated by the lack of availability of functional clothing for women who did physical work, she invented and produced a line of trousers for women. These "Putnees"—sturdy pants for working women in wartime and agriculture, were manufactured by a company in Massachusetts under Marjorie's patented design. She liked to work with her hands and find innovative ways to teach and motivate young people. Disheartened by the unreal form of many dolls then produced for children, she designed for sale wooden dolls that she felt should look like real people and tiny doll houses. Her work created a new line of rubber dollhouse dolls, "True

Family Real People Dolls." She applied for her first patent in 1936.[59] "I hope both as toys that children may play with, and as material for artistic, creative work, my own dolls will someday be important,"[60] Marjorie wrote.

Richard loved Marjorie and sent letters to her frequently, especially during her illness a year or so before her death. According to Katy Thompson (Richard's grandniece), Marjorie was quite a character and a fixture in South Tamworth.[61] She was deeply committed to working with local schools, and supportive and involved in an array of local activities. She never married and died in 1968.

Faith Mary Gregg: Family Organizer (1877-1958)

Richard's older sister Faith taught kindergarten before marrying and set-tling into the conservative social scene in Chestnut Hill, Massachusetts. The kindergarten where she taught for a year was at Chicago Commons, an early settlement house founded in 1894 on Chicago's northwest side to help immi-grant families (modeled after Jane Addams' 1889 Hull House.)

Faith was affectionate and cheerful, with a good sense of humor. She remained close to her brother throughout her life and often looked after him when his first wife was ill and when he was between work and homes—which was quite often the case.[62] She had just turned twenty-two when she married Albert Farwell Bemis in Colorado Springs. Farwell (he used his middle name) Bemis was the son of Judson Moss Bemis, founder of Bemis manufacturing, which began as a producer of manufactured packaging. The company still exists.[63] Faith and Farwell set up home in Louisburg Square in Boston and, later, moved to Chestnut Hill in Brookline, where she remained and provided an anchor for Richard and his brothers and sisters. Farwell purchased two mills in South Tamworth, New Hampshire, and developed a local industry of mill working and furniture making. Faith dedicated herself to helping local families in the area.

Faith was a statuesque beauty. She never pursued a professional career and was a practical and conscientious wife and mother. Like her mother, she had seven children. Her grandniece, Nancy Wirth, described her as "very much a family person" and an "organizer of things." She was friendly and generous—but not good with money.[64] Faith was, perhaps, the most traditional of all the siblings. Her large family, and her marriage to the head of a large corporation, insured a very comfortable existence. Her stability and financial security provided a bedrock for her brothers and sisters. It also allowed her to travel widely, including a trip to India to see Gregg during his time with Gandhi. She died in 1958.

Richard's brothers and sisters constituted a remarkable group of siblings. Several of them went on to play significant roles in a varied number of fields. Fifteen years separated the eldest from the youngest, and all would come into their prime in the first decade or so of the new century. Richard was the fifth child. This large and successful family nourished him early on. Alan served as a mentor and sounding board to Richard until his untimely death in 1957. Faith provided guidance and support, emotional and financial. Marjorie was dear to his heart, and Elinor was a constant correspondent and very close to him. He was less close to Don and James. His parents' determined quest to ensure that their children would grow up as educated readers was critical to who he became. The context of his upbringing and his work after graduating from Harvard would prime his engagement with social and political concerns and define his role as a social philosopher.

Most importantly, he never lost the drive toward education instilled by his mother and the love of learning she had inculcated. Ironically, when Gregg's mother received his letter about his plan to move to India in 1925, she could not see how deeply she had instilled education and religion into her son. She decided he must be going to India to be an agricultural missionary.

CHAPTER FOUR

Law, Labor, and Disillusionment

Western peoples cannot escape their competitive capitalist net of ideas.
Holders of power will hold it...Even though...breakdowns go on all
around them they will try to hold to their power. Power is what they want.
No matter how appalling the win, no matter how much crime, disorder,
unemployment, starvation and war exists, they will cling to their power.
—Richard Gregg, Notebook XXIII, 1935, 52-53.

THE NEW CENTURY HAD JUST STARTED, and Richard Gregg was thinking about college and getting out of Colorado Springs. Like his brothers, he was anxious about his readiness for the challenges. His oldest brother James had completed his Harvard days and was teaching at St. Georges School in Newport, Connecticut, an Episcopalian private school just established. James was one of their first hires. His other older brother Don at Harvard seemed to be doing well. His sister Faith had married in 1899; Marjorie was starting at Radcliffe; and teenaged Elinor was at home with ten-year-old Alan. Richard was the oldest sibling remaining at home, but this still left plenty of children to fill the days of the preacher and his wife.

As he contemplated college Richard often wrote to James, expressing his concerns and trepidation about leaving home. Just fifteen when the twentieth century started, he proudly told his brother that year that their older sister

Faith was teaching him to waltz, a grown-up thing to do. He wanted his father to buy him a guitar.[65] Mainly, science and engineering occupied him, and he reminded Don about his time with Tesla and asked whether Don thought he had taken enough science courses to prepare him for college.[66] Like many teenagers of his class and time, he worried about his academic potential and the challenges he would face in college, even with excellent teachers at the Cutler Academy in his hometown and a stellar home education until he was ten. He was nervous about his size and weight: did Don think that his 135-pound frame was too small for the sports and male culture of Harvard? Should he try to put on weight?[67] Despite these adolescent worries, there wasn't much doubt that Harvard was where he was headed. He matriculated in the summer of 1903, joining fellow undergraduates of the Class of 1907. It was exciting for eighteen-year-old Richard (and not a little intimidating) to be at Harvard, following older brothers and his father.

As cosmopolitan as Colorado Springs was, it was not Cambridge and certainly not Boston. With its prestigious universities and sophisticated elite, its wealth and old connections to Europe, Massachusetts was beyond anything that the western states had to offer. Gregg found himself, as undergraduates do, excited and intimidated. But Gregg strode into his new life and became fully engaged with the university. Elected class treasurer, he joined the music club and threw himself into his studies. He was happy as a student and he did well. Gregg wrote the words for the baccalaureate hymn for his graduation.[68]

Fresh out of Harvard and twenty-two years old, Gregg, like many before him and since, got a job teaching. He joined the faculty at the Milton Academy in Massachusetts and taught high school level mathematics and science. The driven students at Milton were helpful (if not intimidating) to the young new instructor, and he felt that they taught him almost as much as he taught them. The affluent and ambitious students were on their way. In Gregg's day, it was considered a premier institution and, later, counted among its many noted graduates such luminaries as T.S. Eliot, Buckminster Fuller, Douglas MacArthur, and Robert and Edward Kennedy. Gregg stayed for a year, unsettled about a career. Despite its prestige, Milton didn't pay well, and Gregg supplemented his salary with private tutoring during the summer.

After Milton, Gregg decided to join the legal profession, and he applied to Harvard Law School in 1908. Now twenty-three, he still had an interest in science and engineering, but the turmoil of the era had begun to awaken his social conscience. This included the continued militancy and activism of the reformers of the Progressive Era, the growing female suffrage movement and struggle for the right to vote (the Women's Trade Union League was formed in 1903), and the formation of the Industrial Workers of the World (IWW)—in 1905, in Chicago. Gregg had seen the consequences of the devastating Colorado Labor Wars on workers and his home state. Some of these issues became more real to him during his last year as an undergraduate when he served as a teaching assistant for a course in Government. The course exposed him to the significant challenges America faced at the beginning of the new century, and this would begin his questioning of the brutal consequences of capitalism, questions that would remain with him for the rest of his life. And, of course, during these early years of the 1900s, technology and American capitalism generated enormous technological advances. The first movie theater opened in 1902, the Wright brothers made their first successful flight, and Marconi had transmitted wirelessly across the Atlantic. Very soon, Henry Ford would start production of the Model T automobile. It was an exciting time to be a young graduate in Cambridge and in America. Throughout the period, President Teddy Roosevelt challenged the big trusts and promoted some of the Progressive Era politics and demands for reform.

He graduated from law school in the spring of 1911 just as the Mexican Revolution was boiling over and the colonial powers were settling disputes in Africa, conflicts that would be the harbingers of war in Europe in a few years.

In the U.S., the Progressive Era rolled on, and demands for reform arose everywhere, a social and political storm without precedent. Upton Sinclair's *The Jungle*, published in 1906, exposed the horrors in meatpacking plants and resulted in tougher regulations for factories, especially in meatpacking and for food safety. The Women's Political Union was founded in 1910. Demands for an income tax and a more democratic Congress rallied social reformers, unions, and workers. The Triangle Shirtwaist fire in March 1911 shocked the nation and underscored the often poor working conditions for Americans, resulting in calls for immediate reform.[69] Although the Progressive Era was never a fully coherent movement, it represented widespread concern about poverty and urban slums, with the corruption of local and state politics, the exploitation of laborers and children, and the failure of capitalism to serve the collective good. Eventually, it mobilized workers and unions, social reformers and progressive churches, and muckraking journalists to demand government reforms, better regulations, and helpful programs.

Although the state of the poor and the conditions in the factories and mines were the focus of huge conflicts and moral outrage, manufacturing in the U.S. had become enormously productive and profitable, so much so that the American economy outpaced that of Great Britain, producing more iron, coal, and steel, and manufactured products than ever before. Gregg graduated into a world where America was poised to replace Europe as the dominant economy and most powerful state, its dark underside of corruption and corporate domination already evident and troubling.

For now, however, these issues, although alarming, were far removed from Gregg's life in Cambridge. After studying and teaching for the best part of seven years, he did what many graduates of elite schools did in those days—he took the summer off and traveled to Europe for the first time.[70] This trip was simply a vacation and adventure. When he got back, he needed a job, and as a young, newly minted lawyer in Boston with good social connections, it wasn't hard for him to find work. He landed a position that September at the firm of Gaston, Snow, and Saltonstall in Boston. Even in those days, this was a large and prestigious firm that had built its reputation on corporate and real estate law, deeply involved in contracts for corporate restructuring and finance. For Gregg, this was a long way from the gentle life of Colorado Springs, his religious and socially conscious family, even from the excitement of turning coils for Nikola Tesla. He worked with the firm for three years, living in an apartment on Beacon Hill, about a twenty-minute walk across the Boston Common, past Frog Pond, and down towards Congress Street. It was a pleasant stroll in summer but cold in winter when the wind whipped across the Common.

The job at Gaston, Snow, and Saltonstall was a good position, in an influential firm, and most young lawyers would have been happy to be there: a powerful practice, lots of useful connections, all in a sophisticated city. Despite the prestige of the firm and the convenient location in downtown, corporate law was not where Gregg wanted to be. The novelty of his job with Saltonstall wore off, and, after a couple of years, he began to think about more socially valuable and relevant work—at least work more in line with his emerging beliefs about the world.[71] He left the firm just as Europe was getting ready to plunge into the horrors of WWI.

Gregg's older sister Faith, married, lived a couple of blocks from his apartment. They had always been close, and Faith's husband Farwell Bemis was President of the Bemis Bag Company. Farwell's father Judson Moss Bemis founded the Bemis Company in 1858 as a manufacturer of bags for food products. After inventing a way to sew bags and print on them mechanically, the Bemis Company expanded rapidly. Bemis opened a slew of plants in the 1890s and began paper bag manufacturing at the turn of the last century. The company developed packaging techniques just as the U.S. was growing as a major manufacturing and trading center.[72] By the start of

WWI, this was already a valuable multinational company.

Faith and Farwell moved easily in the Beacon Hill social scene, and Gregg was a frequent visitor to their home. Farwell, in his early forties, was building his company's international connections and needed someone he could trust by his side as the business expanded. His brother-in-law was perhaps an obvious choice, or maybe he was responding to Faith's suggestion that they should look after Richard. Whatever the motivation, in the spring of 1913, Farwell offered him a position as his private secretary and, after learning the ropes of the business, Gregg went with him on a business trip to India. It would be the first of many visits Gregg was to make to his soon-to-be adopted country.

Farwell wanted to examine the jute manufacturing process, since jute had become an essential component of the sacking and packaging for which the company was famous. He had founded the Angus Jute Company in India the previous year and needed to visit the plant to explore further expansion and business connections. The jute mills were well developed in India by this time, and the trade had been part of the activities of that old colonial edifice, the East India Company. As the Industrial Revolution progressed, jute became a valuable commodity, and British trade with India in jute essentially built the city of Dundee in Scotland, where jute mills peppered the landscape by the end of the nineteenth century. In short order, many mills had been moved to India to exploit cheaper Indian labor. Jute was enormously profitable, and the Bemis Company was there working the sources.[73]

Richard and Farwell set off for India in December 1913 by way of England, reaching India in January 1914. The trip took them to Calcutta and the Angus Jute Mill, one of the biggest in India.[74] While Farwell negotiated business with Gregg's assistance, there was time for sightseeing, and Gregg took the opportunity to see as much as possible. He found India completely different from the rushing, conflict-ridden, industrialized and rapidly urbanizing U.S., and the intellectual-and-corporate world of Boston/Cambridge.

But this was a business trip, and he spent much of his time there working with local businesspeople, and with American and British managers and investors who had little regard for either the native population or the intricate culture and society in which they lived. For them, as Gregg would recall later, "Indians and their whole civilization were distinctly low and of no account."[75] Gregg thought otherwise. He saw a sophisticated and fascinating society, trapped under the yoke of imperialism and serving only to supply the industrialized west, especially Britain and the United States, with the raw material for their factories that churned out wealth.

Farwell and Gregg got back to the U.S. in May 1914, just a few months before the Great War would break Europe apart.[76] This trip would be the start of a lifelong love for India and its people. At the time, Gregg recalled he was "an ignorant tourist with the usual ideas as to the superiority of the white man."[77] He did write a lovely piece, however, ("A Monument to An Ancient Love.") about his visit to the Taj Mahal. He published it in *The Bellman* (a small literary magazine in Minneapolis, Minnesota) in September 1915.[78] In it, he describes his visit to the great temple: "Having seen it, I know that very rarely in this world has tender human feeling been so perpetuated. I was so subtly and deeply stirred that the wonder of it will never leave me." The Taj Mahal was indeed a wonder of the world, and Gregg would find many others in India when he returned to live there a decade or so later.

Law, Work, and Conflict

Back from India, Gregg stayed in Boston and decided to try the law once more: this time at the offices of Warner, Warner and Stackpole.[79] Founded in 1874, the firm specialized in real estate and corporate law. Again, though, this was not what he wanted to do with his life. He now had a taste for both India and the alternatives it suggested. But lawyering offered interesting encounters. One acquaintance, in particular, exposed him to perspectives that would put him in the thick of the burgeoning industrial conflict causing him to examine deeply the nature of American capitalism: Robert Grosvenor Valentine.

Gregg met Valentine in Boston in the fall of 1915 while associated with Warner and Stackpole. When Valentine offered to have him work with him at the law offices he was opening with Ordway Tead in Chicago, Gregg gladly accepted. He had had enough of corporate law, and the team of Valentine and Tead offered a tantalizing new view of law and society. Valentine's intellect and credentials fascinated Gregg. Also from Massachusetts, Valentine graduated from Harvard in 1896. Valentine became Commissioner of Indian Affairs after working at the Bureau of Indian Affairs in Washington, D.C., for several years as an inspector. Appointed by President William Howard Taft, he held the position until he resigned in 1912 and returned to Boston, joining the Progressive Party. Valentine served as chairman of both the first wage board under the Massachusetts Minimum Wage Law and the Massachusetts Committee on Unemployment in 1914. Supporting unions when he could, Valentine contributed to the development and study of industrial relations, working to resolve conflicts between management and labor. In this, he followed actively the then-popular perspective of Frederick Winslow Taylor, whose work on scientific management was a critical part of the "efficiency movement," founded a decade or so earlier. Valentine published in the field of labor relations and about the precepts of the new ideas of scientific management. He died of a heart attack in New York City in November 1916 at the age of forty-three.[80] He had an enormous influence on Gregg.

Like his colleague Valentine, Ordway Tead was from Massachusetts, a graduate of Amherst College. Tead saw the science of labor relations as a way to mitigate conflict and to use the ideas of the scientific management school to increase efficiency and rationalize labor relations. For Gregg, Tead and Valentine's work on the industrial audit and innovative ways to resolve labor disputes suggested a whole new approach to the field of labor/capital relations. Valentine,

Tead, and now, Gregg, embodied many of the ideas to which Gregg was just beginning to pay attention. While working there, Gregg got to know Tead, whose work and writing shaped some of Gregg's later thinking. Like many others at the time, Gregg was at first uncritical of the implications of the "industrial engineering" techniques that Frederick Winslow Taylor advocated to improve efficiency and to promote his scientific management movement.[81] Gregg saw it as a rational alternative to the conflict and exploitation ubiquitous in American capitalism. Perhaps those lingering affections for "science" colored his judgment at the time, but he was certainly not alone in viewing this new field as a progressive contribution to labor-management relations.

Tead left the firm in 1917 to join the Bureau of Industrial Research in New York and started teaching industrial relations at Columbia University. He went on to be a leading advocate for equal rights for women, a promoter of civil liberties, and later chaired the New York Board of Higher Education from 1938 to 1953. Tead wrote more than twenty books on history, economics, and education, and many articles on labor conflict and higher education.[82] Clearly, working with Valentine and Tead energized Gregg and helped him think about labor relations differently.

The firm specialized in what Valentine called the "industrial audit," which surveyed working conditions and paid attention to how employers provided a channel for workers to resolve their grievances.[83] Gregg favored this scientific approach to dealing with the complex relations between employer and employee. Valentine's work was not only about applying the law or making work more efficient or establishing a new welfare system for workers who earned too little to survive, or who had been laid off. Rather it was a holistic vision, based on gathering data and knowledge. At the time Gregg believed in this approach:

> The human factors, the psychology, the problems of science, organization, group action and democracy are fascinating. When you get close to men in

their work, you see them at the heart of their ambitions, disappointments, and hopes and fears. An opportunity to gain special insight into human nature is ascribed to the medical profession, but my experience in industrial counseling makes me believe that more than any other profession it affords an absorbing and interesting view of human nature.[84]

The school of scientific management would later be much criticized and come under both attack and scrutiny by union leaders and progressive reformers. Today "scientific management" is seen as a way in which early owners sought to enforce and co-opt workers' discontent, to increase efficiency at the price of a worker's autonomy, and to deskill them. But there's no doubt that these ideas would play an essential role in the development of business administration and labor relations throughout the twentieth century. In this framework Gregg reconsidered the causes and nature of conflict, especially in industrial settings.

His time with Valentine and Tead built Gregg's interest in psychology and work organization. The literature then emerging around these ideas got him thinking about how labor conflict could be better resolved and, more importantly, how industrial engineering might serve as a model for dealing with conflict in general. The work excited him in a way that corporate law never did, and his experience at the firm sowed the seeds of his lifelong concern for resolving conflict, working for justice, and his antipathy to modern industrial capitalism. But that experience was to be relatively brief: Valentine died in 1916, Tead left the firm in 1917 and, with the entry of the U.S. into WWI, Gregg had to seek other work. He moved to another job, one that began to make him question even further the state of labor and human relations in capitalist America.

Between Labor and Capital

When America joined the allies in the fight in WWI, Gregg took a position with the U.S. Shipping Board in Washington. The Board came about as a result of the passage of the U.S. Shipping Act of 1916, a response to the weak U.S. merchant and naval ship production in the face of European dominance in the industry. The work became much more critical when the U.S. entered the war, and the Board developed and expanded to help improve U.S. shipping resources since most foreign ships were now tied up in the war. Gregg's job was to arbitrate conflicts between ship manufacturers and carriers and their workers, to reduce possible threats to production. Given his background with Valentine and Tead, his legal training, and his interests, this was a good fit for him. He threw himself into the job.

Immediately, Gregg became involved in a contest between ship owners and seamen and longshoremen of the Great Lakes. At the time, U.S. Steel dominated the Lake Carriers Association. As Gregg recalled later:

> There was a dispute between the ship owners and seamen on the Great Lakes. My immediate boss in this division of the shipping board, ex-governor Robert P. Bass of New Hampshire, who had been a good been a friend of Valentine's, took me with him on an investigation of the labor situation in Chicago, Buffalo, Cleveland and some of the great big ports and we found that the seamen had some just grievances that deserved a discussion between them and the ship owners. The war effort required the continuous carriage of iron ore on the lakes. So, Mr. Bass called a meeting of the representatives of both parties in Washington. On the appointed day, the representatives of the Lake Carriers Association, dominated by the U.S. Steel Corporation ore-carrying boats, refused to come into the same room with the representatives of the seamen. Mr. Bass sent me to the head of the U.S. Shipping Board to ask him to compel the representatives of the ship owners' association to meet with the seamen's representatives to talk over the situation and to try to reach an agreement. The head of the shipping board declined to do so. It was clear then where the power lay. In all innocence I had been going to various meetings of seamen and longshoremen and telling them that the government would give them justice. When I saw that was not so, I resigned and joined the National War Labor Board of which ex-President Taft was a member.[85]

After a few months of conflicts like these, Gregg was disenchanted, but things were not much better for him when he moved to work at the National War Labor Board (NWLB).[86] At the NWLB, the government assigned him as examiner-in-charge during a dispute at the Bethlehem Steel Company. Gregg investigated the complaint and had to administer the award once the Board handed down a ruling. Since Bethlehem Steel was the primary manufacturer of guns and shells for the U.S. war effort, the conflict received priority with the Board.

The complaint originated with ten thousand electrical workers and machinists in a dispute over back pay owed to them by the company, and issues involving overtime pay and working conditions. The Board ruled in favor of the workers and expanded coverage to include all thirty thousand employed by the company.[87] At the time, Bethlehem Steel ignored these rulings, claiming that the end of the war negated any agreements they had made to restore pay. Head Examiner Gregg, in a document written in December 1918, "Ways in Which the Bethlehem Steel Company is Derelict in the Award," stated that the plant had "discriminated against committee men in the matter of layoffs," violating its "professed principle of retaining its steadier, more efficient, and longer employed workers." Despite NWLB and Gregg's efforts, Bethlehem Steel procrastinated in implementing reforms. As the war ended and the high demand for steel collapsed, the company laid off workers. This action severely weakened the union. It would take until the 1930s for steelworkers to once again fully unionize and get a voice in protecting their working conditions and pay.

For Gregg, the Bethlehem Steel dispute was yet another example of the intransigence of big capital in the face of the needs of ordinary workers and symbolic of the ability of large corporations to defeat even government demands for reform. The desire to maintain and increase profitability surpassed any concerns for the wellbeing of workers. Despite his efforts, Gregg realized that corporate interests were able to rig the system against workers and were uncontrollable. His deep involvement in this dispute only served to increase Gregg's sympathy for labor.

Gregg understood the profound challenges of trying to create a better life for workers under the systems then prevalent in the U.S. He mistrusted not only the corporate bosses but also the nature of industrial production itself. It was clear to Gregg that capitalist industrial production, as it was emerging in America in the early decades of the twentieth century, was not sustainable, equitable, or capable of any real humanity. His views were not enhanced when the 1918 armistice ended his job at NWLB and, forced to look for work, he reluctantly took a position with the Clothing Manufacturers Association (CMA) in New York City in the spring of 1919. He lasted a few months, but the CMA, and the way it ran, only served to underline his previous experiences. Shortly after quitting the Association in October that year, he wrote to his brother Alan that the organization had "such a tremendous proportion of SOBs that it became quite unbearable."[88]

By the fall of 1919, thirty-four-year-old Gregg was out of work and despondent about the state of labor relations in the country. Leaving behind the "SOBs" at the CMA, he decided he needed to get back to basics by spending a couple of weeks cutting wood and farming at a friend's place in Vermont. He told Alan that this was an opportunity to get back to being "full of health and do the job of chopping down ash trees, sawing and splitting them...."[89] He thought that a few weeks in the country doing honest manual work would purge him of the toxic residues of his encounters with corporate America, and the challenge of physical activity and closeness to nature would restore him. The pull of physical work on the land would be a choice and driving force for him throughout his later life.

After a few weeks in the woods, Gregg returned to New York City in November. Thinking about how to document and write about his experiences in labor relations, he played with the idea of a book. As the concept began to develop, he sought some advice. Leveraging his Harvard connections, and those of his brother Alan, he was able to arrange a lunch with two noted British academics, Harold Laski and Graham Wallas, at the Harvard Club in the city. These two were colleagues and, by then, well-known scholars. Wallas was a leading Fabian (the Fabians, committed to democratic socialism, were founded in 1884) and socialist in the U.K. A social psychologist, he co-founded the London School of Economics and Political Science (LSE) with Sidney Webb and George Bernard Shaw. Although he left the Fabians in 1904, he was a lecturer at LSE and at Harvard (where he first met Gregg). LSE created the Graham Wallas Chair in his honor (later occupied by Harold Laski).[90] Laski was also well-known by the time Gregg had lunch with him as both a journalist and an emerging political theorist. Like Wallas, he was teaching at Harvard and an editor of the *Harvard Law Review*, and he, too, would end up at LSE. He would go on to become a leading political theorist and a significant force in the British Labour Party in the 1930s.[91] His work on pluralism would become the dominant perspective of political science as a discipline, especially in the U.S., for much of the twentieth century. As pluralism promoted an image of a multiplicity of competing forces in an open society, it provided an ideal model of the political functioning of a market economy, and of liberal government.

There was a further later link that would bring Gregg and Laski together again in a few years: one of Laski's students at LSE in the late '20s was Krishna Menon, leader of the revamped India League in the U.K. and a member of the Labour Party. Menon worked tirelessly for Indian independence throughout the '30s and was close to Mohandas Gandhi and Jawaharlal Nehru (whom he helped bring to the U.K. in 1935).[92] All of this would, in the future, connect Gregg to India. Gregg's lunch meeting with these two British academics was pleasant and, while Wallas liked Gregg's idea for the work he proposed, the book never materialized.

As November drew to a close Gregg's brother-in-law Farwell once again stepped in to offer him work, researching the state of housing and of working conditions in England and France; Bemis was looking to set up a company in both countries. Gregg was happy to take up the offer as it allowed him to travel to Europe and gain a better understanding of post-war social and labor conditions across the Atlantic. He would also be able to get first-hand experience of the devastation caused by the war. He sailed for England just after Thanksgiving 1919, having spent the holiday with Faith and Farwell in Boston, where he got the chance to talk with Farwell and get some clarity about what he hoped he could achieve with the trip.

Gregg stopped first in France and visited a couple of towns north of Paris, witnessing the unimaginable destruction wrought by the war.[93] The trip did little to relieve his sense of the problems facing the industrialized economies. When he got to England it was in a sorry state: the conflicts around Ireland and women's suffrage were tearing the nation apart and, with the economy entering a severe depression and unemployment rates rising rapidly, industrial strife abounded. And France, too, was still recovering from the enormous economic and physical costs of the war. Gregg, surprisingly, gave no indication of being concerned about the global Spanish Flu pandemic that was devastating the U.S. in 1918-19, especially in Massachusetts. The disease killed between fifty and one hundred million worldwide and nearly three-quarters of a million people in the U.S. Nor was he concerned, apparently, about travelling to flu-ridden France. Collapsing from sickness, Europe churned as monarchies fell and revolution scented the air.

After a couple of months in Europe, Gregg returned to the States. Needing work, he accepted a position in the summer of 1920 at the Railway Employees Department (RED) of the American Federation of Labor (AFL), headquartered in Chicago. Created in 1905, RED brought together seven of the national craft unions of the railroads. These included, among others, the

Carmen; the International Association of Machinists; the Blacksmiths; the International Brotherhood of Boilermakers; Iron Shipbuilders and Helpers of America; the Electrical Workers; and the International Brotherhood of Firemen. RED bargained on behalf of these unions on a wide range of issues affecting their wages and working conditions.[94] At the time, Leland Olds directed the Research Bureau at RED. An impressive figure whom Gregg had met while working at the National War Labor Board, Olds got him the job at RED.

Olds shared many of Gregg's values: both were deeply spiritual and committed to social justice issues. Olds became convinced of the need to link social justice to his religious beliefs and spent some time working in a social settlement in Boston soon after he graduated from Amherst College. Later he studied economics at Harvard and Columbia universities and became a Congregational minister at a church in Brooklyn, New York.[95] He went on to serve as industrial editor of the Federated Press, a labor news service, and as an economic consultant to labor organizations. In the early '30s, he worked on power utility regulation in New York State, pushing for greater public control of power utilities. President Roosevelt appointed him Federal Power Commissioner in 1939, a position he kept for ten years.

A key figure during the New Deal, Olds played a significant role on a commission studying European cooperative enterprises for Roosevelt. When he was being considered for reappointment as Commissioner during the Harry S. Truman administration in 1949, Texas Senator Lyndon B. Johnson (then Chair of the confirmation sub-committee) worked to remove him with a vicious campaign of red baiting (citing his radical writings from the '20s). It was not one of Johnson's finest moments.[96] Olds had been a leading advocate of regulating the oil and natural gas industries and, at the time, was deeply critical of American capitalism and interested in collective ownership and cooperatives, especially for power production. Gregg's association with Olds exposed him to someone of high intellect who shared Gregg's developing views. Olds' interest in cooperatives resonated with Gregg, who would later see the connection to the work of Gandhi.

Gregg was pleased with the move back to Chicago, but the work was hard. The intense struggles around the railroads necessitated many sleepless nights and long, intense periods of work. The job required that he prepare testimony and arguments for the unions to present to the U.S. Railway Board, write publicity, and appear on behalf of the unions at the Interstate Commerce Commission.[97] This required a lot of traveling to towns where the disputes were most intense. Here, too, Gregg found that corruption and injustice reigned. For example, in November 1921, he went to Louisiana to investigate the complaints of the railroad workers in Bogalusa, a small town created and constructed in 1908 by Goodyear to house workers for the Great Southern Lumber Company, which, when completed, was the largest lumber sawmill in the world. The sawmill was the site of the Bloody Bogalusa Massacre in 1919, where Black workers who had attempted to form a labor union were shot and killed by a private militia, the Order of Self Preservation and Loyalty League, paid for by the lumber company.[98] The sawmill manager who worked for Goodyear was also the town's mayor until he died in 1929 and had almost complete control of the town. The killing of both Black and white unionists became a national scandal and tragedy. Gregg arrived there only a year or so after the Massacre.

Gregg's visit made him even more acutely aware of how bad things had become. He wrote to Alan:

> The town where I had to make my investigation is ruled body and soul by a big lumber company. As you get out of the RR station you are greeted with a big sign about fifteen feet high—lighted at night by two arc lights—reading "Bogalusa wants 20,000 good citizens by 1925. Advice to Bolsheviks and Agitators, This is No Place for You. Get Out. By Order of the Self Preservation & Loyalty League." Cordial, isn't it! They killed 5 labor leaders there in the

autumn of 1919 in cold blood in their own yard. The congregation will now rise and sing "My Country 'Tis of Thee, Sweet Land of Liberty!" The poor devils there have had their hearts nearly ground out. It's a grand life, if you don't weaken.[99]

This experience, and others like it, gave Gregg yet more education in both the state of labor and capital relations and of Black Americans, especially in the South. Conflicts increased further in the early 1920s, while Gregg was at RED, especially with the Great Railroad Shopmen's Strike of 1922. This massive confrontation involved nearly all the existing railway unions—some 400,000 railways workers put down their tools. The initial cause of the strike was an announcement by the Railway Labor Board that it was going to cut wages by seven cents an hour as of July 1, 1922. That summer, the Railway Shopmen were joined by other railroad workers, making it the most massive strike in the U.S. since the great Pullman Strike of 1894. Owners hired strikebreakers, and the state deployed more than two thousand deputy U.S. Marshalls (bolstered by the national guard) to clamp down on protests and union meetings. Company guards and hired cops killed ten strikers. Strikers and picket lines were initially peaceful, but eventually the railroad companies put together an "army of armed guards" and "Major confrontations ensued on July 8 when shopmen were fired upon by railway guards."[100] Marshals and troops responded. Violence escalated.

This was the summer that Gregg, on a casual visit to a favorite bookstore in downtown Chicago, happened to pick up and open a copy of *Young India*, the pages full of news and comment by Mohandas Gandhi, also a lawyer, who was pushing for social justice for the millions of men and women in his country. By that time Gandhi was already a leading activist in India and had already been imprisoned for sedition because of articles he wrote in the journal. Gregg recognized in Gandhi's method of nonviolent resistance an innovative strategy of resistance to oppression and to conflict resolution. These stories and ideas resonated in his bones, especially in contrast to the chaos Gregg saw in front of him. The propitious encounter with Gandhi's writing would send him on a life's journey.

But this was for the future. For now, the shopmen shut down railroads across the country. The strike was notorious for the acts and sentiments of the then U.S. Attorney General Harry Daugherty in the Warren G. Harding Administration. Virulently anti-union, the AG persuaded the courts to issue an injunction against strikers and other forms of union activity; this became known as the "Daugherty Injunction," and represented one of the most sweeping acts against fundamental constitutional rights in the U.S. As a result, the workers were forced to capitulate, and most were back at work at less pay by the late fall of that year.[101]

This strike and the violence of its repression affected Gregg deeply, making him even more conscious of the injustices prevalent under capitalism. His close-up experience during the strike was undoubtedly the straw that broke the camel's back and helped launch him on a very different path. Having experienced two of the major labor conflicts of the twentieth century and seen, at first hand, the amount of labor unrest, corruption, and exploitation that marked the century's first two decades, it is hardly surprising that Gregg became increasingly disillusioned with American industrial capitalism.

After the railroad workers lost the strike, and Gregg his job along with it, he spent some of the rest of 1922 and 1923 in fixing up the house he had bought in Chicago so he could rent it. During this period, he worked in a doctor's office and a free medical clinic, while doing a brief stint reporting on labor issues for a Washington paper.

Having discovered Mohandas Gandhi's ideas and story in the summer of '22 on that bookstore run in downtown Chicago, such a catalytic event, Gregg filled any spare time reading about his new hero and the culture he came from, one he found increasingly attractive. His letters to his mother during this period speak to his sense of alienation from America and what he saw going on around him. In August 1923 he told her that he no longer went to church and was now much more interested in "individual spirituality." He let her know that he had found someone to rent his house so that he would be free to go look for work on a farm in Wisconsin.[102] By October, Gregg had quit the clinic and the doctor's office in Chicago and was focused on selling his house. In early November he moved temporarily to Madison, Wisconsin, and enrolled in agricultural classes at the university. He would soon take work at a small farm in rural Wisconsin, about two-hundred-and-fifty miles north of Madison.[103] His father's death added to his sense of disillusionment with the world. He was not as close to his father as some of his brothers and sisters—there were often moments of disagreement between the two, especially over Richard's support for unions and his generally progressive politics, and they sometimes had conflicts.[104] His father wrote to him, criticizing the unions and their acts of resistance and expressing concern about where his son's life was going. The exchange of letters reveals some of the differences between father and son. Gregg chided his father:

> The manual workers are, so to speak, living in the shallows, on the margins of existence. Their wages are so low and the conditions of living so narrowed by the steady, unrelenting economic pressures that their infant death rate is so high, their disease and accident rate is higher than that of other groups, they have little or no leisure in which to develop their minds and spirits, and by all other groups in society they are looked down upon either with contempt or pity,—chiefly the former. So the manual workers instinctively have formed organizations for their mutual self-protection and for the enlargement of their lives. And tho [sic] there is plenty of self-seeking and politics and imperfection in these unions, I find in them more real brotherliness and spirit of mutual service than I do in the church or any other organization.

For Gregg, these were unusually strong and assertive words, especially to a father who was a minister and whom he loved, despite their political differences. Responding further to his father's complaints, Gregg continued emphatically:

> You urge me to go into business or possibly engineering or some other activity. I have been in business, I have been in law, I have seen and talked with many kinds of men in many occupations and stations and with many modes of living in many different parts of the world. I have had wider experiences of men and the ways of the world than you have, Daddy, even though you have lived so long. And the way you and Mother brought us up made me able to discern different qualities and values, physical, moral, mental and spiritual, more closely perhaps than many other people.[105]

These tensions went beyond politics and their competing worldviews. Gregg's mother and father were also concerned that he had not yet married and wanted him to find a wife and settle down. Gregg rebuked his father in the letter for the demand that he marry and for not allowing him to wait for someone he loved or someone who loved him. In one of only a few comments he made on the issue of his personal relationships, Gregg made it clear that he adamantly refused to marry just for the sake of being married or having children. He wanted to marry for love. Obviously, at the end of that challenging year, critical issues were troubling and engaging Gregg, ones that would not go away.[106] He was disillusioned with the law, horrified by the impact of capitalism on workers and becoming increasingly alienated from church-based institutional religion.

During these changes and challenges in his life, he struggled to figure out his next steps. The encounter with the ideas and work of Gandhi had planted the seed. The job in the doctor's office, the readying of his small house in Northbrook for sale, the move to the small farm in Wisconsin were all preparations for the next stage in his life—even if that was not yet clear to him. Gregg saw around him the harmful effects of contemporary capitalism: pollution, commercialism, alienation— and he wanted no more part of it. He was thirty-nine, with few financial resources, no wife or partner, and limited prospects for a job or career that he could tolerate.

Looking for Answers on the Land

Wanting a way out of Chicago and needing to prepare for India by learning about farming and other manual skills, in Spring 1924 Gregg took a job on a tiny farm in the small town of Phillips, Wisconsin, about one one-hundred-and-fifty miles southeast of Duluth, Minnesota, classic farm country, far from any large city. Founded as a logging town, Phillips earned a mere speck on the map, home to fewer than two thousand souls. The seat of Price County, surrounded by fields, forest, and farmland, was a long way from a life lawyering and arbitrating in the buzzing core of Chicago. The simpler life, working with his hands, had become a serious goal. Gregg wanted to be a farmer.

Gregg got to the farm in mid-April. He worked there through the fall, looking after pigs and cows, and helping bring in the harvest. He recounts in a letter to his brother Alan an interaction with the farmer's wife that made him think more deeply about social hierarchy and class:

> Shortly after I came here the farmer's wife dropped a line that started a train of thought. When about to ask me to do something, she hesitated and then naively said, "It's much harder to order you to do things than it used to be with Pete" (their last year's hired man) which, being interpreted, was something like this as I heard it. She knows I was a Harvard graduate and an ex-lawyer and that neither she nor her hubby and friends had anything on me in way of education or experience with the world. The inferiority idea thereby being extracted from the employer-employee relationship left her feeling all lost and awkward. It made me realize how false the association of that idea and that relationship is. There is really no inferiority in being an employee or a servant. In reality the servant is often the superior because of being a source of more total energy (compare Christ saying, "He who would be greatest amongst you be the servant of all"). The fact of having an employee usually means either that the employer is too weak or incompetent to run a man's (or woman's) job alone; or that the employer has (knowingly) tackled a job too big for one person (in which case the employee is a helper and not thereby inferior). The matter of the division of labor (where one does more hand work) gives a false sense of superiority to the white-collar end.[107]

Gregg, cleaning out manure from a barn on the farm, dwelled on the issues that consumed him for the rest of his life: the value of farming and the production of wholesome food, the nature of inequality, the relationship of employee to employer, and the impact of capitalism and its divisions. In the same letter, he recommends a book to Alan that he might profitably read on his forthcoming trip to Italy: Franz Oppenheimer's *The State*.[108] The work was then widely read as a combative alternative to social contract theorists who saw the State as subservient to society. Oppenheimer would go on to promote collectivist alternatives to capitalist production, such as cooperative farms and versions of kibbutzim. He was a great admirer of the American social reformer Henry George whose book *Progress and Poverty* was hugely popular in the 1880s and helped provide economic arguments that fueled the Progressive Era.[109] Oppenheimer's ideas spurred Greg's thinking and were ones he would elaborate on in his later writing. Gregg was already reading and contemplating these alternative social and political ideas—especially those that integrated simple farming cooperatives with new forms of political organization. These are themes he would return to in his later work in India and in his life as an organic farmer.

Gregg spent most of the late spring and summer happily working the farm in Phillips. The honest, manual work was appealing, and he felt healthy and restored by being outside working the soil and tending to the animals. Those few months gave him the chance to breathe and to read. It was also a time for him to plan and think about studying with Gandhi. His mind was made up: Gandhi had much to teach him about conflict resolution and a better way to live in the world. In the fall of 1924 he left the farm to take further courses in agriculture at the University of Wisconsin in Madison.

The Letter Home

It is October 1924, frost sparkling on the morning grass. In Madison, students are in classes and professors at lecterns. Gregg has finished up at the farm near Phillips and moved to Madison to take courses in agriculture. It is a Saturday, and Gregg has completed the couple of courses in agriculture he took at the university. He has taken a class or two on Swedish massage, thinking it was a way to get a skill that pays. But Gregg has no job and no career. As the semester gathers speed and students settle in for a weekend free of classes, Richard Gregg, almost forty, sits at his typewriter. But this is not a term paper or an exam he's writing: it's a letter. A letter to his family. Long and complicated and heartfelt. He has been thinking about it for months, considering what to say and how to say it.

He sits and thinks about his life so far. He has grown up in a close and supportive family, where all the children were afforded the education and opportunity to enter professional careers. And Richard has also gone that route, training as a lawyer and practicing law in Boston and Chicago. He has taught. He has tangled with labor law, labor negotiations, arbitration, and conflict resolution. Indeed, Gregg has seen and done a lot, and, by any standard, his life was full and rewarding. In the America of the Twenties, he could look back and say life has been kind to him. So, what troubled him? Why agonize over his life and his times? Why write a letter to the family about the state of his world and his life? Why now?

By the time Gregg finished, the letter stretched over six pages of dense single-spaced argument. Clear, structured, and full of self-reflection, the letter reads like a critique *and* a manifesto. It is an elegant and thoughtful statement. It must have been hard for his family to read and, perhaps, impossible for them to respond. The letter gives a unique insight into both the man and his motivations. The words he wrote that day captured much of who Richard Gregg was and what he would become. The fact that he composed such a letter to his family suggests the closeness and responsibility he felt towards them. Yes, it was a justification for the actions he was about to take, but it was also very much a statement about how he had processed his whole life experience up until that crucial moment. He wanted to share this with his family.

It explains why a middle-aged man, already committed to justice, was to embark on a journey that would radically change his life and lead him to become a significant figure in twentieth-century pacifist thought. At the start of the letter, he remarks: "I am going to continue farming and do some community work and try, if possible, to spread a few of my ideas by writing articles or perhaps a little teaching. For the place to settle in I have decided on India, not as a missionary, but with an entirely different attitude and purpose, as you will see...." Gregg recognized that this was more than just about the direction he wanted his life to take. He knew then that what today we called a "holistic" experience was for him a matter of integrating work, thinking, and firmly held spiritual, moral, and political beliefs. In the letter, he tells his family that he wants to "Choose a job that is in harmony with your most important beliefs and convictions; one that will give you a distinctive sense of being useful to other people; one that is healthy and one that you can continue into old age. For a place, go where the institutions, customs, habits, beliefs, and feeling-tones of the people coincide with those that you care for or want to acquire. Life in such a community makes real freedom of opinion, discussion possible and permits you to be much more serviceable than you could be otherwise."[110] Perhaps having moved a lot and being still unmarried led him to stress this need for community; perhaps, too, there was loneliness and more than a little despair in the frosty air of Madison as he wrote. More likely, for Gregg was not a man to make snap judgments, these concerns grew from his reading and reflection, and the unique experiences in labor relations he had encountered. And there was always the drive to see and do more:

> I want to live an interesting life with some real risks and adventure and pioneering in it. I want to live very simply and as naturally as possible. I want to have a job much bigger than myself, which I can thoroughly believe in and into which I can throw myself without any reservations. I believe in and want

to live my religion and I want to be with people to whom religion is a living reality and not convention or Sunday formality.[111]

This last comment may have been his critique not only of organized religion in general but also of the customs of his father and what he stood for. Gregg speaks of the desire to "live naturally." Much later, after his time in India, this search for natural living would constitute the goal of the last third of his life.

Gregg wrote that, during the past ten years, in his professional legal experience acting as a liaison between industry, government, and labor, he had worked in at least a dozen positions across twenty industries. Gregg, the reader, had mined much of the classic and contemporary literature that spoke to his concerns. As he said in the letter:

> All that time I was reading all I could lay my hands on, piling up and comparing facts and opinions of every shade and kind, and thinking all the while. It is an experience that not so very many men have had. It makes a fairly intricate mixture, together with my previous and subsequent work. The resulting feelings and beliefs may be warped or prejudiced, but that, doesn't bother me, for as William James says: "Anyone who pretends to be neutral writes himself down here as a fool and a sham." My ideas may be mistaken, but they are not based on a wholly inadequate foundation. To show you another part of the foundation, I'll add to this letter a list some of the books that have influenced me most.

Perhaps the strongest statement he makes in the letter from Wisconsin is this:

> I am opposed to our government and to most existing governments. Government is founded on and exists by violence . . . . its legislators, judges and administrators are frequently corrupt and usually stupid and ignorant of the real meaning of their problems and results of their actions . . . . I am against machine industry and commercialism . . . . I'm against newspapers, movies, phonographs and radio, and the increasing passivity and standardization of knowledge, thought and feeling they create. I'm against war . . . . I don't believe in the germ causation theory of disease . . . . I'm opposed to capitalism and banking credit control of industry. I think most American food and cooking are the causes of tremendous physical deterioration . . . . And, by the

way, I am not a socialist or communist . . . . though both these doctrines have been mighty useful in making all sorts of people think deeper . . . . Trade unions accomplish little for they simply work within the existing order, not attempting to change it but merely to get a fairer division of the profits.

With a final, dramatic, flourish, he concludes, "You see these beliefs don't fit into modern America. They don't fit at all into any place, but I think more of them fit into India than into any other country.[112]

Gregg tells his family that he intends to leave for India very soon. He is direct and emphatic, yet, as the letter unfolds, he writes of his self-doubt and contradictions ("I'm not especially articulate.") and he admits he can ". . . work and act out my beliefs better than I can talk about them." He describes both the difficulties and opportunities he believes exist in India while writing glowingly of the value of the simplicity of life there. At the same time, he acknowledges the immense suffering arising from its colonial status, poverty, and inequality. Gregg finishes his letter with a confirmation of his love for his family and his plans to see most of them before he leaves, in Chicago, New York, or Boston. In these closely spaced pages, he barely mentions Gandhi.

While Gregg spent nearly a year debating whether farming would become his permanent occupation, his heart was now set on India. He told his family that he would shortly move back to Chicago and to send any letters care-of his friend Leland Olds, whom he would stay with briefly. In that letter, Gregg listed the books and authors that had the most significant impact on his thinking. Among those he mentioned are (and it is an eclectic list): Sidney and Beatrice Webb, Gandhi, Tolstoy, Veblen, the Bible and Bhagavad-Gita, Thoreau, Bertrand Russell, Franz Oppenheimer, J.A. Hobson, and William James. Gregg was a voracious reader, a habit he would continue throughout his life. In a handwritten note at the top of the letter, he asks his mother to be sure that the letter circulates to all family members. It remains a most elegant statement of why he chose to go to India and how he saw the rest of his life.

By the fall of 1924, Gregg had penned and mailed a letter to Gandhi explaining his desire to go to India to meet him and gain a deeper understanding of his philosophy and ideas. There was no reply from Gandhi, but Charles Freer Andrews, Gandhi's friend, and English missionary, did respond. Gandhi was in jail at the time, arrested and accused by the British of sedition in 1922, a charge based on the articles he authored in *Young India* and for inciting an uprising against the British Raj, the direct rule of Indians that Britain had imposed since 1858.

The charges followed from the British colonial administration's concern about Gandhi's increasingly effective role in the growing independence movement and his "non-cooperation" campaign launched in 1920. The campaign set out to create and establish self-rule of India.[113] One central goal was to have Indians stop buying cloth made and manufactured by the British in the textile mills of England. Gandhi saw the importation of such cloth as the key vehicle for maintaining India's dependence on Britain.

The campaign also called for a refusal to participate in the British "educational, legal, and representative institutions [as well as] a symbolic refusal... to participate in colonial system of rewards and honors."[114] Gandhi also urged Indians to engage in *ahimsa* or direct action and civil disobedience through nonviolent action. After November 1921, one hundred-and-eighty-eight Indian cloth merchants signed a three-part pledge in which they promised to sell *khaddar** or *khadi* (home-spun rather than machine-made cloth). Thousands pledged to practice nonviolent civil disobedience and reject

*Khadi or khaddar is the term conventionally used in North and Central India to refer to varieties of coarse cotton cloth hand woven using hand-spun yarn. This was the cloth commonly worn by peasant and artisan groups in pre-industrial India. It was made from locally grown cotton which would be harvested by peasants and laborers, spun by local women, and woven into cloth by men from various specialist weaving castes. Although hand-spun, hand-woven cotton cloth of this kind was common throughout India, it was not until the early twentieth century, when its production and use were in severe decline, that the term "khadi" entered nationalist vocabulary and the cloth became a key visual symbol of India's struggle from colonial rule. See: Tarlo, Emma, Ferguson Centre for African and Asian Studies, the Open University.

untouchability. The pledge asked that signers wear *khaddar*, oppose untouchability,[115] and uphold religious unity in a multi-religious society.[116] By the end of 1921 thousands of volunteers across the country were engaged in regular acts of civil disobedience.

In early 1922 the independence campaign came to a halt in the Indian city of Chauri Chaura. A procession of some three thousand peasants marched to the local market and on to the local police station to protest price gouging by merchants and the recent arrest of one of their leaders. In the confusion police fired warning shots into the air and the crowd turned on the police, eventually burning down the local police station, killing twenty-two officers. Gandhi called for an immediate halt to the noncooperation campaign and said of the event:

> God has been abundantly kind to me. He has warned me . . . that there is not yet in India that truthful and nonviolent atmosphere which and which alone can justify mass disobedience which can be described as civil which means gentle, humble, knowing, willful, yet loving, never criminal and hateful.[117]

Within a month British authorities arrested Gandhi for inciting violence against the Raj.[118] During his trial Gandhi pleaded guilty and requested he be sentenced to the harshest sentence. The judge obliged and gave him six years.[119] He was released two years later, as he had appendicitis and required an emergency appendectomy.[120]

After his release and while Gregg was with him, Gandhi refocused the campaign for independence away from civil disobedience and mass direct action to what he termed the "constructive program." The program meant "increased power from within through the development of personal identity, self-reliance, and fearlessness," for the individual and, "for the community, it meant the creation of a new set of political, social, and economic relations."[121] It placed emphasis on social justice and economic self-reliance rather than simply self-rule, especially the production of *khadi*, village education, the elimination of class differences and antagonisms, and the removal of the practice of "untouchability."

Gandhi wanted to stress that the production of *khadi* would encourage organization, self-discipline, and break down the class barriers which had hindered true nonviolent protest. He described it as the "symbol of unity of Indian humanity, of its economic freedom and equality." Gandhi envisioned education for village children, particularly in agriculture and science, which would "develop both the body and mind, and keep the child rooted to the soil."[122] This set of ideas took shape just before Gregg's arrival in India. In a fortuitous moment, Gregg's letter to Gandhi arrived detailing the kind of experience and skills that became of great use in Gandhi's new quest, and Gandhi later enlisted Gregg to help him understand and document the promotion of *khadi*.

When Gregg's letter arrived, Gandhi sat in prison for the Chauri Chaura incident. His campaign for Indian Independence had just begun to recover from that historic low. Despite Gandhi's incarceration, Andrews invited Gregg to come to Gandhi's ashram (the Indian term for a religious retreat or meditation center and community), knowing that Gandhi's release was imminent. Once Gregg had the invitation, he headed east, first to Chicago and then for a round of family visits in New York, Boston, and New Hampshire before he embarked on his new life. On January 1, 1925, Richard Bartlett Gregg left New York Harbor for India and for the experiences that would change his life and influence the lives of many.

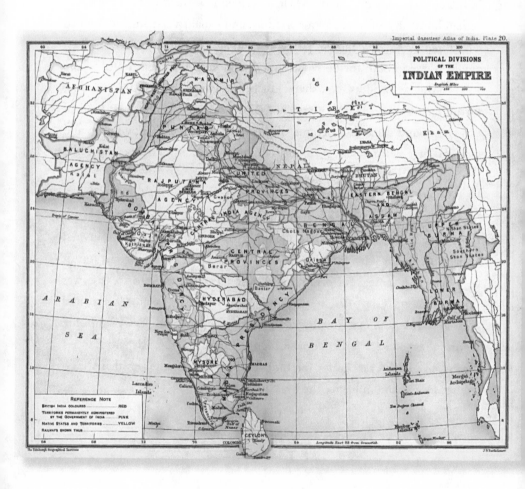

CHAPTER FIVE

India

If there is one place on the face of earth where all the dreams of living men have found a home from the very earliest days when man began the dream of existence, it is India.
—Romain Rolland

To India

HAVING SAID HIS GOODBYES to family and friends in Boston, Gregg set off from the port of New York on a cold, blustery morning in early January 1925. His brother Don came to see him off and stood on the dock, believing, as did Gregg, that they might not see each other for a very long time. Gregg was pleased to have his brother waving goodbye but, in his fashion, he wrote to his sister Elinor on the first day after leaving New York that he was deeply concerned about Don's health. As they waved their farewells, Gregg saw his brother as a man with some potentially severe health issues. He thought that Don looked unhealthy and pleaded with Elinor to take care of him and to ensure that Don paid attention to his diet and got more exercise. On food and health, he was always something of a nag.[123] Indeed, if Gregg had any concern about his trip, it was about leaving his siblings.

The voyage to India took about six weeks, plenty of time for him to think and read and prepare. As was his custom, he had a suitcase full of books to keep him company. But this was also a chance to visit Europe, and Gregg used the trip as an opportunity to stay with his brother Alan who was then stationed in Paris working for the Rockefeller Foundation. Gregg stopped off in the City of Lights for a few days to be with Alan and his wife, Eleanor, and then traveled on to Napoli and Genoa, Italy.

The long leg of the journey was from Genoa to Bombay. Gregg settled in for three weeks at sea and spent time on the boat talking to people and, of course, reading. He wrote to Alan from the *S.S. Genoa* that he was deep into Bertram Russell's *ABC of Atoms* and some of the science behind quantum theory in Eddington's *Space, Time, and Gravitation*, leading him to a long discourse in the letter about how reality is "framed" and how the new science of quantum physics made him reflect on alternative realities.[124] He wondered about versions of reality formed from experience and culture and how they affected encounters between people, especially when those encounters held the possibility of violence. His interests were increasingly eclectic.

As always, he wrote to his mother frequently. In a letter he sent before he reached Genoa, he told her of his excitement and anticipation about getting to India. He also let her know that he had done some soul searching, especially about his father, and how sad he was that politics had created a bit of a rift between them. Gregg told his mother that, while he had tried to explain to his father what he was doing in Chicago and what working with unions meant to him, he never felt he was able to convince him of the value of unions. With his father dead, he regretted the fight and told his mother that the man she had married was always good, kind, and "wholly unselfish." As always, Gregg tried to make peace.[125]

At the age of forty, he was embarking on an adventure that would change many of his assumptions about the world and would reinforce others. A seasoned traveler, but apprehensive about the trip, he knew he would see India in a different way than on his visit with his brother-in-law more than a decade earlier. He had planned this move for a year. He was eager to meet Gandhi, travel across the land, and learn more about the practical and spiritual elements of Gandhian philosophy. He was going not as a tourist but, he thought, as an immigrant. Gregg felt confident that this would heal his wounds of the past decades and give him the experience and knowledge he craved. He didn't know, but may have wished, that he would be tied to India for the rest of his life.

After over a month the boat docked at what was then Bombay (now Mumbai) at the beginning of February 1925. Bombay was the busiest port city in India and home to the Indian National Congress, which was founded there in 1885. Long the center of Indian textile manufacturing, the city was home to the first university in India. The first railway line in India was established in Bombay in 1853, and Bombay built the first electric railway the year that Gregg arrived. In the early part of the century Bombay was a thriving city and port, home to one-and-a-quarter million people, alive with commerce and traffic, and very cosmopolitan.[126]

Gregg had the chance to spend a few days in this vibrant port city, getting the lay of the land, picking up his belongings, and exploring. He then traveled to Ahmedabad—a journey of a day or so by train. He was met at the station by Gandhi's friend and colleague, Charles Freer Andrews, always known as Charlie. Andrews was bearded and angular, and Gandhi affectionately called him Christ's Faithful Apostle—CFA from his initials. He had answered Gregg's letter to Gandhi and encouraged him to visit. Their first meeting marked the beginning of a long friendship.

Andrews was a significant figure in the struggle for Indian independence. A priest in the Church of England and a Christian missionary, he had met and worked with Gandhi in South Africa, where Gandhi organized against the racism and exclusion of Indians living and working there. In England, Andrews was recognized as a new breed of Christian socialist, combining the teachings of the church with the new ideas of the socialist movement in Britain and the programs proposed by the growing Labour Party. In 1904,

Andrews went to India and spent four years teaching at Saint Stephen's College in Delhi as a missionary with the Society for the Propagation of the Gospel.[127] He grew appalled at the presumed racial superiority of the British and by the indenture system imposed on Indians in South Africa and elsewhere. He renounced his role as an Anglican priest in 1914.

Andrews went to South Africa to help with the treatment of Indians and met Gandhi that same year. He was instrumental in convincing Gandhi to return to India with him in 1915. Andrews went on to be a significant force in fighting for the rights of India's poor. He traveled widely in India and throughout the world, lecturing and writing. He authored numerous books and articles and maintained a lifelong friendship with both Gandhi and the Indian mystic and poet Rabindranath Tagore, whom he had met in England in 1912 and joined at his school in Santiniketan in 1915.[128] Tagore would later call him *sadhu*, meaning monk and friend of the poor. Andrews condemned the treatment of Indians by the British and supported the Indian National Congress Party. He was one of Gandhi's dearest western friends and he once said of him. "I do not own on this earth a closer friend."[129]

Gregg and Andrews shared somewhat similar backgrounds: Andrews's father was a bishop of the Catholic Apostolic Church in Birmingham, England. Andrews became enamored, as did Gregg, with India, and with Gandhi. Both Gregg and Andrews struggled with their religious and spiritual beliefs as they encountered the inequality and injustice of the capitalist systems in the United States and England. For Andrews, his critique of the western powers found form in his work against the British Raj and his engagement with the Indian independence movement and the Indian National Congress. He worked tirelessly through the 1920s and '30s, advocating for Indian independence and the plight of Indians resident in Fiji, British Guiana, and Kenya.

This was the man who greeted Gregg at the train from Bombay. After brief introductions, Andrews led him a little way out of central Ahmedabad and across the Sabarmati River to Gandhi's ashram. It was a beautiful spot, built on the banks of the river and covering about fifty acres, sitting between a jail and a crematorium. Gandhi once said of the site: "This is the right place for our activities to carry on the search for truth and develop fearlessness, for on one side are the iron bolts of the foreigners, and on the other the thunderbolts of Mother Nature."[130] The idea of an ashram was a core part of Gandhi's vision, nurtured in the struggles in South Africa, the creation of the Phoenix Settlement, and modelled on Tolstoy's concepts of communal living. Having returned to India, and eager to build upon the work in South Africa, Gandhi joined others from the Phoenix Settlement now at Tagore's School in Shantiniketan. Seeking better accommodations and a permanent location, Gandhi and his followers settled on Ahmedabad, establishing the ashram on May 25, 1915.[131]

By the time Gregg arrived, the ashram was already a working farm, a retreat center, and a destination for the many visitors who wished to learn from Gandhi. Built on the Sabarmati road, the ashram featured schools on the left side and orchards on the right.[132] Gandhi had selected these fifty acres of land because it could support orchards, as well as cattle and agricultural plots. Nearby sat a temple to Deadheechi, a saint known for his self-sacrifice.[133] Standing on the west side of the ashram, across the Sabarmati River, the cotton mills of Ahmedabad were clearly visible.

At the Ashram

The ashram had about one hundred-and-twenty people in residence—many of them students doing work with the peasants, others being teachers and their families, and some, visitors like Gregg. There were few buildings: a cottage that Gandhi lived in; dormitory-like buildings for visitors (Gregg lived in one of these for a few months); and small cottages for other residents and teachers. There was a library, a dairy, a small school, and sheds for spinning and weaving. Through all this, the Sabarmati river ran north to south, broad, and wide in the rainy season.

It was reduced to a shallow stream when the rains ended. Water for cleaning came from the river, and residents washed themselves and their clothes at the same time, as was the custom. Drinking water came from a big well not far from the river's edge, collected for personal use in large earthenware pots.[134]

The ashram was founded as a place "to learn how to serve the motherland," where individuals learned how to "live as equals and without fear."[135] Those living at the ashram could not accumulate material possessions, had to grow their own food, make their own clothes, build their own homes, and run their own schools.[136] Also, everyone had to take part in chores such as latrine cleaning and kitchen duty.[137] Most importantly, however, the ashram required that members practice *swadeshi,* or learn to hand-spin cloth.[138] But surrounding this was the profound belief of *satyagraha** and the role the ashram played as a retreat. In this, Gandhi followed Henry David Thoreau. Walden Pond was a retreat to refresh the soul, as was the ashram. But the ashram was also about mutuality and community and living in harmony with nature.

When Gregg got to the ashram, Andrews introduced him to people working there and showed him to the small room in the dormitory that was

---

*"Truth (Satya) implies love, and firmness (agrapha) engenders and therefore serves as a synonym for force. I thus began to call the Indian movement Satyagraha, that is to say, the Force which is born of Truth and Love or nonviolence, and gave up the use of the phrase 'passive resistance', in connection with it, so much so that even in English writing we often avoided it and used instead the word 'satyagraha' itself or some other equivalent English phrase." M.K. Gandhi, *Satyagraha in South Africa,* Navajivan, Ahmedabad, 1111, 109-10. Or, more broadly: "Satyagraha or nonviolent resistance, as conceived by Gandhiji, has an important lesson for pacifists and war-resisters of the West. Gandhiji showed that nonviolence to be effective requires constructive effort in every sphere of life, individual, social, economic, and political. These spheres have to be organised and refashioned in such a way that the people will have learnt to be nonviolent in their daily lives, manage their affairs on a cooperative and nonviolent basis, and thus have acquired sufficient strength and resourcefulness to be able to offer nonviolent resistance against organised violence. The practice of nonviolence in the political sphere is not, therefore, a mere matter of preaching or even of establishing arbitration courts or the League of Nations, but involves building up brick by brick with patience and industry a new nonviolent social and economic order. It depends ultimately on banishing violence from the heart of the individual and making of him a transformed disciplined person. Gandhiji's contribution lay in evolving the necessary technique and showing by example how *all* this can be done." Bharatan Kumarappa, Editor's note, M.K. Gandhi, *Non-Violent Resistance (Satyagraha),* New York: Schocken Books, 1961 [1951].

to become his home for the next few weeks. He had a cot made of ropes and a thin mattress; there were no chairs. A shared toilet was behind the communal room in the dormitory, but Gregg did have a verandah that looked north across the ashram, and this was the place where he would sit in the evenings, writing letters home and filling his notebooks. Gregg learned to sit cross-legged on the floor though it took a while for his legs to get used to the position and then getting back up.[139]

When he had settled himself into these modest accommodations, one of the first people he met was Gandhi's nephew (and then heir apparent), Maganlal Gandhi, a sweet and kind young man and the competent manager of the ashram. Maganlal always had time for visitors and he took to the serious and erudite American. While Gandhi usually called Maganlal his nephew, he was the older son of Gandhi's cousin Kushalbhlai Gandhi (himself the orphaned son of Gandhi's father's sister, who was raised by Gandhi's parents as one of Gandhi's elder brothers).[140] Maganlal had joined Gandhi in South Africa and later looked after Gandhi's Phoenix Settlement there. Some claim that Maganlal could be said to have invented *satyagraha* at that time and that he essentially created Gandhi's ashram at Sabarmati and managed it.[141] This may be an overstatement, but there is no question that Maganlal was at the core of the day-to-day running of the ashram and very close to Gandhi.

In addition to being the heart of the ashram, Maganlal was a very able mechanic. It was he who taught many of the ashram's residents how to spin cotton and fix things; he also dedicated himself to the exhausting manual labor at the ashram. His mechanical abilities mirrored Gregg's own, as both were good at thinking about solutions to problems confronting everyday existence: how to improve the latrines, how to ensure access to clean water, and the many common but critically essential challenges of running a farm and a retreat. It was no wonder that Gregg and Maganlal became firm friends.

Gregg spent the first couple of days resting and settling himself at the ashram, getting to know the layout and the customs, and talking with Maganlal. Gandhi arrived a few days after Gregg (having been released from prison) and came immediately to meet his new American guest.[142] Meeting Gandhi face-to-face was a wonderful moment for Gregg, and seeing the gaunt and willowy figure for the first time was something that he never forgot. Despite his diminutive size and being in his mid-fifties, Gandhi was fit and robust and a great and dedicated walker. His slightness was deceiving—his chest was very deep from front to back, giving him tremendous endurance. He usually only slept four hours per night and was notorious for taking long and exhausting (for his companions) walks. He was bald with beautiful brown skin and, Gregg thought, sad eyes.[143]

As was Gandhi's custom, he asked Gregg to walk with him in the evening air and to talk as they strolled (Gandhi was educated in England and fluent in English). It was an opportunity for Gregg to explain himself, and he did so at length. He told Gandhi of his background and experience and that he thought, passionately, that western civilization was on the wrong track. He made it clear that he had come to India to learn from Gandhi and was committing himself to Indian ways. At first, Gregg was intimidated to be in the presence of his hero, but Gandhi was patient. Gregg noted much later, "Knowing what I did about his ideas and what I had done, I felt at first awed by his presence, but he listened attentively and made me feel entirely at ease."[144] Impressed by the quiet and serious American, Gandhi immediately accepted Gregg as his student. And so began one of the most remarkable relationships of the early twentieth century: a forty-year-old former labor arbitrator and lawyer became one of the very first Americans to study and become friends with Mohandas Gandhi.

After his initial talks with Gandhi, Gregg plunged into the work and life of the ashram. As he described it, daily life began with a series of customs, arising before the sun at 4 a.m., and going with the rest of the ashram's students, mostly Indian social workers, to a prayer ground. Usually, Gandhi, along with a musician, sat at the front of the room facing the students, who sat in rows. Only one lantern, positioned next to Gandhi, burned in the dawn. Together, the students and Gandhi recited prayers in Gandhi's native Hindi. Gregg's first prayer on his first day came from Chapter II of the Bhagavad Gita, the central text of Hinduism. While Gregg remained a devout Christian all his life, after six months in India he noted that he was convinced of the "validity of Hindu spiritual experience and insight."[145] As daylight broke the prayers ended, and students dispersed to their daily tasks. Gregg returned to his room where he sat in the window, facing the early morning sun, to practice using the spinning wheel.[146]

The place was a hive of activity; Gregg did not see Gandhi every day by any means, but his close and blossoming friendship with Maganlal proved a precious substitute. It was Maganlal who got Gregg his first spinning wheel and taught him to spin and weave. He also introduced Gregg to the many customs of India and began teaching him the rudiments of Hindi. Gregg learned how to spin, sitting by Maganlal's side, and observing him. The two new friends spent much time together during Gregg's initial few weeks, both engaged in the day-to-day tasks of life on the ashram, much of it involving cleaning, cooking, and, of course, spinning. Working like this with Maganlal felt to Gregg like coming full circle, enabling him to integrate his beliefs in the physical and intellectual benefits of manual work with the spiritual and educational environment for which he longed. He got to know Maganlal, "better than anyone else in the ashram."[147] In Gandhi, too, he found someone who believed that manual work and the simple activities of day-to-day living were critical to a life well-lived. He was impressed by Gandhi's embrace of the most mundane chores. Gandhi was always willing to do simple tasks, peel vegetables, and clean the latrines. Years later, Gregg remarked, "... during WWII, I used to sometimes smile to myself at the contrast between Gandhi and two other great leaders of their peoples, F. D. Roosevelt, and Winston Churchill. One could not imagine either of them peeling vegetables in the kitchen as examples to their people of the value of manual work."[148]

Within a few days, under Maganlal's careful guidance, Gregg slowly began to master the spinning wheel and the elements of *khaddar*. It took Gregg a while to become adept. Still, he quickly appreciated that spinning was more than the creation of *khaddar*, the homespun fabric for Indian clothing. It was the essence of Gandhi's conception of how resistance to British imperialism and Indian self-sufficiency could develop. Soon Gregg would understand and write about the whole *khaddar* movement. For now, he tried to figure out how to operate the *charka* (spinning wheel). In all of this, Maganlal would be his guide and mentor.

Gregg spent his first months in India at the ashram. A lot of that time, he was with the handsome and delightful Maganlal (who spoke excellent English). Their friendship quickly led them to collaborate on writing a short manual on home spinning using the simple hand spindle, which could be made and used by the very poor. The little instruction book, co-authored by Gregg and Maganlal Gandhi and printed as *The Takli Teacher*, was Gregg's first publication in India. *Takli* is an ancient and straightforward system of spinning; it does not require the larger spinning frame (the *charkha*), just a small rod and a source of raw cotton. It has been used for generations to create fine thread. Very much at one with the beliefs and philosophy that Gregg had been developing, the booklet taught users how to create a homespun cloth that could be used by anyone, even those without a good command of the language, practical skills, or formal education. The manual was completed and published in March 1926, less than a year after Gregg had first arrived at the ashram. Gandhi said of it, "I hope that every *takli* teacher in municipal and national schools where *takli* has been introduced will procure the book for his own guidance and that of his pupils."[149]

Within those first six months of his arrival Gregg began to lay out his goals in India. Above all Gregg wanted to learn about Gandhi's method of nonviolence and the philosophy that underpinned it. At the same time Gregg felt he had something he could give to India. He hoped, particularly with his writing, to "help destroy the glamour of the West in the minds of Indians."[150] He hoped to teach Indian children and prepare them to "meet and conquer western culture."[151] Importantly, Gregg imagined himself as a cultural liaison, someone who could go between East and West to synthesize the best of both.[152]

For Gregg, the experience of this simple life and the deep spiritual beliefs he encountered at the ashram were a reassuring contrast after the labor strife and difficulties he had experienced back home. His friendship with Maganlal taught him much, and when Maganlal succumbed to typhoid in April 1928, it was a terrible loss for Gregg and an even greater one for Gandhi. Indeed, Gandhi was profoundly and tragically affected by losing his most devoted follower, stretching back to South Africa in 1903. Gandhi wrote of his death: "He whom I had singled out as heir to my all is no more… He was my hands, my feet and my eyes. The world knows so little of how much my so-called greatness depends upon the incessant toil and drudgery of silent, devoted, able and pure workers, men as well as women. And among them all Maganlal was to me the greatest, the best and the purest." Gandhi went on to say: "… And but for a living faith in God, I should become a raving maniac for the loss of one who was dearer to me than my own sons, who never once deceived me or failed me, who was a personification of industry, who was the watchdog of the ashram in all its aspects—material, moral and spiritual."[153] Nevertheless, this was later. For now, it was Maganlal who became Gregg's most important contact in India and to Gandhi's work.

Khaddar

While Gandhi mostly mentored Gregg, it was not long before the roles were somewhat reversed, and Gandhi recognized that his new friend had a considerable amount of experience in American industry and was well acquainted with research and assessment of work and work activities. Gregg was, after all, a researcher, arbitrator, and evaluator. After a couple of months at the ashram, Gandhi asked Gregg to go to the province of Bihar to observe the spinning programs in the villages there. The trip would not only help Gregg to understand the spinning program in action and serve as part of his education in the workings of *khaddar*, but it would allow Gregg to assess the efficacy of the program for Gandhi.

Bihar was a study trip for Gregg, and he happily set out to understand *khaddar*. However, this was an arduous journey, some one thousand miles across India by train. Such travel rarely daunted Gregg. He had crisscrossed the U.S. in his job as a labor arbitrator and had undertaken extensive sea journeys in prior visits to Europe and India, so Gregg set off with enthusiasm and anticipation, once again using the extensive rail network that covered India, courtesy of the British. To get to Bihar comfortably, Gregg broke the journey with an overnight stay at the home of Jawaharlal Nehru in Patna. Patna sits on the banks of the Ganges, one of the oldest cities in the world. By the time Gregg got there it was a local hub of the British Raj and a seedbed for the Independence movement; the thirty-six-year-old Nehru was already a key figure in the movement and one of Gandhi's most notable protégés. The highly educated Nehru (he grew up in a very privileged environment, went to the very selective Harrow public school in England, and studied law in London) would soon become president of the Indian National Congress Party. He had the manners and carriage of his class, and Gregg found Nehru courteous but aloof. Gregg stayed with Nehru for one night. The second night in Patna Gregg spent at the home of Rajendra Prasad, who, in contrast, Gregg found to be a "… devoted follower of Gandhi and his program. He was gentle and modest, with a deep interest in the welfare of the peasants."[154]

Prasad would go on to become the first president of the newly independent India. These two central figures of the Indian independence movement were among Gregg's first contacts with influential Indians; they would be followed by many more.[155]

Gregg spent a week or so observing *khaddar* in the villages around Patna, taking notes, and talking in halting Hindi with the people there. He then set off three hundred miles southeast to visit the school at Santiniketan founded by Rabindranath Tagore, the great Indian writer, poet, musician, and polymath. While there, he became good friends with Kahitimohan Sen, who traveled throughout India, recording the poems and sayings of the medieval mystic Kabir (these were translated and published by Tagore as *Songs of Kabir*.). This visit to Santiniketan was his first encounter with the poet. By then, Tagore was already a legend and, in his '60s, extremely active as a teacher and writer.

Tagore was very close to both Andrews and Gandhi. Born in 1861, the son of the religious reformer Debendranath Tagore and leader of Brahmo Samaj (Society of God). Despite his social and economic advantages, Tagore, the youngest of fourteen children, had a difficult childhood (his mother had died when he was quite young, and his father traveled widely and was not often home.) He did not last long in any of the several schools in England he attended and consequently received little formal traditional education.[156] In 1880 he returned to India and married Mrinalini Devi with whom he had three daughters and two sons.[157] His father had hoped he would go into law, but he never completed his degree at University College in London. Despite, or because of this, his father sought to engage him in more practical activities, asking him to return to India and manage his extensive estates in eastern Bengal. While there, Tagore established an ashram at Santiniketan in 1901. Seeking to develop progressive and innovative education for Indians, in 1907 he founded a school firmly based on the "guru to mentee" model derived from ancient Indian spiritual teaching relationships.

Deeply involved politically, Tagore had been part of the Indian nationalist movement, but he withdrew in 1907 to focus on his school, always short of money. The search for financial support eventually required him to make several fund-raising and lecture trips to the United States, Great Britain, and Europe. These very successful endeavors established him as an ambassador to the West—a role he found much easier to fill after he won the 1913 Nobel Prize for Literature.[158] Like Gregg, Tagore became one of the intellectual bridges between East and West and traveled across continents visiting more than thirty countries in as many years, arguing against nationalism, but for Indian independence, and seeking funding for his school. Later, Gregg got to know Tagore well through his repeated visits to the school and their many conversations. They remained correspondents until Tagore's death in 1941.[159]

While he was at Santiniketan, Gregg also met G. Ramachandran, the social reformer and teacher who had studied with Andrews, Ramachandran's lifelong friend. A significant supporter of Gandhi, Ramachandran founded the *Gandhigram* at Madurai in 1956, a rural college based on Gandhian principles. He played an essential role in the fight for Indian independence throughout the 1940s, and in 1959 invited Martin Luther King, Jr. to India. Much later, Gregg returned to teach at the school that Ramachandran had founded. They remained steadfast friends.

On this first trip across India, Gregg met some of the key players in the Indian independence movement and educated himself about the country. He was achieving his goal of getting to know India, and readily embraced as much of the culture as he could. He met Indians in their villages, wore native clothing, and ate local food. At the end of April, he traveled north, going deeper into the subcontinent.

Stokes's School at Kotgarh

After spending time in the villages and at Tagore's school, Gregg traveled to the small village of Kotgarh, fifty miles north of Simla (the former summer seat of the British Raj, now known as Shimla). Set in the foothills of the Himalayas over six thousand feet above sea level in a beautiful valley, Kotgarh overlooks the Satluj River and snow-clad sub-Himalayan Range. The village offers a marvelous panorama of the range with breathtaking views of the slopes of the Himalayas. Its wonderfully cool climate and stunning location Gregg found refreshing and calming, and, mercifully, free of mosquitos. He traveled there to visit another school, this one founded by Samuel Evans Stokes. The school buildings looked out on those snowy mountains that separated India from Tibet.

Gregg was impressed with Stokes, yet another critically important figure in the Indian independence movement. Stokes (who adopted the name *Satyanand*) was the son of a wealthy American family (his father, a Quaker, owned a company that manufactured elevators). He came to India initially to work at a leper colony at Subathu, a village in the state of Himachal Pradesh. After a brief period as part of an Order of Franciscan Friars dedicated to frugality and poverty (where C.F. Andrews joined him), Stokes renounced the Order and married a local Indian woman. He bought land close to his new wife's village and, in 1916, began growing apples (he introduced the American Red Delicious variety to India). The village stands amidst acres of apple orchards, which today are the source of nearly all domestic apple production. Significantly, Stokes was also the only non-Indian to sign the manifesto of the National Congress Party (1921) and the only American to be arrested by the British government for acts of sedition. He converted to Hinduism in 1932.[160] Stokes was the only American to become a member of the All India Congress Committee of the Indian National Congress.

Stokes's journey to India was not unlike Gregg's. He came in 1904, and it was unclear where the trip would finally take him. Stokes was twenty-two when he first set foot in the country. He had been convinced to take on this trip by Marcus Bradford Carleton, who ran a leper colony at Sabhathu and whom he had met a few months earlier in Philadelphia, Pennsylvania. Carleton was full of missionary zeal, and his words, when Stokes heard him preach, inspired him to think about a life of service, and to do that in India. It also gave him an excuse not to take over his father's company, which he very much did not want to do.

Stokes started his school in 1924, not long before Gregg got there, to provide an education for his five children and those of local farmers and peasants. Stokes's children were being taught at home because he was dissatisfied with the education available in the local schools. Stokes believed that his children should have a complete Indian education, not built around Western ideas, such as those available at the boarding schools far from his farm and primarily based on the British system. He committed, therefore, to construct a school in the winter of 1923, and, by March 1924, he had his first building finished. Stokes founded the school because he believed the school years were the ones in which "the foundations of character, intelligence, and ability are laid." The children worked the orchards surrounding the school to pay their way, and Stokes created a curriculum designed to build their character because he believed that the purpose was to "to turn out men with ideas of their own, a developed personality and character, a clear conception of the world in which we live . . . a clear idea of the problems and needs of [their neighborhood] and a sense of responsibility to do their part in solving the immediate problems."[161] He did not want to rely on outside funding for the project or be beholden to the curriculum and rules of the Indian Education Board (then under the control and influence of the British), so he funded the work from his resources, which were not insignificant given his family's wealth. His primary school opened in April with a dozen children, including his first three sons.

By the time Gregg got to Kotgarh, there were nearly seventy students at the school, including a class for local girls. Stokes emphasized the education of girls (neglected at the time) and focused on necessary skills, including science and math, as he saw these as critical to the future development of India. By 1928 the school had some eighty children attending, nearly all of them from peasant families from around Kotgarh. As Asha Sharma, Stokes's granddaughter, noted: "To this school Stokes brought the best of both the East and the West—an emphasis on reading and independent thinking which had been so much a part of his education and the disciplines and values of the old Indian system for which he had great regard."[162] Stokes also emphasized play and sports and taught older students such skills as masonry and carpentry.

It was an educational model that Gregg admired, and which reflected many of Gregg's beliefs about what education should look like. He wrote to Stokes's mother:

> In your son's philosophy I see the promise, for myself anyhow, of a spiritual road along which I can travel with a renewed sense of security, serenity, and enthusiasm. Around his central ideas I think I will be able to group other ideas and conceptions and feelings which hitherto have been fragmentary, disconnected, inconsistent and puzzling. Also I can discard some parts of my thinking which were used as scaffolding, but are now in the way. Hence, as you can imagine, I am grateful to him.[163]

Stokes was immediately impressed by Gregg and offered him a job as a teacher. But Gregg was not prepared to move to the school at that point. There was still so much he wanted to do in India, not the least of which were the possibilities and lessons to be learned from his investigation of *khaddar*. A year later, however, he moved to Kotgarh, taking up Stokes's offer to work full time at the school. In the meantime, however, Stokes and Gregg got to know each other while Gregg spent the summer working and living with him at the school. It was then that Stokes asked Gregg to teach math and science—an experience that would result in one of Gregg's first publications, *A Preparation for Science*. All in all, Gregg delighted in the location and was impressed by Stokes and the work he was doing. The school embodied much of what Gregg had been thinking about and what he had come to value: gardens and vegetable growing, progressive education attuned to the intellectual and cultural needs of the children, and, mainly, Stokes's efforts to make sure young Indian girls got the benefits of decent schooling.

After a couple of months of living at Stokes's school, Gregg headed out on yet another lengthy journey. Leaving Kotgarh in the middle of July, he went to Allahabad (a British colonial administrative center, and, later, a center of the Indian revolutionary movement), about seven hundred miles south of Kotgarh, and then back to visit with his new friends in Patna. From there, Gregg spent a few days again at Tagore's school before traveling south to Calcutta (Kolkata). In Calcutta, he did some research at the Imperial Library for his work on *khaddar* and then headed back across the country to Bombay (Mumbai) and back to Ahmedabad and the ashram at Sabarmati at the beginning of September. All told, this is a journey of some three thousand miles by train: a formidable adventure even by modern standards, but especially impressive because Gregg insisted on traveling third class with poor Indians.

By this time, most of India had an extensive network of rail lines, especially along the corridor from Calcutta to Rawalpindi, making such a journey possible, if not always pleasant or comfortable. If there were any benefits to British imperialism, one might have been the creation of the India railway system that was built across all of India and was already extensive by the mid-nineteenth century. Gregg rode the rails across the entire country. He was adept at making new contacts and friends and finding places. On this first long journey he visited and met many people, most connected to or supportive of Gandhi and his movement.

Somewhere on this route (or just after he arrived back at the ashram),

Gregg contracted malaria. It was unclear, even to him, what ailed him at the time, but it put him out of commission for a couple of weeks, and complete recovery took a while, probably hastening his decision to move to the hills (back to Stokes's school) during the hot season the following year. After he had recovered a little, he spent a few weeks in October up at Mt. Abu, about seventy miles northwest of the ashram, where he worked on the booklet on spinning. Mt. Abu was a hill station and a popular destination for those fleeing the heat of the plains; it was not Kotgarh, but it was colder than Sabarmati and not infested with mosquitos. While recuperating, he wrote to his mother at least once a week, letting her know in chatty terms what he was doing, describing his living quarters, and asking for socks and subscriptions to the *Nation* and the *Christian Science Monitor*. Gregg excitedly told her how much he had learned from the Bhagavad Gita and recommended that she read it. In late November he told her that Gandhi had visited his cottage that morning and brought Gregg some flowers.[164]

Back at the ashram in November 1925, Gregg met Madeline Slade (who had just arrived), the daughter of a British admiral, whom Gandhi called Mirabehn (or Mira). Slade came to India to study with Gandhi and ended up staying for some thirty-four years. She became a colleague and friend to Gandhi and was a ubiquitous presence at the ashram. Not unlike Gregg, she had discovered Gandhi through reading—only, in this case, it was via the biography of Gandhi written by Nobel Prize-winning author Romain Rolland. Slade had met Rolland through his writing on Beethoven, about whom she was deeply passionate. Rolland was a lifelong pacifist, novelist, and playwright. The story of Gandhi so took her that she moved to India and became a fixture in Gandhi's life, promoted Indian independence, and went with Gandhi when he visited London in 1931.[165] She worked actively promoting India's independence both in the country and abroad, meeting with Winston Churchill in England and Eleanor Roosevelt in the U.S. She was imprisoned by the British in 1932 for sedition. On meeting her at the ashram, Slade told Gregg that her father said to her: "Well, now that you have chosen your leader, stick with him through thick and thin." Gregg thought this was "pretty sporting of an English Admiral."[166] Slade remained in India after Gandhi's death and continued to promote sustainable agricultural practices and community development. Later, she received the *Padma Vibhushan* medal, the country's second-highest civilian honor. Gregg and Slade kept in touch throughout the 1930s.[167]

At the end of the year, and now mostly recovered from his illness, Gregg returned to Bombay. There he met up with Farwell and Faith and their daughter, Faith, who were visiting together. This was the first visit by any of his family since Gregg had made his move to India. He loved being with them, as he was always close to Faith. Less close to Farwell, Gregg had some ambivalence in his feelings for his brother-in-law. When he wrote to his mother after their visit, he complained about how Farwell was flaunting his wealth by renting a big, expensive car while the family was in Bombay. He did, however, spend a week or so sightseeing with them, and he brought them to the ashram so that they could see where he lived, meet Gandhi, and give them an education on why the life he was now living was so important to him.[168]

Gregg's concern with the prejudice and racism that separated Western white civilization from the East took a personal turn during this visit. He was embarrassed not only by his brother-in-law's big car but also by his manners. He told his brother Alan that he was appalled by his sister and her husband's etiquette while guests of local families:

> And to see the way they refused to eat the tea and food offered them by their Brahmin hosts at one of the villages was a picture of the contrast between Oriental and Occidental manners. A Brahmin's kitchen, barring flies, is as clean as any place in India, outside of a few operating wards; whereas the kitchens of the "European" hotels are pretty damned dirty. But the tourists seem to think

that if the food comes in a china plate and that they sit at a table with a white cloth on it then they are safe.[169]

This failure of manners by his sister and her husband (and the prejudice it represented) reminded Gregg of the enormous amount of education necessary to change attitudes in the West about India and Indians.

After the visit with Farwell and Faith, Gregg stayed at the ashram until the second week of February 1926. He had been in India for just over a year and had built a relationship with Maganlal, Gandhi, Tagore Rabindranath, C. F. Andrews, and Stokes, and had made many more new friends and acquaintances. Gregg felt good that he had learned some Hindi, and now knew how to spin. He had already seen a lot of the country and, during this first year, he had learned to wear Indian clothing, to do some gardening and cooking, and had explored ways in which he could help with sanitation and food production at the ashram. Gregg had also been able to spend more time with Gandhi. All in all, it was an enormously productive year. Gregg recorded much about this time and its impact on him in his notebooks, which are full of ideas, records of conversation, and his extensive lists and quotes from the books and articles he was reading.

Gregg began keeping these detailed notebooks in the first year he was in India. In Notebook 1, he outlines his goals as he saw them then:

My job in India (1) In writing: to help destroy the glamour of the West in the minds of Indians and to criticize the foundations of its civilization constructively so as to help both East and West to rebuild something better. Such ideas as industrialism, machinery, the pride of its unduly positive science (e.g., medicine) . . . To help undermine and destroy the false pride of the West . . . To help establish the self-confidence of Indians in their own culture. To help make the culture contact more fruitful to both E and W. To work out application of love to its problems. To help the West to see the real value of humility, (2) in agriculture to stimulate productivity not by machinery but by adaptations of old customs.[170]

It was a heady time for Gregg, and, it seemed, everything he had hoped for had begun to play out. He had taken a risk by dedicating his life to India. The troubled soul who haunted the streets of Chicago in the summer of 1924 now studied with Gandhi. The exposure to these many new experiences filled him with joy. There was so much to learn about his adopted country: its language and customs, yes, but also the politics of the nationalist movement, the life of a subjugated colony and, not least of all, Gandhi's philosophy and ideas. He entered the second stage of his time in India, returning to Stokes's school and to what became his home for most of his remaining stay.

CHAPTER SIX

Teaching and Writing

RICHARD GREGG HEADED EAST to join Samuel Stokes or Satyanand in late winter 1926. The journey took him by train first to Santiniketan to renew his contact with Tagore, then on to Calcutta, and up to Delhi, where Stokes met him, and they went north to Kotgarh. For Gregg, this was another formidable journey. He crossed India towards the Himalayas, a train ride of more than two thousand-five hundred miles through the varied countryside. When he and Stokes reached Kotgarh, he unpacked his bags and moved in with the Stokes family in the main house on the site, welcomed by Stokes's wife, Agnes, and taking his meals with them. Much later Gregg recounted an amusing story. Stokes referred to his wife as "my dear" and would call out to the garden "my dear" when he needed her. Once, when Gregg was out walking, one of the men of the village asked him whether he had a "mydear" at home, thinking "my dear" meant wife.[171] He was safe and secure in their delightful home but was soon busy building himself a modest cabin. He felt at home there, and his health improved despite his continual issues with malaria.

Gregg felt lucky to be in this beautiful village surrounded by gorgeous scenery and people whom he greatly respected. But there was work to do. Knowing that Gregg had a background in science and engineering, Stokes suggested again that he teach at the school. Gregg accepted and rigorously prepared, reading extensively about science, pedagogy, and curriculum development, and taking comprehensive notes about old and new ideas in math and physics. He had brought materials with him, but constantly struggled to get newspapers and journals delivered to the village. As he had discovered in Boston, he was not a natural teacher or a comfortable speaker, so the classroom role was a challenge, as was the lack of material he had for the students. The old schoolbooks were those given to English students thirty years before. Where they were even vaguely relevant, they assumed that students would have experience of Western, industrial, and sophisticated science. The general textbooks could say little to the children of Indian peasants who had never seen a factory or an airplane or had even the rudimentary tools by then common in Western classrooms. Gregg told Gandhi about the problem: "These children here have never seen automobiles, steam engines, electric lights, pumps, water pipes, or even bullock carts. So the assumptions, pictures, technical terms and arrangements of textbooks of physics, and even of much of mathematics can have no reality and therefore no interest or educational value for them."[172]

The teaching came hard to Gregg. He had little experience in teaching young children who had only limited skills, and this was not, after all, Milton Academy. He was also teaching in a language in which he was barely competent. Gregg's notes are full of class preparation ideas and not a little self-doubt about how he was to proceed. He cared very much that his teaching would give the children what he thought they needed and in a way that was accessible and engaging. He knew exactly what the problem was: teaching demands a kind of theater, and Gregg was not a theatrical man. Standing in front of a class, being (if only briefly) the center of attention did not sit well with him.

While he prepared his classes, he was working on his book on *khaddar*, using his investigations and notes for the work. He divided his time between the book and teaching preparation. With his efforts to finish his cabin and tending his vegetable garden there was not much time for recreation. When he could, he spoke with Stokes and ate dinner with the family or took walks across the beautiful hills surrounding the school. The hard work served him well. The ideas he investigated and considered to make him ready for the classroom would later be fleshed out and turned into *A Preparation for Science,* his second publication in India.[173] At this time, he was also reading, learning, and writing about *Satyagraha,* the Gandhian project, and considering how to make the concepts accessible and appealing to a Western audience. Those ideas eventually formed the backbone of the series of books he wrote that culminated in *The Power of Non-Violence.*

While teaching at Stokes's school, he developed a philosophy on education. His notebooks contain pages and pages of writing about how to teach physics, math, algebra, and chemistry. He pasted clippings of articles and book reviews that interested him, or that he thought relevant to his teaching and writing. These were annotated with discussions of cause-and-effect in science and the scientific method, data on electricity and atomic theory, and numerous references to possible books or articles that he had either read or thought might be useful. The notebook he kept on education reads like an extensive course on how to teach science to young children.

It is impressive that Gregg could engage with these endeavors while living in a remote area with no electricity, no immediate access to communication of any sort, and writing by the light of an oil lamp at night. But Gregg was always focused and, despite these handicaps, was able to continue his research and writing. While he was analyzing *khaddar* and refining his science-teaching text, Gregg studied Hindi with Stokes, maintained a vegetable garden, and wrote often to family and friends. He filled seven notebooks while he was in India, covering 1925 through 1927, most of them consisting of more than three hundred pages of closely spaced handwritten notes, pasted newspaper clippings, and reviews. To read them now is to stand at the side of an erudite researcher and thinker, one working in the most primitive circumstances.

The vast majority of his notes are transcriptions from works he considered essential and relevant to his thinking and writing. They document the writers and ideas that provided the basis for much of his work and occasionally reflect personal observations.

In one of the first notebooks, from early 1925, it is clear that Gregg was thinking about his life, even as he immersed himself in the country he loved:

> In considering any near or remote return to the U.S., remember that I must pay a price for what I get in India or in U.S. Shall that price be loneliness here of something else? Balance clear conscience, simplicity, spiritual growth vs. mental comfort of old habits and environment, and the more disquiet of compromises there. Will have to be lonely in either place, probably, in order to live as I believe right. Least probability of loneliness, though, in India."[174]

The concern with loneliness reflects not only the absence of friends or family, but the absence of more intimate companionship. There is little mention, throughout his early letters to family, of any possible love interest. Over the first twenty years of his adult life, in Boston or Chicago, or his travels, he never refers in writing to any intimate relationship.

A year or so later, in a letter to his sister Faith, he admits:

> Often, I incline to come home again, but I'm letting that grow into its own solution, meanwhile balancing all the pros and cons as carefully as I can. If I come back it can be only because I have learned to find a different basis of living & a different attitude toward people and surroundings from what I had before.

He went on to tell her:

> All my former assumptions, beliefs, attitudes & ways are being pretty thoroughly shaken. Tested, re-valued, illuminated, enriched, deepened, altered, or discarded. It is a wonderful kind of education and I wouldn't have missed it for anything. I am getting a far more intimate contact with Indian life and ideas than even the missionaries or officials who stay here many years (with very rare exceptions).[175]

Already his experience had challenged his foundational beliefs, and he began to question what he had learned from his family, from Harvard, and his life in labor relations in the U.S. While he harbored some doubts about staying in India, for the time being he threw himself into his daily routine. By the fall of 1926 he had settled into his life in the hills, but he was shaken one day by bad news: returning to his cabin from a walking tour of the district he found a cable from his brother Alan telling him of his mother's death. Gregg was a long way from home and had no way of immediately contacting his family or any real hope (or intention) of coming home. He was close to his mother, and while she never fully understood what motivated her son, her loss hit him hard—alone in India, with poor command of the language, and thousands of miles from his brothers and sisters. He took a great deal of solace in the Bhagavad Gita, its words and wisdom about death and life. In a letter to Alan acknowledging the news of his mother's passing, he told him how much comfort he had gotten from the Gita, and he quoted it at length to him. Gregg took comfort in knowing that his mother died while with Alan, his wife, and his sister Elinor.[176]

The Economics of Khaddar

Despite the hardships of living and working at the school, late 1926 saw the beginning of Gregg's serious writing. In a relatively short time he completed *A Preparation for Science*, providing a guide for teaching science to Indian children not based on Western concepts and ideas. The book is not only a preparation for learning science, it also illustrates Gregg's efforts to translate Western science concepts for Indians as well as Gandhian beliefs and values for a Western audience. This all came to fruition in his later work and reflected Gregg's deep respect for science in all contexts.

While at Stokes's school during the summer and fall of 1927, Gregg also completed *The Economics of Khaddar*.[177] In early 1926 he had written to Gandhi about his goal of writing a book on Gandhi's economics and on the practice of nonviolence. Gandhi wrote back to Gregg approvingly, and expressed his willingness to answer any questions Gregg had.[178] As he wrote in the beginning of the book, it drew on "seven years of practical work and study in industrial and labor relations in America (much of it in cotton mills)."[179] Gregg opened *The Economics of Khaddar* with a discussion of the extreme poverty in India. He recognized *khadi* is often dismissed in the West as "misguided zeal," "reactionary," "an antiquated and unprofitable method," or "flying in the face of all modern scientific knowledge and progress."[180]

Khadi could not compete with machines that produced cloth at a rate over two hundred times that of hand producers but, Gregg argued, that was not the point. The point was what should an economy be for? Rather, he argued, "The ultimate object of all economic activity is the actual complete supply of food, clothing, and shelter and other needs of mankind."[181] *Khadi* offered work to vast numbers of rural peasants and was, therefore, much more likely to improve standards of living and give Indians more control over their lives.

His time learning to spin and his investigation of spinning activities in several villages motivated him to bring this experience to a broader audience, with Gandhi's encouragement. As Gregg explained later:

> I became so interested in the hand-spinning program that in 1927, I wrote a book about it, using my experience in American textile manufacturing as a background. That pleased Gandhi . . . (T)his writing was due to the stimulus of the situation, new to me, and the contact with Gandhi's original mind. I am not a professional writer, and I did not go to India in order to get material for writing. Such an idea never occurred to me. I just got steamed up over the whole idea and possibilities of the program and felt compelled to explain it in Western terms. This was true also of the book I wrote later, called *The Power of Non-Violence*.[182]

In addition to *A Preparation for Science* and *Khaddar*, Gregg found time to write a short piece for the Indian journal *Modern Review*—a significant magazine for Indian nationalists and a source of information on political, social, and economic issues. Gregg's work here set out to praise *charkha* (the hand spinning wheel, central to Gandhi's constructivist program) and *khaddar*. Although the work was written and published very early in Gregg's stay in India, it shows the beginnings of his thinking around issues of exploitation and peace: ". . . it is not difficult to see how the universal adoption of Charkha and Khaddar would promote peace. It would reduce strife between classes by reducing and eventually removing one great area of exploitation of the masses by their industrial masters. That is, it will reduce the total amount of industrialism which creates classes, and their concomitant discontent, bitterness and strikes."[183]

These were themes that Gregg took up more fully in the *Economics of Khaddar*. They reflect Gregg's work experience in the decade before he left for India and his exposure to industrial strife in Colorado at the turn of the twentieth century. *Khaddar* was not only about decentralized production, distribution, markets, and empowered local producers, but also the potential that local manufacture had for reducing conflict. For Gregg, as for Gandhi, simplicity was a way to peace, a means of connecting the practical process with spirituality. As Gregg wrote in *Modern Review*:

> Khaddar is also simple and pure in the sense that it involves a satisfaction
> of desires out of one's own self-reliant strength and ability. Such simplicity is
> not the simplicity of harsh poverty, of niggardly asceticism, or unlovely austerity,
> of a low, sluggish, ignorant or static form of life, incapable of beauty, growth
> or great developments. It is the simplicity of the person who refuses to have his
> desires played upon so much that he becomes enslaved by them.[184]

These ideas did not find a favorable reception in the West at the time, and most Indian leaders did not embrace Gandhi's enthusiasm for programs that called for everyone to spend time spinning. They do represent, however, Gregg's commitment to the value of both manual labor and simplicity. Gregg took this a little further in the article he published in the journal *Current*

Thought, "The Morals of Machinery." The work began Gregg's exploration not only of the superiority of traditional handcrafts but also decentralized production. This thinking led him to emphasize that such forms of work were not only more efficient but also morally superior. Again, this was Gregg seeking out the connections between local, small-scale, and non-industrial production and a life that is spiritually, ethically, and environmentally superior.[185] There is in this work, however, one of the few places where Gregg challenges Gandhi's emphasis on the core issue of machinery and automation as the source of humankind's problems (a position with which Gregg used to agree), noting in the conclusion of the *Economics of Khaddar*, "On further thought it seems to me that most of the evils involved . . . are due *more to capitalism than machinery*." Gregg argued that "if capitalism as a motive and mode of industry . . . ceased to exist, much machinery would disappear also."[186] After *The Economics of Khaddar* was published, Gandhi commented, "Richard B. Gregg has been studying the Khadi movement in the most minute manner ever since his arrival in India. After a year's labor, he has written a book on the movement which treats khadi in the most original manner." Maganlal told Gregg the work had been written with the "insight of a master."[187] One Indian critic called the book "the view of a long-sighted economist who...has enough intelligence...to look a few years ahead."[188] From the point of publication on, Gandhi dedicated significant time to finding scholars able and willing to further develop his radical economics.[189] For Gregg (as for Gandhi) the promotion of decentralized, labor-intensive production was humane—it leveraged the availability of labor in countries such as India and was more efficient.

This time was one of Gregg's most productive periods, and ideas and analysis flowed from his pen. Not only had he completed the small instruction manual with Maganlal and the book on *khaddar*, but he also started three other significant works: *Gandhiji's Satyagraha or Nonviolent Resistance* (published in India in 1930),[190] the very similar *The Psychology and Strategy of Gandhi's*

Nonviolent Resistance (also published in India in 1930),[191] and *Gandhism and Socialism: A Study and Comparison* (first published in India in 1931).[192] This was a lot of writing for someone who was not, by his admission, "a professional writer." While there is some overlap among the works, it was these books that began to focus his thinking about Gandhi's philosophy, especially in *Psychology and Strategy*. The last two works principally provided drafts for *The Power of Non-Violence* which Gregg revised and developed back in the States, to ultimately be published there in 1934.

Writing *The Power of Non-Violence*

In *Gandhiji's Satyagraha*, Gregg set out the basis for his vision of nonviolent resistance as he then understood it from Gandhi. He added Gandhi's work by incorporating ideas in the then-current literature and analysis of psychology and the study of human behavior. Unlike pacifists before him (who mostly cast pacifism in terms of religious beliefs and imperatives), Gregg argued that nonviolent resistance was a tactic and a practical maneuver that could throw a would-be violent attacker off his guard. By not responding violently to an aggressor, it made the perpetrator of violence a victim of "moral jiu-jitsu," as he memorably put it. Gregg explained this as:

> The nonviolence and good will of the victim act in the same way that the lack of physical opposition by the user of physical jiu-jitsu does, causing the attacker to lose his moral balance. He suddenly and un-expectedly loses the moral support which the usual violent resistance of most victims would render him. He plunges forward, as it were, into a new world of values. He feels insecure because of the novelty of the situation and his ignorance of how to handle it. He loses his poise and self-confidence. The victim not only lets the attacker come, but, as it were, pulls him forward by kindness, generosity and voluntary suffering, so that the attacker loses his moral balance. The user of nonviolent resistance, knowing what he is doing and having a more creative purpose, keeps his moral balance. He uses the leverage of a superior wisdom to subdue the rough direct force of his opponent.[193]

Here Gregg drew on the works of a range of writers and theorists, including the behaviorist J.B. Watson, the psychologist I.P. Pavlov, the philosopher W.E. Hocking, and the community organizer and, later, management and organizational theorist Mary Parker Follett. The first part of the work set up Gregg's view of the psychological dynamics of violent encounters by positing two antagonists. An attack by one is met with violent resistance by the other, and both become trapped in a similar moral universe where violence is the only possible outcome. But Gregg argued that changing the situation to one where the attacker meets nonviolent resistance throws the attacker off-balance, having to confront a different set of values and norms. The response is unanticipated and confuses the attacker. This "converts" the attacker or, at very least, bewilders him. For Gregg, this was all about psychology and performance. In a threatening encounter between two people, where one practices nonviolent resistance, and when there are witnesses, they will feel sympathy for the nonviolent resistor, and make the violent attacker feel ashamed for his or her actions.[194] These ideas were refined and developed in *The Power of Non-Violence.*

What was unique about Gregg's argument, although it drew from Gandhi and other thinkers of the day (and Gandhi drew heavily on the Hindu doctrine of *ahisma*, the work of Leo Tolstoy, and that of Henry David Thoreau, among many others) was that, first, the strategy of nonviolent resistance operated at the level of human psychology and played into the psychological basis of violence. Second, it stressed the importance of such resistance as a performance, one that informed and educated the audience. Last, he emphasized that violence and change are inevitable but can be combated by this moral jiu-jitsu. Most importantly, Gregg goes on to argue here (and, again, more fully in *The Power of Non-Violence*), that nonviolent resistors can be trained in these responses and that such training can draw many lessons from military preparation and discipline. This position was controversial among pacifists and brought a whole new dynamic that lifted the actions of pacifists out of the moral universe (and, indeed, the moral high ground) by advocating direct nonviolent action.

In his next work, *Gandhiism Vs. Socialism*, published in 1932, Gregg argues that institutions are the superficial manifestations of control. For Gregg, the real power came from the ideas and sentiments underlying the institutions. Whoever controlled the meaning of words, numbers, ceremonies, and costumes exercised the actual control. He would expand on this much later in *The Big Idol* (1965), a work that contains prescient ideas about the use of imagery and belief in creating forms of social manipulation and control. *Gandhiism Vs. Socialism* represents a critical step in Gregg's work. In *A Preparation for Science* and *The Economics of Khaddar*, Gregg offers focused studies of particular aspects of Gandhi's movement. *Gandhiism Vs. Socialism*, on the other hand, is Gregg's first published work to provide a broad synthesis that rejects both capitalism and socialism. Here Gregg is concerned with establishing the central components of the Gandhian project. He starts the piece with his statement about how control is exerted in the world:

> Most people think that the world is governed by institutions and organizations such as political governments and banks, or by laws, or by certain ruling classes. But really the control is deeper and more subtle. Governments, banks, laws, and ruling classes are only the exterior instruments of management. The real control comes from ideas and sentiments—a scheme of values, a set of ideals or activities which people are induced to desire or accept as right, fitting and praiseworthy. The most important adjunct of this control—even more important than organizations—is a set of symbols which indicate and arouse emotions about the given systems of values.[195]

He points out that Gandhi's philosophy will weaken the five critical ways in which, as he puts it. ". . . the ruling class have been able to govern, retrain and thwart the masses" through the use of ". . . money, physical violence, social divisions and flatteries, parliamentarianism, large-scale organization."[196]

Gandhiism Vs. Socialism established his critique of liberal capitalism, and his words would find an echo in the post-WWII analysis of the role of ideological hegemony that emerged from some of the New Left and, particularly, the work of Antonio Gramsci.[197] Here Gregg began to address how people came to believe what they believe about the world, a question that, in the '50s and '60s, neo-Marxists struggled to explain. Gregg's concern about the control of "ideas and sentiments" and the use of powerful symbols, predates the work of many radical academics, who puzzled over the quiescence of the working class in liberal democracies, and the seeming effectiveness and legitimacy of the liberal capitalist state.

As Gregg began to form these concepts in the first year or two of his time in India, he sought a wider audience for his emerging ideas. In the late summer of 1926, Gregg wrote to W. E. B. Du Bois, the great historian, and civil rights activist, to introduce himself and give him a copy of the *Economics of Khaddar*. In response, Du Bois sent Gregg a copy of his *Darkwater: Voices from Within the Veil*, the first volume of what was to become Du Bois's autobiography.[198] He also sent a sample copy of *The Crisis*, the journal Du Bois founded in 1910 as part of the early development of the National Association for the Advancement of Colored People (NAACP). Gregg wrote back to him in the fall of 1926 from Kotgarh. It was a long letter, and, in his usual decent and polite way, Gregg expressed his concern that it might take him some time to pay for the book that Du Bois sent. He went on in the letter to recognize the fundamental similarities of the struggle caused by, ". . . (t)he false pride, blindness and the exploiting selfishness of the white race or nations. More than ever I am convinced that in essence it is a spiritual and moral attitude which is at fault, and that the only real solution must be in the realm of the spirit."[199] Later, this aspect of his thinking faded into the background as he focused on the consequences of industrialization and laid out the argument for simplicity. But the spiritual realm would always be a touchstone for Gregg the Christian.

While the *Economics of Khaddar* laid out the practical case for adoption of *khadi* as part of India's economic development, the book also represented the culmination of broader theoretical and philosophical discussions between Gregg and Gandhi about the nature of machinery, capitalism, and the desirability of industrialization. Gregg wrote and published *The Economics of Khaddar* in India, but wanted it to reach a much wider audience, particularly in the U.S. This, in part, was why he sent a copy of the book to Du Bois. But, while Du Bois expressed admiration for Gandhi, he did not consider Gregg's economic ideas applicable to the situation in the U.S. Other critics expressed similar sentiments. While many admired Gregg's views, they had significant reservations as to their applicability in the industrialized West, where capitalism and large-scale industrial production were firmly established. The criticism was at times harsh as noted above, using terms like "misguided" and "antiquated."[200] In general, the advocacy of simple homespun textiles by both Gregg and Gandhi was met with derision by radicals and pacifists alike. It did not seem to them to be appropriate for those living and working in mature and industrial societies in the U.S. and Europe. The lack of enthusiasm disappointed Gregg but did not dissuade him from trying to get the work to a broader audience. He was determined to see his book published in the West. The work was only published much later in the U.S. and had little impact at the time. It did contain the foundation of what Gregg would build on later in his life.

Homesick

The experience of working at Stokes's school, and with Gandhi, from 1925 until 1928, exposed Gregg not only to Gandhi's overall philosophy and commitment to nonviolent social change, but also to all aspects of life in India. He relished the beauty of the country, the warm and loving people, and their connection to the earth and the natural world. His fascination with

India became profound appreciation and turned to deep love for the country and its people. While these were critical and productive years for Gregg, in his personal life there remained a gap. He was not married, and wondered and frequently worried, about what a future alone would look like. While he said he wanted to be in a relationship, or be married, his travels and his commitment to work made that unlikely. In his notebook for 1926 Gregg wrote, "I want to marry so as to experience love more fully, as an aspect of reality. I have talked art, philosophy, and science fairly deeply, but of love I know and have lived too little."[201]

Like anyone a long way from home, he was a little bit homesick, missing his brothers and sisters and the ability to communicate quickly and fluently. He also missed more mundane things. In May 1927, he told Farwell in a letter how much he would love to eat "some vanilla ice cream with chocolate sauce, johnnycakes and butter and maple syrup, cheese crackers, ginger snaps, a chocolate malted milk shake etc."[202] It is a startling admission by him about missing the very ordinary. The homesickness, the recognition that he was, and would always be, a Western man, and the struggle to become fluent in Hindi troubled him. He fretted about this in his notebooks and in letters home. He admitted to Alan, in August of 1927, that he still had real problems with his "bone-headedness" when it came to language. He was able get by in limited conversational Hindi but found himself longing for more regular and more in-depth conversation. It was the language barrier and loneliness more than anything else that led him to think about going home.[203]

Throughout 1927 Gregg exchanged letters with Gandhi on many issues: helping Maganlal at the ashram, ideas about diet and nutrition, the progress of the resistance to British rule, and some comments by Gandhi on Gregg's work on khaddar. In several letters, they write about diet. Once Gandhi complained about a box of apples Gregg sent from Kotgarh (they were too hard for him to eat!). Both Gandhi and Gregg had a deep interest in food, and there were some lengthy exchanges between Gandhi and Gregg describing their efforts to improve their nutrition, as well as that of the world. In one letter, Gregg strongly recommended uncooked goat's milk and a diet of pulverized nuts to Gandhi; in return, Gandhi told Gregg that he was trying neem leaves to combat high blood pressure and flatulence. Gandhi also gave a lengthy description of his many dietary adventures in the three-page letter. Both men suffered from hemorrhoids, as did Charles Andrews, and Gregg needed to do something about the severity of his ailment but could not afford an operation and did not know where to go to get relief.[204] Gandhi suggested a doctor in Bombay who had operated successfully on him and on Andrews.[205] Gregg took his advice and traveled the one thousand-two-hundred miles by train from Kotgarh to Bombay for the operation in the winter of 1927. He had the surgery in January 1928. After the operation, he spent some time recuperating with friends in Poona (now Pune), a six-hour train ride southeast of Bombay. Gandhi arranged for the operation to be without cost for his American friend.[206]

Feeling better, Gregg set off back to the Stokes school for what was to be his last few months in India. The decision was made despite having moved that spring to a new cabin that Stokes help him build. By the early summer, the longing to go home was more and more occupying him. But he also realized that, if he wanted to get his ideas and values to a Western audience, that could only happen if he were back in America. There he would have easier access to materials for his work and the ability to connect to American thinkers, activists, and a Western audience directly.

That summer, Gregg made plans to return home in the fall. But before he set off, he wrote a long letter to Gandhi detailing his desire to bring Gandhi's message to the West and arguing that this was important: "Your message and work brought me here: I have learnt what I came for. It has given me a poise and a sense of inner peace which were lacking before: Your friendship and love have been very precious to me."[207] Gandhi wrote back saying he found the argument convincing and wished him well. He was insistent that he get a chance to say goodbye, "On no account should you go away without our meeting."[208]

Gregg told his brother Don that it was a "jolly fine prospect" to be thinking about going back and could not find enough words to express his anticipation of the trip. Once the decision was made, Gregg booked his passage on the Italian liner *Aquileia,* due to leave Bombay in early November 1928. His mind and itinerary set, he began to make plans for the trip. He would stop off to see Alan and his wife in Paris, and then head for New York, hoping to get there by December 15. With the prospect of returning home now a reality, Gregg decided on a final train trip through India, from the hills of Simla back to Bombay and then on to the ashram. In September, Gregg packed his bags and collected as many of his books and belongings as he could. He said his very fond goodbyes to Stokes and his wife, to the children he had been teaching and, with mixed emotions, he took his leave of Kotgarh and the beautiful Simla Hills and headed south to stay at Santiniketan for a couple of weeks. While there, Gregg again met with Tagore and other friends and headed north again to Patna, before going back to the ashram. At the ashram he reconnected with old friends and, briefly, with Gandhi. After traveling south to stay a few days in Poona, Gregg set off for Bombay.

India had changed him profoundly. Most important of all was the relationship he formed with Gandhi, a friendship that would shape not only his philosophical and social ideas but also his struggle with his spirituality and existential concerns. He had met many people and made several friends, many of whom became his correspondents and colleagues for the rest of his life. In India, he had taught, studied, and traveled. He had seen the hubbub of Bombay, the tranquility of the northern hills of Simla, and the crush of people in Calcutta. He had met Nehru and Rabindranath Tagore and, most important to him, had become Gandhi's American friend.

His experiences and relationships in India put his past in perspective and allowed him to understand those years with Ordway, Tead and Gregg, the work with the railway unions during the strike, the difficult negotiations with Bethlehem Steel and the Lake Carriers Association, and the strife around him as the war ended. India also framed his experience, from a distance, of the horrors of WWI. His brother Alan had been in France during the carnage, as had his sisters Elinor and Marjorie. They described the devastation, and he had seen it with his own eyes on his trip in 1919. All the decades after 1918 are in the shadow of that war, which claimed twenty million lives, with over twenty-one million casualties. There was no historical precedent for such a human cost of war. Nevertheless, it was his years spent in labor relations, at a time when the American labor movement was so in conflict with American capital that no amount of arbitration could heal, that most deeply troubled and affected Gregg. It was a violent period in U.S. history, and it was this, more than the catastrophe of the trenches in France, that had led Gregg to a sense of hopelessness for the future of industrial society and spurred his motivation to seek an alternative: Gandhi and India.

Gregg always kept labor and the plight of the working class and the poor central to his concerns. In that way, his thinking reflected the core values of the American Old Left activists, with their focus on fair labor conditions and wages and other class issues. But his antagonism towards industrial production, corporate power, consumerism, and the seemingly inevitable alienation caused by the materialistic mass society was very much the center of what was to become the New Left. Gregg, although he did not know at the time, was one of the bridges that connected the two. The combination of his experience in America, his friendship with Gandhi, and his time in India brought everything into focus for him. He became convinced that nonviolence was more than an ethical and religious principle; it was also a method of social action with its own logic and strategy.

In all of this, Gregg was extraordinarily prescient. His concern with the cultural, psychological, and sociological impacts of modern technology had developed through experience and extensive reading. His recognition of the many adverse effects of contemporary work (the inequality, drudgery, the alienation), of the mindlessness of the growing consumer society, and of the environmental and health consequences of rapid economic and technological growth sat heavily on him. He struggled with these issues. The solutions he sought in simple living, farming, and the rejection of the consumer society grew from his time in India. These ideas would be taken up in the West by the New Left some thirty years later at the core of the counterculture movement of the 1960s and '70s, and, today, in the growing interest in organic farming, self-sufficiency, and environmental awareness—the emerging concept of being "green." These, too, came to him in part from his encounters with Gandhi, with Tagore, and with Stokes. They came to him, too, from his love of the country that had been his home for nearly four years.

Before leaving he cautioned himself: "In returning to life in America don't go in for reform movements. Don't join organizations for reform. Stay hidden and quiet. Trust to example. If you write, do so by way of explanation and not as exhortation . . . Accept all things. Don't strive. Conquer by love and help . . . Live with commitment to ideas. Homespun, farm (i.e. solar power development) little use of money, simplicity, friendly to all. Simplicity."[209]

He left India on November 7th. After the long voyage, he arrived in Paris to see his brother Alan and his wife Eleanor at the end of the month. A week or so later, Gregg took a steamer across the Atlantic Ocean and was back in Boston by Christmas. He was now forty-three, owned almost nothing, had no reserves of cash or savings to speak of, and no real career or job prospects, save as a writer.

CHAPTER SEVEN

Peace, Love, and Understanding

"The unity of the human species is not only a biological and physiological fact; it is, when wisely and fully asserted and acted upon, a great power. Human unity is actual in man's universal capacity to think, feel, will, understand and act, and to apprehend spiritual truths. Human unity is a power that can overcome all differences of race, nationality, ideology or culture. Military leaders have aroused partial unity by means of fear, pride, anger, hate and lies. But unity can also be aroused, more fruitfully and enduringly, by love and the desire for justice."
—Richard Gregg, Preface to 1959 edition of *The Power of Non-Violence*

AFTER MORE THAN A MONTH in transit, Gregg arrived in a cold and bustling New York City in mid-December 1928. Happy to be home and eager to reconnect with his family, especially his sisters Faith and Elinor, he looked forward to reintegrating into at least some of the life he had known. In his years away, the Roaring Twenties drove on mostly unabated, fed by new inventions and the development of automobiles, the radio, movies, airplanes, and all the marvels of the age. In 1927, Charles Lindbergh had flown the Atlantic, capturing the seeming promise of technological progress and American individualism. After some headway on social reform, the Progressive Era began to fade as labor unions and workers fell victim to Red Scare tactics, lack of leadership, and a generally buoyant economy. The women's movement gained momentum, too, over the '20s, and changed much of the cultural and political mores of the country, at least on the east coast and among the more privileged classes. In New York City, the Harlem Renaissance continued making vibrant contributions to music, art, and literature. However, racism and the Ku Klux Klan still made life extraordinarily difficult, and often deadly, for Black Americans. Herbert Hoover won the presidential election and would formally take office at the beginning of 1929. In October, The *Hindenburg* Zeppelin crashed and burned in New Jersey. Internationally, the Kellogg-Briand Pact was signed by most nations, outlawing war and calling for the peaceful settlement of disputes. In Boston, James Michael Curly was still mayor, and the Boston Garden had just opened. The Boston Red Sox finished last in the American League that year.

This was the America to which Gregg returned. He had been gone for the best part of four years and had traveled to the other side of the world, having experiences few Americans could understand or appreciate. He had absorbed an enormous amount about the life and culture of India and seen first-hand the consequences of decades of colonialism on the sub-continent. He had learned Hindi (sort-of), studied *khaddar*, taught school, grown vegetables, and crisscrossed the country, forming relationships that would last. All of this had contributed significantly to his life's goals, but he still had some pressing personal problems: he was single, solidly into middle age, and yet with no visible means of support or a home to live in. These were issues he had to confront, and soon. And Gregg was desperate to reach a wider audience for his ideas about peace, simple living, and his critique of modern consumer society. Most importantly, he wanted to interpret what he had learned from Gandhi and compile and promote his ideas for an American audience. Gregg wanted to publish at home.

The long journey home gave Gregg time to catch up on his letter writing, and he made a point of keeping Gandhi informed of his progress. He wrote from the ship on the way to Europe and from his stopover in Paris (where he once again got the chance to meet up with C.F. Andrews, who happened to be in France). Their letters dealt with a range of issues from the impact of Prohibition in the U.S. to Gandhi's proposed visit to England, possibly in 1930. Gregg wanted to discourage Gandhi from taking the trip, fearing that it would be used to the detriment of India's independence struggle and by the British to co-opt Gandhi.

Despite concerns for Gandhi and events in India and the rest of the world (the rise of fascism in Italy troubled him deeply), he had other things on his mind. Heading up to Boston on that December day, he was mostly thinking about just settling back into life in the States and seeing Faith and her family again at the house in Chestnut Hill. Although he took great joy at the prospect of being back in the streets of Boston that he knew so well, he kept thinking about the work he wanted to do. His writing in India had paved the way for this, and *Preparation for Science* and *Economics of Khaddar* had laid out the practical views he held for making science and production in what we would now call "appropriate technology." These studies, released in India, provided only the broadest outline of his thinking on nonviolent resistance and his advocacy of pacifism.

Coming Home

Faith was delighted to have her brother back, and he stayed with her through the early winter of 1929. He enjoyed being back among all the comforts of Faith's home, a far cry from the ashram. While he was there enjoying American food and a comfortable bed, his personal life took a different and unexpected turn: he met an interior designer from Charleston, South Carolina, named Nonie Tupper.

Nonie, a designer and artist, had worked on projects around Boston, notably the rehabilitation of the Lyman House in Waltham in the 1920s.[210] She had a studio on Boylston Street from which she ran her business. After a whirlwind romance, Gregg married Nonie on April 14, 1929, in New York City. Nonie was fifty-three and Richard ten years younger. After the wedding, he and Nonie spent the spring and summer at South Tamworth and in Jamaica, Vermont, enjoying the countryside, being with his sisters, and hiking. South Tamworth, and Faith and Farwell's home there, would be a place he and Nonie returned to often. For the time being, however, it offered an idyllic setting for the newlyweds and a chance for Gregg to be with his family.[211] He was finally married, and, at last, the loneliness he had felt during most of his life dissipated. But Gregg didn't settle into married life in any traditional sense. After the wedding and brief honeymoon, always active and engaged, he threw himself back into his writing, eager to distill his experiences and acquired knowledge into a statement about an alternative social and political vision.

Yet, even then, the call of India was loud and insistent. Gregg longed to return, especially as he knew that the Indian independence movement was growing in strength and British oppression with it. He also wanted to show Nonie some of what he had experienced over the last few years. So, that summer, Gregg made plans for a return to India, this time with Nonie.

Back to India

The couple left the U.S. at the beginning of 1930, barely eight months after getting married and a little over a year after Gregg returned. As they left, the catastrophic Wall Street crash was just beginning to bring down the American economy. Yet, this was hardly noticeable to Gregg and Nonie, who were full of anticipation about returning to India. After booking passage and packing for the trip, they left New York in early January, arriving in India in February. Gregg was excited to be back and eager to show Nonie the country and introduce her to his many friends. They planned an extensive itinerary that took them across India to Madras, Bombay, Calcutta, Simla, and, of course, to the ashram at Sabarmati. They stayed with Gregg's friends and colleagues along the way, sometimes sleeping on a mat on the floor, always connecting with and immersing themselves in everyday life. They went to Santiniketan and stayed at Tagore's school, allowing Gregg to introduce Nonie to Tagore and his colleagues.[212]

The primary goal of this trip was for Gregg to return to the ashram to see Gandhi. Their timing was perfect. They got there shortly before Gandhi embarked on the Salt March, a critical moment as Gandhi's proposed action would change how the world saw India and British colonialism along with it. The Salt March (also known as the Salt Satyagraha or Dandi March), a great act of nonviolent civil disobedience as a campaign against British taxation and salt monopoly, served as the beginning of Gandhi's specific leadership of the independence movement. It quickly became a model of nonviolent resistance to oppression and the most significant act of rebellion against the British since the non-cooperation movement of 1920-22. Gandhi started the Salt March on March 12, 1930, leaving from the ashram. Gandhi, with some eighty initial marchers, cheered on by ten thousand onlookers, walked more than two-hundred-and-forty miles and arrived at their coastal destination, Dandi, on April 6, after twenty-four days. At the various stopping places and near the end of the March the crowd exceeded eighty thousand. In a dramatic climax on April 6, 1930, sixty-one-year-old Mohandas Karamchand Gandhi picked up a lump of salt and proclaimed, "With this, I am shaking the foundations of the British Empire."

The Salt March, the first and most stunning example of how Gandhi approached nonviolent resistance, initiated the country-wide civil disobedience movement, and gained worldwide attention. The March confounded the British authorities and left them confused about how to respond. It would become the first and most compelling example of the effectiveness of civil disobedience in history and be a model for the tactics of the American civil rights movement thirty years later.[213] As Gregg wrote in an article for *The Nation*, not only was the Salt March a significant challenge to British authority, but it was also remarkable in that it mobilized thousands of Indians and saw the first real mass engagement of Indian women in the struggle.[214] Being with Gandhi just before the historic March had a profound impact on both Gregg and Nonie. Gregg would later use the Salt March as an example of the proven effectiveness of nonviolent resistance in much of his writing, lectures, and workshops.

The ashram buzzed with excitement as Gandhi and his followers prepared for the March. Although this was an intense time, Gandhi and Gregg did find the opportunity to catch up and for Nonie to meet Gandhi. Nonie was a big hit with Gandhi, and the couple spent every afternoon and many mealtimes with him during their brief stay.[215] From that time on, Gandhi would remain very fond of Nonie, always calling her Radha (a Hindu goddess and lover and companion of Krishna) and, later, in his letters to Gregg, always asking about her health and sending her his love. And for Nonie, meeting Gandhi was an exciting experience, as was the whole trip: the exotic countryside, the members of the ashram, the food, and the excitement and passion of the struggle against British imperialism. How could it not be? An interior decorator from the South who had never left the country now found herself in the personal company of someone who was already one of the most well-known figures of the twentieth century. In a rare entry in one of Gregg's notebooks, she described being at the ashram on March 8, 1930, just as Gandhi learned of the arrest of the politician and independence leader Sadar Patel (a prominent activist, leader of the National Congress Party and, later the First Deputy Prime Minister of India) in the village of Ras while giving a speech. The arrest was for breaking the prohibition on addressing large crowds, but the act was designed to stop Gandhi and the March. She and Gregg joined a procession to visit the imprisoned Patel, expecting the arrest of Gandhi himself very soon.[216]

The British arrested Gandhi later, in May, after he led trained members of his ashram and many thousands of Indians in the Salt March protest. At the end of the March, the marchers (without Gandhi) protested peacefully. They were met with brutal force, as the American journalist Webb Miller reported at the time:

> In complete silence the Gandhi men drew up and halted a hundred yards from the stockade. A picked column advanced from the crowd, waded the ditches and approached the barbed wire stockade . . . at a word of command, scores of native policemen rushed upon the advancing marchers and rained blows on their heads with their steel-shot lathis [long bamboo sticks]. Not one of the marchers even raised an arm to fend off blows. They went down like ninepins. From where I stood I heard the sickening whack of the clubs on unprotected skulls . . . . Those struck down fell sprawling, unconscious or writhing with fractured skulls or broken shoulders.[217]

As Gregg pointed out, this was a clear example of the power of nonviolence, despite the horrendous acts of the police: "But the voluntary non-violent suffering by Nationalists for the cause is too much for the moderates to endure. It touches them too deeply, as indeed it must touch all men, including the British themselves. The West understands violence, so the cables are full of the stories of violence; but the much greater amount of nonviolent resistance is not understood and so does not get reported. But nonviolent resistance is the great power that is moving events in India."[218] In the end, the British arrested over sixty thousand of the participants in the month after the March.

This was Nonie's first experience of any significant political action, and in another entry in Gregg's notebook, she reflected on how impressed she was with both Gandhi's commitment and the passion and power of his disciples.

For Gregg, being this close to Gandhi just before he embarked on the Salt March and witnessing its immediate effects, gave him a direct experience of the application of the ideas of nonviolent resistance. Later, with extensive knowledge of how the Western press presented news, Gregg was in an excellent position to report promptly and accurately about what was going on. In the two pieces he wrote for *The Nation* upon returning to the States, Gregg was at pains to point out the real situation in India. As he stressed, regarding the nature of British colonial rule and the possibilities presented by the independence movement: "The political liberation of one-fifth of the human race is a momentous event. Primarily it is a moral and spiritual affair, and it touches all of us. In forming our opinions and reaching our decisions we can no longer limit our loyalties to any one nation or one civilization. We must be loyal to the highest interests of humanity as a whole."[219] This article established Gregg as one of the leading commentators on the Indian independence movement for the progressive press in the U.S. It drew widespread attention from activists and progressives across the country.

Back to America

Despite the excitement of reconnecting with Gandhi, and being at the ashram during the Salt March, the Greggs had to return to the States. They left India in mid-April, arriving home in May 1930. After his long and eventful trip, Gregg was again facing practical questions of where to live and how to support himself and Nonie, while he continued to write. Nonie still had her work as an interior designer, and, in her small studio on Boylston Street, they managed to eke out a living for a couple of years, living there together until they were able to buy a small house in Natick in 1934. Gregg revised much of his earlier writing and finished the manuscript that would be published in the U.S. as *The Power of Non-Violence (PNV)*.

The Great Depression began to devastate the U.S. economy. Between peak and trough, industrial production declined by forty-seven per cent, Gross Domestic Product dropped by thirty percent, and unemployment reached twenty percent. In Britain and Germany, too, jobs vanished, and economic growth and trade collapsed. The Smoot-Hawley Tariff Act, signed that year to protect American industry and agriculture from foreign competition, heralded widespread economic nationalism. That year saw the first major electoral success of the Nazi Party in Germany. At home, Gregg watched these events with increasing concern, and they added urgency to his work on nonviolence. It was clear, even then, that another war in Europe was likely, and, given the developing economic crisis, the impact would be global and devastating. Prompted in no small part by the success of the Salt March, events in India were also coming to a head. In January 1931, the Indian National Congress declared Indian independence, and the British were deeply concerned about what they saw, from their perspective, as a rapidly deteriorating situation, forcing them to consider negotiations to give greater rights to the movement.

Gregg knew that Gandhi had been invited to London for the first Round Table Conference on India that spring. He cautioned Gandhi not to undertake the trip, showing concern for his safety and fear that the British government would distort the meaning of the meetings. Gandhi went to London in October, however, despite his friend's concerns, and began the delicate negotiations with the British. Worried about British motives and the safety of his friend, Gregg wrote to several Indian leaders and also to Harold Laski, who was then serving as a chief secretarial assistant at the Conference, so that Gandhi and Laski could connect, and that Laski could provide support.[220] The formal meetings with the U.K. government officials were mostly a failure but, even so, Gandhi was able to give lectures and talks to large crowds in London's East End, in Lancashire, and to a packed audience of students at the London School of Economics. Later in the year, Gregg wrote several letters to

Gandhi arguing strongly against any plan for him to visit America, arguing that the time was not right for such a visit.[221] Gandhi did not come.

The economic collapse and rise of fascism showed how powerful forces were threatening the stability and peace of the major capitalist powers and the international system. Gregg believed that conflict in India was inevitable and more extensive global war loomed. The question of how to deal with these conflicts had become yet more urgent and pressing for Gregg.

Writing *The Power of Non-Violence*

In his efforts to write about approaches to the nonviolent resolution of disputes, Gregg had already completed two books, which made up something of a trilogy with *The Power of Non-Violence.* The first of these, *The Psychology and Strategy of Gandhi's Nonviolent Resistance,* he completed in 1928, and it was published in India in 1929. Here, for the first time, Gregg began to elaborate on his ideas about nonviolence and elucidate Gandhi's insights. The work introduced the concept of nonviolent *action*, stressing the possibilities of training and discipline, of strategy and tactics, and, most tellingly, the idea that nonviolent resistance was akin to a military campaign, both physical and spiritual. The work also developed Gregg's ideas about the importance of the psychological aspects of nonviolent resistance, building on the then-recent work in psychology that he had read in India, and that had informed some of his thinking in Chicago, working with Tead.

In *Psychology and Strategy*, Gregg described for the first time his concept of moral jiu-jitsu—the idea of putting an opponent off balance by passive resistance and treating the moment as a kind of theater, educating, and mobilizing an audience. He developed these perspectives extensively in his later work, and several chapters derived from *Psychology and Strategy* formed the core of *PNV*. Published in India in 1930, the second work, *Gandhiji's Satyagraha or Nonviolent Resistance*, revised and extended many of the arguments Gregg had made in his previous book on nonviolence. This revision was a massive undertaking, and the work ended up being close to five hundred pages. It provided all the core arguments that he would later use for his most significant and widely read book.

Gregg knew about the resistance to Gandhi's ideas even among pacifists in the U.S. To counter these, he was at pains to make Gandhi accessible and relevant, and to move beyond simple explication. As he wrote in the foreword to *Gandhiji's Satyagraha*:

> It seems to me that in the West it is time that the subject of pacifism, in
> both individual and collective use, should be removed from the profitless
> atmosphere, on the one hand, of warm adjectives, and on the other, of vague
> mysticisms, futile protests, or confused or incomplete thinking. We need to
> understand this thing much more clearly and fully.[222]

Gregg's distaste for "warm adjectives" very much embodied his practical side; he understood and believed that social transformation must be deeply rooted in personal transformation and a commitment to a nonviolent way of life. For him, this was no abstraction, and it demanded concrete action. Without such a transformative commitment, a real understanding and application of nonviolence was not possible. Gregg's view drew on his experience in American labor relations, his time with Gandhi, his teaching, his farm work, but also on his extensive reading of psychology, history, and philosophy, and, of course, his Christian beliefs.

This was a very productive time for Gregg, as he revised *Gandhism and Socialism* (first published in India in 1931, republished in 1932 as *Gandhiism Vs. Socialism* in the U.S.) and working on *PNV*. He also worked on a draft of *The Value of Voluntary Simplicity* (first published by Pendle Hill in 1936).[223] Here he sought to connect the philosophy of nonviolence to the development of a nonviolent, ecologically sound way of life, one that rejected modern consumerism and industrialism. In the revisions to *Gandhiism Vs. Socialism*,

Gregg wanted to emphasize the value of a decentralized, nonviolent society over leftist collective economies. He laid out the argument that the real control of society (and thus the root of power) lies in the fact that, "governments, banks, laws, and ruling classes are only the exterior instruments of management"[224] whether they claimed to be liberal, conservative or, especially, socialist. This argument that socialism relies on the same forms of production and uses the same symbols of power as capitalism reflects Gandhi's perspective. Gregg's distrust of large organizations (capitalist or socialist), bureaucracies, and their use of symbols and violence to maintain legitimacy and control threads through his work. In *Gandhiism Vs. Socialism*, therefore, he laid out his critique of socialism and, especially, the Soviet model as he understood its development from the decade or so since the Russian Revolution. Gregg argued that money served as the most potent symbol of the capitalist order. Financial capital, not elected officials, was the "invisible government of nations."[225] For Gregg, physical violence is the second most potent sentiment underlying the capitalist order, physically symbolized by uniforms, martial music, and military parades. These things control "people by fear of violence…and prestige of power." The people who participate in the parades, and laud those wearing the uniform, give their tacit approval for violence.[226] In *Gandhiism Vs. Socialism* he stressed that socialism was not the only alternative to capitalism and that socialism embodies many of the ideas and features that both Gregg and Gandhi found detrimental to true equality and human emancipation.

Eventually, Gregg was able to combine much of this thinking into *PNV.* Once the manuscript was complete and back from his typist, Lippincott Press in New York agreed to publish it. The Quaker leader (and co-founder of the American Friends Service Committee) Rufus Jones wrote the foreword, stressing and admiring the practical approach the work took. The book got noticed quickly. *The New York Times* did a brief, favorable review in December 1934, noting that, "His extensive application of the principles of psychology to the question at issue is one of the important and very interesting features of the work, while another is the extent and astuteness of the copious quotations and references with which he substantiates his arguments." The reviewer concluded that "Mr. Gregg brings out into the open field a workable theory of a substitute for war and demonstrates practical methods by which each individual can take part in its realization."[227] Others were even more generous: the renowned pacifist and activist John Nevin Sayre called it the "bible" of nonviolence. Others lauded its practicality and pragmatic approach. There was one voice of dissent, however. The theologian Reinhold Niebuhr was skeptical and concerned that the work, while authoritative, ultimately contained the contradiction that a practical nonviolence did not or could not exclude the use of force in the final analysis.[228] In general, however, *PNV* was received extremely favorably. It became a training manual and argument for pacifists across the world.

More Like War Than We Imagined[229]

With its publication, Gregg gained the audience he sought, particularly in the United States and Great Britain. The first edition of the book is complex and multi-faceted. Gregg tackled the problem of how to deal with violence and conflict and laid out why he believed that nonviolent forms of conflict resolution were the *only* ways to make the world a better place. Gregg argued that this could only result from cooperation and that, where violent contestation occurs, nonviolent protesters should engage in "moral jiu-jitsu." This notion became one of the most quoted terms of the pacifist movement. Gregg built this idea of "moral jiu-jitsu" on psychological insights into human sentiments, similar to the argument he made about the differences in beliefs that underpin socialism and Gandhism. He argued that the cruelty of the assailant was rooted in fear, anger, and pride. In nonviolent protest, the actions of the protester suggested to the assailant that he might be in the morally inferior position and unable to conquer the protester. This realization would put the aggressor off-balance, unable to continue the attack.[230]

Having established the dynamics of nonviolence between individuals, Gregg turned to the issue of mass nonviolence, setting out an argument that showed nonviolent resistance in military terms and as a substitute for war. No pacifist before him had invoked the military metaphor to inform and advocate nonviolent resistance. Gregg was presenting a unique perspective: that nonviolent resistance was a public and collective performance designed to gain the sympathy of opponents and observers. Moral, spiritual, and political principles could be dramatized in a way that would be extremely effective theater. Gregg had seen this in the Salt March and, later, this public showing of nonviolent resistance would add tremendous power to the civil rights protests of Martin Luther King, Jr., and others like young John Lewis, perhaps most notably in the confrontations on the Edmund Pettus Bridge in Montgomery, Alabama, on that tragic Sunday in March of 1965 when countless marchers many were beaten and bloodied by police.[231]

In addition to advocating for nonviolent protest as a media spectacle, Gregg argued that nonviolence is passive resistance, requiring intense training. He emphasized the importance of onlookers seeing the violent assailants as "excessive and undignified—even a little ineffective." In this way, nonviolent protest, "wins for its users the support of public opinion." Gregg repeatedly invoked martial metaphors and indeed argued that peaceful protest represented a war of its own.

But for Gregg, as for Gandhi, acts of nonviolent resistance, while critical theater and essential forms of confrontation against power and violence, are temporary manifestations of a more profound, cooperative, nonviolent way of living. True nonviolence, he asserted, required a way of life that embraces peaceful, collaborative relationships and that respects both humanity and nature. Gregg saw this approach as a way to transform the use of power over people, countries, and nature to the power of cooperation and harmony in all aspects of life. To put this another way, as Gregg indeed did, this is the power of love, one that extends and is in harmony with nature, human relationships, and social interaction. These beliefs derive directly from *satyagraha* and its core tenet that all life is interdependent.

In *PNV*, Gregg asserted that it is the power of love that drives all nonviolent ways of life. Gregg firmly believed and expressed throughout the work that human beings must find a way to tap the persuasive power of nonviolence, by building and sustaining cooperative relationships through constructive practices in all aspects of material life, and through all aspects of human behavior. These encompass not only government and institutions but also the development and use of technologies, economic systems, relations with nature, and all efforts to promote the health and well-being of people and the environment. In one notebook he wrote, "If we who are privileged and yet believe in nonviolence do not simplify our lives and go to help and then to lead the underprivileged then the communists...will win their trust by other kinds of service."[232] With this he made clear that he rejected communism and wished to embrace simplicity as the core of radical social change. In all his work, and especially in *PNV*, Gregg consistently claimed that cooperation and harmony are the normal and defining state of the world. It is the creation of competition, distrust, and individualism (all very Western in their origins) that corrupts the unity of life. The power of an individual, group, or country over another is a constraint that drives a violent social system.[233] The book was not by any means only about international conflict. It reflected Gregg's experience and concern with labor and social struggles for justice. It is not surprising that it became a guide for the civil rights movement decades later. Of course, Gregg recognized that nonviolent resisters needed courage and fortitude and insisted on training and group support before undertaking nonviolent action. Specifically, he recognized that the discipline of the military, which seeks to replace fear with courage, is equally relevant for the nonviolent actor. For Gregg, the human psyche is malleable. People can be taught to overcome their fear.

Gregg was a careful writer, and he developed his arguments with modesty and restraint. This reserve is something Gregg always struggled with, and he writes about it in his private journals and notebooks, remarking on his tendency towards shyness and diffidence while at the same time being keen to get his ideas out. He was, however, unrelenting in his advocacy and his righteousness. His concern with these aspects of his personality, especially his lack of openness, was clear from very early on. In his notes from 1925, as he journeyed to India to join Gandhi's ashram, he remarks: "It has long been one of my defects not to share my thoughts and feelings with others or to do so far too little. Has constricted my personality, the quality and richness of my friendships, and my happiness and usefulness. Consider this in relation to my stay in India."[234]

These self-doubts sometimes left Gregg feeling reticent about what he could contribute to the critical issues. They also drove his belief that change must come from within, and, although Gregg would never say this of himself, it is his self-doubt and introspection that make his work all the more compelling. There is an openness in his writing that was certainly not typical of many of his peers. He expresses humility, writing carefully and with constant alternative viewpoints to ensure that his readers do not feel attacked or alienated. His presentation of ideas follows that of Gandhi, with many admissions of doubt and openness to alternative perspectives. Not only does this reflect who he was, but it was a deliberate and carefully considered component of how Gregg thought people are persuaded and convinced. It reflects a deep belief, drawn from Gandhi, of the need for creating empathy and, indeed, love.

In *PNV*, Gregg explicitly seeks to take from Gandhi the clearest of his expressions of nonviolent resistance. For Gregg, all life should be nonviolent—in our relationships with each other, our daily conduct, and in our connection to nature and the natural world. This was not just a set of ethics for Gregg, it constituted a way of being in the world and how the world might be transformed. Over the ten years between his decision to move to India and the publication of his major work, he had read deeply into the literature on psychology, philosophy, and social sciences. All this built on his past, as it defined his future.

Gregg completed his revisions to the *PNV* while he and Nonie were living on Boylston Street. Again, it is remarkable how much scholarship he produced in this short period. In fewer than ten years, Gregg had written four books, traveled twice to India, written countless articles and letters, and taught himself the rudiments of Hindi. He had developed considerable skills at organic farming and gotten married. Throughout, he remained wholly engaged with the pacifist movement, giving talks on his experience and ideas, and advocating for and defending pacifists throughout the United States.

A Home at Last

With *PNV* now on the shelves, Gregg took the time to find a better place to live. He and Nonie had bought and moved to a house in Natick in the summer of 1934, their first real home. The house gave them relief from the cramped quarters of Nonie's studio and the noise and traffic of downtown Boston. Modest and cozy, the typical New England home had a covered porch that sheltered the front door and main entrance. A small garden in the back got plenty of sun and provided a great place to grow vegetables. The house was not far from Boston, but affordable, at a stretch. It was comfortable, and it gave Gregg and Nonie a base from which they could pursue their interests—not least of which was the creation of an organic garden. It was here that Gregg honed his skills as a gardener, some of which he had developed while living in India. He used his garden to experiment with different soils and ways of growing vegetables. As he gardened, he made copious notes on his ideas, experiments, and outcomes. And the garden in Natick provided them wholesome food.

Being settled was very much a new thing for Gregg as he approached fifty. He had barely lived in one place for more than a few months and certainly never with a partner. Being in Natick gave him a sense of place and stability for the first time in his adult life. He used these years to continue his reading, writing, and correspondence to his friends and colleagues in both India and the United States. As Gregg worked, Nonie's interior design jobs brought in much-needed money.

Gregg kept writing while remaining active in many prominent organizations in the U.S. He had joined J.B. Matthews and Roger Baldwin in starting the American League for India's Freedom in 1932. Matthews was a linguist, educator and pacifist, and member of the Socialist Party. Baldwin was a founder and executive director of the American Civil Liberties Union (ACLU) who had been a conscientious objector during WWI and a member of the International Workers of the World. The League provided information leaflets about India and the independence struggle, many written by Gregg. The organization gained prominence in the 1930s before declining, but it connected him with significant figures in the progressive and pacifist movements in the U.S.

In 1933, Gregg began a correspondence with John Nevin Sayre of the Fellowship of Reconciliation (FOR). Formed as a pacifist organization during WWI, FOR was, perhaps, the most important and most effective pacifist organization developed in the early twentieth century. Sayre was one of the founding members of FOR and, in 1935, became the Chair of the International Fellowship of Reconciliation (IFOR), holding that position until 1955. One of the foremost pacifists of the period, he and Gregg became fast friends.

During the 1930s, Gregg helped lead FOR. He joined the War Resisters League, established in 1923 in response to the horrors of WWI and American militarization. The League focused on international war. FOR was internally conflicted about violence and nonviolent resistance and the relevance of Marxism to the cause, and Gregg took part in these debates. This conflict led to passionate and vibrant discussions, intensified by the growing economic crisis. And the debates were part of a profoundly ideological and religious schism that would have implications for the future of pacifism, the development of the American civil rights movement, and for Gregg himself. Protestant pacifists who dominated FOR admired Gandhi, but some had reservations about the confrontational nature of Gandhian nonviolent resistance. John Nevin Sayre, then co-director of FOR, had concerns about strikes and boycotts as potentially violent forms of resistance. John Hayes Holmes, who deeply admired Gandhi, was also ambivalent about advocating non-cooperation with governments, whether in India or the United States.[235] Perhaps most influential was the great theologian Reinhold Niebuhr, whose *Moral Man and Immoral Society* argued that some coercion would be necessary to change society and American pacifists needed to be much more realistic in their approach to nonviolence.[236] Gregg responded to these conflicts by emphasizing that FOR should have as its core the goal of promoting nonviolence, and that any political stripe committed to that goal should be welcomed. Gregg believed this was critical. While never a socialist, and certainly no Marxist, he welcomed these viewpoints so long as nonviolence was primary. In part, working and arguing for peace as a Christian, one who based his thinking on science and practicality, he consciously advocated and wrote in a way that made his arguments appealing to a secular and Left audience. He was equally at home with Dorothy Day's Catholic Worker Movement (started in 1933) as he was working with Gandhi and his followers. He never lost his commitment to workers. And, in many ways, despite sharing

Niebuhr's emphasis on action and realism for pacifist action, Gregg's position stressed that real change could only come about by changing ideology, values, and beliefs—and creating new, peaceful, and positive attitudes.[237]

The early '30s was very much a Gandhian moment. After Gandhi's appearance in London in 1931 and all the attendant publicity, the struggle for Indian independence gained extensive coverage in the U.S. Leaders of the American pacifist movement and social reformers paid close attention to Gandhi. Several of them traveled to India to meet with the Indian independence movement leader. These included important figures, such as W. E. B. Du Bois and Rufus Jones. Jones, the Quaker historian, was one of the founders of the American Friends Service Committee (AFSC), and, like Gregg, one of the few Americans to visit Gandhi in the 1920s. They and many others began to mobilize and respond to what was going on in India. One of those discontented with the more conciliatory position was A.J. Muste, who became a leader in the post-war pacifist movement and FOR, and one of the few leaders of FOR closely allied to the American labor movement. Later he renounced his Christian beliefs, became a Marxist, and quit the organization. And Niebuhr resigned from FOR's national council.

After he became a leader with FOR and after *PNV* was published, Gregg led study groups and communicated extensively with many in the embryonic civil rights movement, labor leaders, and pacifists. His writing was widely disseminated among members of FOR and the War Resisters League. At last, Gregg was getting traction in bringing Gandhian ideas, shaped for a Western context, to the U.S.[238]

Richard Gregg, 1949.

Richard Gregg,
Colorado Springs,
1903.

Richard Gregg (left) with Albert
Farwell Bemis, on a ship during their
Indian trip, c. early 1914.

Richard Gregg, 1920. Location unknown.

Richard Gregg and Maganlal Gandhi,
Gandhi's ashram, December 1926.

Richard Gregg, Calcutta, 1928.

Richard Gregg at
Santiniketan, 1950.

Richard Gregg,
Scott and Helen
Nearing. Forest
Farm, Vermont,
c. 1950.

Richard Gregg and Scott Nearing. Forest Farm, Vermont, c. early 1950s.

Richard Gregg and Scott Nearing. Forest Farm, Vermont, c. early 1950s.

Richard Gregg, c. 1947.

Richard Gregg and
Nonie Tupper Gregg.
Place unknown,
c. early 1950s.

Richard Gregg and Evelyn Speiden Gregg's cottage, Chester, New York, c. 1959.

Faith Gregg Bemis and Richard Gregg, c. 1950.

Richard Gregg, c. early 1950s.

Richard Gregg, India, c. 1956.

Richard Gregg, 1966.

Richard Gregg and Evelyn Speiden Gregg, 1966.

Richard Gregg, Cascade Manor, Oregon, 1966.

Richard Gregg and
Evelyn Speiden Gregg,
McMinville, Oregon,
1966.

March on Washington for Jobs and Freedom, Martin Luther King, Jr., front, second from left, 1963.

Mahatma Gandhi, 1946.

Dr. Martin Luther King, Jr., delivering his "I Have a Dream" speech at the March on Washington, August 28, 1963.

CHAPTER EIGHT

The Value of Voluntary Simplicity

Simplicity, to be more effective, must inform and be integrated with many aspects of life. It needs to become more social in purpose and method. It ought to be organically connected with a thoroughgoing program of nonviolence as a method of persuasion to social change, and to be definitely a part of a constructive practical program for the economic security of the masses.
—Richard Gregg, *The Value of Voluntary Simplicity*, 35

WITH THE COMPLETION OF *The Power of Non-Violence* and his active engagement with the Fellowship of Reconciliation, and having become something of a celebrity in the American pacifist movement, Gregg found himself extraordinarily busy. It was the time for him to develop the thinking of many years: how to integrate the strategies of nonviolence into a holistic approach to living. Gregg was very clear in his thinking that nonviolent resistance could be coupled to a life lived in such a way that it reframed or reinvented the self in those terms. A large part of that reframing involved, for Gregg, a recognition of the critical importance of how humans lived with nature and how they stewarded the resources it provided. As he finished *PNV* and argued and advocated in the U.S. for the Indian independence movement, he developed ideas that linked his troubling experience with

American capitalism and labor relations to Gandhi's philosophies and the ideas that Gandhi advocated. This led him, too, towards articulating, more explicitly, the connection between pacifism and simplicity.

Living the Simple Life

Gregg's ideas found fertile soil in the American peace movement as the Great Depression took hold, and many in the peace movement sought to understand what was going on in India and around the world. For Gregg, the advocacy of nonviolent resistance to war and social inequality could not be distinguished from the need to create a new social and economic system. For him, a better, less violent world could only be built on a new foundation, one much less dependent on the technology and industrialism of modern capitalism. These ideas led to his pamphlet *The Value of Voluntary Simplicity*, published in 1936 by Pendle Hill, the Quaker retreat and center founded in Pennsylvania in 1930. The beginnings of these ideas he jotted down in his 1934 notebook:

> The present system uses covert violence (ec pressure) on people. What shall I do about that/ Refuse to accept the evil values inherent in capitalism, viz 1. Money 2. Competition 3. Outer violence 4. Flattery, prestige, and social grades (division as opposed to social unity). Encouraging barter, neighborhood and community and hand labor, mutual aid. These latter encourage real trust instead of money symbols, and also encourage small-scale organization and social unity. Competition is a denial of human unity. NVR will break up these outer props of capitalism and also many of its inner elements. Hand labor will encourage (Swadidis) and small-scale organization. Work this up into a pamphlet while I am at Pendle Hill.[239]

His concern to promote a sustainable, simple lifestyle as a core element in the fight to end violence was built on experience and, of course, from the ideas and model that Gandhi epitomized. Throughout this time, Gregg was thinking about how to frame this perspective. The result was *The Value of Voluntary Simplicity*.

In this pamphlet Gregg outlined his reasons for adopting a simple life. He drew upon arguments based upon the debates he often had with himself in his notebooks and other published works. For example, in his notebook for 1934:

"(c)apitalism is no mere exterior organization of bankers and industrialists. It consists of a spirit and attitude . . . If I wish actively to participate in this transformation [of the capitalist order], I myself must begin to alter my own life in the desired direction . . . No— the way to master the increasing complexity of life is not through more complexity. The way is to turn inward to that which unifies all—not the intellect but the spirit, and then to devise and put into operation new forms and modes of economic and social life that will truly and vigorously express that spirit. As an aid to that and as a corrective to our feverish over-mechanization, simplicity is not outmoded but greatly needed."[240]

After returning from his trip to India with Nonie in 1930, Gregg imagined a future in farming and simple living. He made a note to himself:

Because of the evils and [. . .] of machinery and its implications, and hence those of industrialism and their bad effects on industrial workers, the latter will always be likely to fail in establishing a better world. Farmers and peasants are nearer the ultimate truth, the decentralization of social life is sounder, the farmers have the ultimate power because they create food. Hence it is perhaps more important to do social work among farmers than among city industrial workers. Certainly, it is as important. **Hence my going to live as a farmer is not a desertion of the struggle** [author's emphasis].[241]

But always these ideas and values remained deeply embedded in his spiritual beliefs: "Christianity needs a means of implementing its ideals of human unity into a social program. While simplicity alone is only one element, it would seem to me to be one of the necessary elements in such a program. Simplicity would constitute part of a code of moral hygiene necessary for a healthy and vigorous spiritual life." And this was also part of his way of thinking about beauty: "He who appreciates and understands a song, a symphony, a painting or some sculpture or architecture gets more satisfaction than he who owns musical instruments or works of art." Gregg knew that a call for simpler living could not only be about giving up a materialistic life, but that is must also integrate into daily existence and that people could learn how to do that as part of a constructivist program and extensive training.

As he noted later in *Voluntary Simplicity*, "For those who believe in nonviolence, simplicity is essential." But it should always be connected to a more significant problem of equity and well-being, and to the equal and just distribution of resources. For Gregg this was a moral problem. He began to lay out the basis for simple living as an alternative to the Western, twentieth-century industrialized system in which he lived. Modern industrial capitalism could not be peaceful. He proposed small-scale farming communities that lived in voluntary simplicity. For Gregg, nonviolence and simplicity were inextricably linked. Nonviolence and simplicity operated at the individual level as well as in the complexities of international affairs.

In writing about simplicity, Gregg attributed much social strife to the lack of self-respect and self-confidence in two class divisions, to unemployment, and to the poverty that capitalism generated. The American South was a dust bowl, and across the country unemployment had reached unprecedented levels. Many lived with the abundant misery that capitalism's failures created. These conditions were so unrelentingly awful by the middle of the '30s, they made the search for an alternative urgent.

Gregg believed that the only solution lay in a complete transformation of production and consumption and that a commitment to simplicity and manual labor would not only increase self-respect and self-confidence for those who adopted it, but also reduce violence at the societal level. Gregg struggled to explain this in terms acceptable to secular, scientific Western minds and, in that way, blunted the spiritual and moral content that infused his ideas about simplicity and nonviolence. As he worked on *Voluntary Simplicity*, Gregg proposed a sweeping change in the organization of production and consumption as a prelude to creating a better, nonviolent world. This was not a vision that would be easily accepted. Gregg knew that. As others noted later, he was suggesting the embrace of a "counter modernity."[242]

Gregg did not separate his ideas about simplicity from his wide-ranging critique of the violence and inequality built into modern capitalism and industrialization (and in state socialism in the Soviet Union). He returned regularly to his central theme: capitalism and industrialism are violent systems and cannot be reformed. Gregg's simplicity preceded a peaceful life, self-determination, and the freedom from acquisitiveness. Gregg connected materialism and technology to avarice, the need to protect private property, and modern alienation. In this, Gregg's writing and thinking about simplicity anticipated much of the 1960s "Back to the Land" movement. Many of the ideas about communal living, deeply embedded in several religious movements in America and elsewhere, were given a modern and youthful slant at the end of the '60s in the West. It would not be too much of a stretch to see these ideas in the modern anti-globalization movement and the promotion of local production, small-scale enterprise, locally sourced organic food, and concerns about global warming. There are also echoes of these sentiments in the contemporary maker movement and the sharing or bartering economy.

Gregg's time on the farm in Wisconsin in 1924, the agricultural courses he took before leaving for India, his reading and writing about food and the simple life, all pointed to a desire to live a life on the land. After living simply in India and developing the concepts that led to the *The Power of Non-Violence*, the possibility of being close to nature never left him. In the fall of 1936, he took the job as director of the Quaker retreat at Pendle Hill in Pennsylvania, where he was exposed to both the ideas and the experience of the Quaker belief system, and it was there that he finished and published *The Value of Voluntary Simplicity*. Although his stay there was brief, he got to know many of the Quaker pacifists who came to the camp for classes and workshops, including

Mildred and Wilmer Young, both activists who worked extensively with the American Friends Service Committee, and, later, in the anti-Vietnam War and anti-nuclear movements. Both also taught at Pendle Hill.[243]

His time with the Quakers was short, and he never saw his role as director of Pendle Hill as long-term. He and Nonie did not relocate there but remained in their home in Natick. Gregg admired the Quakers but did not join them. The energy he devoted to Pendle Hill was limited, partly because the positive reception of *PNV* led to calls for him to lead workshops around the country and to further international engagement with the pacifist movement as the threat of war accelerated in Europe.

While Gregg was extremely busy throughout 1936, it was also that year when another tragedy struck his family: his brother-in-law, Farwell, died in Phoenix, Arizona. He fell from his hotel room balcony while taking photographs of the Grand Canyon and died of his injuries. The accident devastated his sister Faith, losing her husband and the father of their seven children. While Gregg felt ambivalent about the wealthy Farwell, his love for Faith, the memories of the many happy times he had spent at her house, and the family place in South Tamworth, became all the more poignant after the accident.

England and the Peace Pledge Union

In the mid '30s, the situation in Europe deteriorated. The re-arming of Germany under Hitler presaged yet another potential worldwide conflict. In Britain, the fear of the impending war had mobilized the pacifist movement, and *PNV's* publication in the U.K. garnered considerable interest and acclaim. Gregg had rapidly become an international figure in the pacifist movement. Central to the movement in England at that time was the Peace Pledge Union (PPU).

The PPU emerged in 1936 from the Sheppard Peace Movement, a group founded by Dick Sheppard, a WWI army chaplain, and by the Canon of

St. Paul's Cathedral. It was formally created in July 1935 at Albert Hall in London.[244] Sheppard had published a letter a year earlier in the *Manchester Guardian* asking men to send a postcard swearing to "renounce war and never again to support another." After only two days, Sheppard received about two thousand-five hundred responses, and within a few weeks more than another thirty thousand took the oath. Membership reached 135,000.

Sheppard was joined in these efforts by other prominent figures such as Arthur Ponsonby, an aristocrat, but a member of the Labour Party in the U.K., and a leading pacifist; and by George Lansbury born working class in the East End of London and an advocate for women's suffrage in the early 1900s and later the leader of the Labour Party in the mid-'30s. Others included: Vera Brittain, the novelist and peace activist; Margaret Storm Jameson, a writer and socialist and one of the founding members of PPU; and Siegfried Sassoon, a writer and poet, socialist and pacifist, best known for his poetry about WWI and life in the trenches. Two or three others brought significant legitimacy to the organization: Donald Soper, Methodist minister, socialist and pacifist, and, much later, a member of the House of Lords; Aldous Huxley, the well-known novelist, poet and pacifist; and the philosopher and mathematician Bertrand Russell. These notables gave the organization a remarkable degree of prominence in the British political and cultural environment of the time.[245] Shortly after its creation, the PPU opened its membership to women and began regular publication of *Peace News*.[246]

Gregg's book had come out in the U.K. in 1934, and his ideas were quickly taken up by Huxley, Sheppard, and others. As a result, in early 1936, Dick Sheppard asked Gregg to come to England to discuss and promote his book and develop a "manual" on training for peace to distribute to PPU members. The invitation was great news for Gregg and Nonie and represented, at last, recognition of the contribution his work had brought to peace movements in the U.S. and Europe. Nonie wrote to her sister-in-law Marge in July about her excitement that Richard was heading to England at the request of "Canon Sheppard." The PPU paid for the trip (Nonie couldn't go with him because "we couldn't afford it"), and Gregg left for England on July 7 aboard the *SS Europa*.[247]

Gregg was enormously excited about getting his ideas out. Enroute to England, he wrote to Nonie every day with news about his traveling companions, the food on the ship, and what he was reading. He spent most of the journey reading and thinking about Gerald Heard's recently published *The Source of Civilization*.[248] Heard was a historian, novelist, and science writer who had gained fame in England after the publication of his *The Ascent of Humanity*. He was a friend of Aldous Huxley's, and both were involved in the PPU at the time. Heard moved to the States with Huxley in 1937 and went on to develop his ideas about evolution and consciousness while living in California. He is perhaps best remembered for *The Five Ages of Man*. Gregg and Heard would remain in touch for many years. During the trip to England, Gregg became much taken with Heard's thinking and was looking forward to meeting him.[249]

Gregg arrived in England in mid-July, landing at Southampton. On his first night in London, he had dinner with Sheppard and Heard, finding both men delightful and intelligent. He wrote to Nonie that Sheppard was: "a most loveable person, medium height, dark hair, smooth round face, spectacles, an excellent sense of humor, utterly unconventional, no trace of clerical manner or appearance, an infectious laugh, and says most astonishing and amusing things against bishops & churchiness." At dinner, Sheppard told him that women were joining the movement at the rate of about "200 a day." Gregg was thrilled to be in this company and somewhat amazed at the reception he received. Gregg excitedly told Nonie, "Sweetheart, the book is really being accepted by people here for action, not just words and debate."[250]

The leaders of the PPU had read *PNV* enthusiastically and were eager for Gregg to discuss it with PPU members and supporters. To that end, they scheduled Gregg to give talks in London, Birmingham, and Liverpool. On his second day in England, Gregg began a series of meetings and planned talks for the PPU all around Britain, including several long personal meetings with Heard—with whom he felt an immediate bond. Gregg found him to be "brilliant, thoroughly filled with history and science and seeing so clearly what an utter impasse Western civilization has reached . . ." Heard told Gregg that his book "was the most valuable now out."[251]

All in all, Gregg spent a busy couple of weeks in England and presented his ideas to several hundred people at halls and Quaker Meetinghouses across the country. He returned home excited and impressed with what was going on with the PPU, and fully committed to writing the training manual they had asked for. This work became *Training for Peace: A Manual for Peace Workers*.[252] When published in the U.K., the PPU began to implement many of its precepts. In particular, Gregg's notion of "moral jiu-jitsu" found enormous popularity among PPU members. Taking their lead from Gregg's supplement to *PNV*, the PPU advocated for and believed in "the efficacy of training highly disciplined pacifists willing to engage in individual nonviolent direct action that would eventually lead to the end of war."[253] Always practical, Gregg wrote in *Training For Peace* that, for the general public:

> . . . [p]acifism seems to consist merely of reading books and articles, going to meetings, listening to speeches, urging people in high places to do something . . . . It's true that education and definite public opinion are necessary before society can act. Nevertheless, for successful pacifism, just as for successful militarism, there must be a way for the individual to translate his beliefs into concrete action.[254]

Gregg encouraged pacifists to form discussion and reading groups where they should seek to develop "sentiments" appropriate to pacifism. According to Gregg, sentiments were "organized systems of feelings, ideas, and impulses to action." Groups, he said, should particularly seek to develop self-respect, unity, and morale. To cultivate these attitudes, Gregg suggested the three marks of later pacifist culture: "singing, folk dancing, and meditation." The development of sentiments should then be combined with concrete action as "action and sentiment always go together and interact." Members could engage in social service, nonviolent resistance, or, favored by Gregg, in manual labor. These ideas were all very much in line with Gandhi's constructivist programs and Gregg believed they were the core of training for peace.[255]

Of his new friends in England, Aldous Huxley really liked Gregg's approach. Huxley was already a prominent figure in England, author of numerous social satires and, of course, the dystopian novel *Brave New World*. Huxley supported conscientious objectors during WWI and later became a vital leader of the PPU, turning his writing to non-fiction, and authored the *Encyclopedia of Pacifism* and *Pacifism and Philosophy*.[256] Concerning tactics and training of peace activists, Huxley wrote to Argentinian writer Victoria Ocampo, "The only hope lies in pacifists being better disciplined than the militarists and prepared to put up with hardships and dangers with a courage equal to theirs. Not easy. But I suppose nothing of any value is easy."[257]

When Huxley read Gregg's *PNV*, he was enthralled. He liked Gregg's perspective and the implicit and often explicit call for action that Gregg had detailed. Huxley drew on the material for his *Encyclopedia*, and in the pamphlet he wrote for the PPU, *What Are You Going to Do About It?*, the first publication of the PPU.[258] Indeed, there are many distinct similarities between Gregg's work on pacifist training and Huxley's. In both works Huxley produced for the PPU he relied on Gregg's *PNV*, and Gregg appreciated Huxley's endorsement. The two kept in touch into the 1950s.

But not all in the PPU were entirely enamored of Gregg's ideas and his training program (what became known, not always in a positive way, as "Greggism"). Some in England dismissed it. While Huxley prominently supported Gregg's training methods, some of Gregg's injunctions did not sit quite so well with other members of the PPU. Indeed, even Dick Sheppard harbored some reservations about Gregg's insistence on music and singing. In his 1936 work, *We Say No,* Sheppard had much praise for Gregg. But this was quickly replaced by doubts about his methods, and Sheppard allowed the publication of *Training for Peace* under the auspices of the PPU only because of his deep respect for Huxley and Huxley's support for Gregg's ideas. The British pacifists found that Gregg's focus on meditation, folk dancing, communal singing, spinning, and knitting made the whole training program look "too Eastern."[259] This is not surprising since, by that time, most in England were staring down the barrel of the Nazi war machine.

Gregg got back from England at the end of the summer, exhilarated but exhausted. In early 1937 he left the directorship of Pendle Hill and returned home to Nonie. He needed to write and reassess where he was and where he was going. Income was a problem, however. Although the *PNV* had sold well, income from sales did not provide much to support two people, and, by this time, Nonie was beginning to suffer slight dementia, losing some control over her physical movements. It was the beginning of a long illness, and she was frequently tired and sometimes irritable and unable to work.

Several doctors who examined Nonie concluded that she suffered from blocked arteries in the brain. Gregg immediately set about researching ways to deal with her ailment and explored ways to improve her diet. He developed a regime for her, focusing on whole grains and minerals. As always, Gregg was tireless in his research, probing the link between nutrition and his wife's condition. He was convinced that changes in diet and reducing her exposure to what he thought of as "toxins" could cure her physical problems and loss of memory. Despite these efforts, Nonie's illness became a significant challenge for them both in the next few years.

For the time being, Gregg found comfort with Nonie, tended his garden, wrote, and worked periodically. He helped Graham Carey, architect and philosopher, set up a religion-based self-sufficient farm in Benson, Vermont. But with all these responsibilities, there was little time for writing. Still, he did keep up a significant course of research throughout this period and continued to write to Gandhi, and to work with FOR and other pacifist organizations. He struggled to find a cure for Nonie, tirelessly researching the latest medical knowledge about her condition. In the little time he had for writing he completed his pamphlet for Pendle Hill, *Pacifist Program in Time of War, Threatened War, or Fascism* in 1939 on the eve of a new war.

In the pamphlet, Gregg set out to explain how pacifists should act to protest the coming war, pointing out "since modern war is so largely caused by the workings of our economic system, a thoroughgoing refusal to support war would have required pacifists to stop using that system long before."[260] Gregg claimed that only those who had ceased to participate in the economic system underpinned by war could sincerely protest. This work was not only an effort to analyze the rise of fascism in Europe, but also a guide on how to resist conscription nonviolently, and how to deal with the legal ramifications of refusing to pay taxes. It is an elegant sixty-one pages on how to be a pacifist.

In that year, as Europe erupted into war, tragedy again struck Gregg personally. His brother Don, who had been ill for several months, died in January from esophageal cancer. Don was fifty-eight and the first sibling Gregg was to lose. The news came just as he was completing a piece about Gandhi and his contributions as a researcher, *Gandhiji as a Social Scientist and Social Inventor*.[261] Despite the upset of his brother's passing, he did finish the work, stressing Gandhi's commitment to science and facts, reporting how Gandhi purposely set out to collect data, test hypotheses, and examine and evaluate the results. Gregg developed this argument specifically to counteract the many claims that Gandhi was an idealist whose arguments were not grounded in science and analysis.

Gregg carefully but forcefully refutes these criticisms and notes that his mentor always based his work on people's day-to-day experience. This commitment was especially evident in his study of diet, sanitation, caste reform, and the many challenges faced by most Indian peasants. Today the work reads like an argument for participatory action research, stressing Gandhi's deep commitment to knowledge, trust in ordinary people, and belief in what today we would term the practical application of theory and knowledge, or "praxis."

Within a year Germany had occupied most of Europe and, by the late summer of 1940, was bombing Britain and preparing to invade. In the summer of 1941 the Nazis began the invasion of the Soviet Union and, that winter, Japan bombed Pearl Harbor and the world was truly at war. In Germany, the horror of the Final Solution was underway. In Italy the fascists were fully in control and many countries were under military dictatorships. As war raged in Europe, Gregg and Nonie carried on as best they could in Natick. Gregg kept reading and writing, working on a new article, *A Discipline for Nonviolence*, to be published through Pendle Hill. The pamphlet was republished in India by Navajian Press in 1941, with a brief foreword by Gandhi. In it Gregg reiterates the value of military-style training for successful nonviolent action: "It is my purpose in the ensuing pages to point out that nonviolent as well as military training requires physical drills and disciplines and that such training can be obtained through manual work."[262] Again, Gregg stresses the connection between peace, discipline, and manual work. For him, manual labor was a kind of military training. It engages the worker, especially if the work is socially useful and of value to the community and provides and encourages physical fitness.

While this period was one of Gregg's most prolific and productive, day-to-day living got harder. He wanted to get out from under the debt of the mortgage on the house and to generate more income, and Nonie wasn't improving. In April 1941, they sold the Natick house. Gregg was "mightily" relieved to get rid of the debt. They took up Faith's offer to move temporarily to her big house in Chestnut Hill and lived there for a while, and then returned to Nonie's old studio near Copley Square in the fall.

Back to the Garden

Amidst war, Gregg's love for gardening and his connection to the land flourished. He focused on sustainable farming practice and read Rudolf Steiner, considered the founder of biodynamic organic farming, and Ehrenfried Pfeiffer's *Bio-Dynamic Farming and Gardening*, published in 1938.[263] This work built on some of the ideas Gregg had encountered at the ashram and his interest in organic soil, composting, and the maintenance of harmony with nature. When the opportunity presented itself in the spring of 1942, Gregg traveled south to begin work as an apprentice at a center for biodynamic farming and gardening at Kimberton Farm, Pennsylvania, working with Pfeiffer. He took courses there and said of them later:

> In addition to very interesting lectures, every morning there were periods for questions and discussion. The afternoons were filled with demonstrations and practice of laboratory and field techniques for soil testing. A number of resident students, who had already been there for a year, were able to help with some of the demonstrations and lectures. Full of intellectual content but also thoroughly practical, they gave one a strong desire to go out and apply the new knowledge.[264]

There he met, for the first time, Robert Swann, who was to become a community land trust pioneer. Swann was a key figure in the community economics movement and a conscientious objector. A committed advocate of nonviolence, Swann was imprisoned as a conscientious objector during WWII. He later recognized Gregg as the man who gave him his first intellectual understanding of nonviolence. Bob Swann would go on to coordinate the Committee for Nonviolent Action with his wife Marjorie. In the mid-'60s, the Swanns helped establish a land trust on a farm they purchased with others in Voluntown, Connecticut. The farm became the Voluntown Peace Trust, which endures today as a retreat and conference center dedicated to nonviolent social change and sustainable living.[265] Swann was a carpenter and designer and shared many of the qualities of Bill Coperthwaite, whom Gregg would get to know and later befriend. Gregg kept in touch with Swann for many years and reconnected when they both worked on the nonviolent action against Electric Boat, in Connecticut, protesting the corporation's manufacture of nuclear submarines in the early '60s.

It was at the farm, too, that he met Evelyn Speiden, who would become his co-author and, much later, his second wife. After leaving the farm, he completed and published a short book on gardening, co-authored with Evelyn. The work, *A Primer of Companion Planting: Herbs, Their Part in Good Gardening*, is still in print and regarded by many as an essential work on organic garden management. The apprenticeship at Kimberton laid the groundwork for changes in Gregg's life, as he delved deeper into organic farming and how it connected to his work on nonviolence. He continued however to work actively for peace, and, to that end, he agreed to give some talks at the School for Nonviolence in Big Flats, N.Y., at a camp for conscientious objectors founded in 1942 and operated by the American Friends Service Committee. The "school" only existed for a few months at the camp. The camp was formally closed in the fall of 1946. Both Gregg and A.J. Muste gave classes at the school.

It had been close to ten years since the publication of *PNV*, and Gregg was eager to get out a new revised edition as the war continued throughout Europe and Asia. The 1934 edition was by now out of print, so it seemed timely to work on a new version. Gregg sought to capture the new reality of global war and the appropriate responses to it. In the latest edition, Gregg cut several chapters and added new ones, including sections on "discipline" and "persuasion." Quaker theologian, historian, and founder of the American Friends Service Committee, Rufus M. Jones, wrote the foreword to the second revised edition, published by Fellowship Publications in 1944.[266]

While he was working on the new edition of *PVN*, Nonie's condition gradually worsened. Gregg thought that the diagnosis of arteriolosclerosis was affecting her brain functioning. He continued to research her symptoms and possible cures and tried a variety of nutritional and medical programs, but her condition did not improve. Caring for her was becoming a round-the-clock commitment that, while Gregg embraced it wholeheartedly, added further stress to his life. And money was still a problem. With Nonie no longer working and Gregg getting only small payments in royalties and some minimal earnings from talks and lectures, their financial situation became increasingly problematic. They were still living in her former studio, but Gregg needed a job, and he felt that getting out of the city would help Nonie's condition. They decided to leave Boston.

In the summer of 1944, Gregg and Nonie moved to Putney, Vermont. Gregg was hired to teach math at the Putney school, where he believed Nonie "would be happier in those surroundings."[267] They lived close to the school, above a "very smelly" barn according to Kate Thompson, Gregg's grandniece, who visited them there when she was very young.[268] But the school and the location seemed right. It was founded by Carmelita Hinton in 1935 and was based mainly on the progressive educational ideas of John Dewey and seemed a perfect fit for Gregg.[269] The school had a progressive philosophy, a working farm, and its founder believed deeply in manual labor, art, and music as part of a complete education—an approach in harmony with Gregg's views. But he was not entirely happy there. As he realized in India, he was not a natural teacher, and his abilities were challenged by the students, who tended to be the offspring of wealthy intellectuals and highly educated parents. The trials of teaching in this environment were not helped by Nonie's chronic illness.

In the fall of that year, Gregg pleaded to his sister Elinor for advice.[270]

In response, Elinor offered space for Nonie at her home in Santa Fe, New Mexico, and Gregg considered this but decided against moving her, thinking it would only add to her discomfort. He taught through the summer of 1946, but the strain was too much, and he eventually quit, losing the apartment above the barn. Also that year, Gregg's eldest brother James Edgar died of a heart attack at the age of seventy, leaving his wife Mary and three children. Gregg had now lost his two older brothers.

By early 1947 it was clear that Nonie was not going to recover. After much soul searching and many consultations with doctors, he committed her to the Fuller Sanatorium in South Attleboro, Vermont. She frequently did not recognize him or know his name when he visited her. She was by then seventy-three and had suffered from the debilitating effects of what we now know to be Alzheimer's Disease for more than ten years. It was a painful decision, but Gregg knew that he could no longer give her the care she needed. At the end of the year, with his wife in the sanatorium, Gregg was without job or home. His family came to his rescue. Faith offered to have him stay at her home, and he moved into the house in Chestnut Hill. Her support gave him a chance to start to think about his next steps.

These steps would lead him back to Vermont and almost ten years living and working on the farm of Helen and Scott Nearing. It was also then, at the end that year, that he had his last correspondence with his mentor and friend. Gandhi was assassinated in January 1948. The next stage of his life would open the possibility of a return to India and a deeper understanding of the social and economic forces controlling the post-war world.

CHAPTER NINE

Mother Nature's Son

I take part in exploiting others. I live on an income derived from it. I am able very easily to fool myself with notions of "division of labor" and then hide to myself the exploiting that I am doing. "Sell all thou hast and give to the poor." If I am to stop exploiting completely or sharing in it, I would have to earn by my own labor of hand or mind or both all my food, clothing, shelter and incidentals. Who is to say what my labor is worth? Only if I live extremely simply can I be reasonably sure that I am not taking more than I earn.
—Richard Gregg, Notebook 23, p. 92

No—the way to master the increasing complexity of life is not through more complexity. The way is to turn inward to that which unifies all—not the intellect but the spirit, and then to devise and put into operation new forms and modes of economic and social life that will truly and vigorously express that spirit. As an aid to that and as a corrective to our feverish over mechanization, simplicity is not outmoded but greatly needed.
—*The Value of Voluntary Simplicity*

The Value of Voluntary Simplicity

GANDHI'S ASSASSINATION BY A RIGHT-WING Hindu nationalist
on January 30, 1948, shocked and saddened Richard Gregg. He had lost
his friend and mentor. Gandhi's death ended the relationship that had
dominated Gregg's life and thinking since that moment in a Chicago
bookstore so many years ago. He drafted a long letter to the editor of the
Boston Globe commemorating his friend and the contribution he had made.
He finished by saying:

> Gandhi's influence will live for ages. But the loss of his physical presence at this
> critical time in India will have grave consequences. The whole world is poorer
> by his going. This alone decreases, I believe, the chances of survival of Western
> civilization; and the survival of oriental culture is rendered much more difficult.
> His utter faith in the immanence and power of the spirit in all people and all
> human affairs is something without which no society or civilization can endure.[271]

With Gandhi's murder and the conflict that would soon engulf India, the
question of the appropriate response to violence became even more central
in Gregg's thinking and writing. The assassination added a tragic personal
dimension to his work, and, to come to terms with his friend's death, Gregg sat
down and wrote "My Memories of Gandhi." In it, he tried to capture his own
life's journey while putting to paper his experiences in India and at the ashram
with his mentor. As always, Gregg was keen to share the human side of Gandhi:

> During part of my stay at the Ashram, after they had begun to have all their
> meals in a large common dining room, Gandhi for a while set an example by
> cleaning, paring and cutting up. He let me join him in this work. I remember
> saying to him on one of those occasions that I was surprised with so many of
> the troubles and sorrows of India on his mind he could nevertheless joke and
> see the funny side of things and people. He answered that if he could not
> laugh sometimes, he would go mad.[272]

For Gregg, this is one of the things he admired and thought gave Gandhi such
strength: the ability to laugh in the face of the world's tragedies. Gregg held on

to this memory of his friend and tried to make it a little bit more real by pursuing a new stage of life, one of which he knew the Mahatma would approve.

Forest Farm

By the last couple of years of the 1940s, the promises of peace rapidly disappeared. The end of the British Raj in 1947 and the division of India into what is now the Republic of India and the Islamic Republic of Pakistan precipitated a civil war and in which millions died or were displaced. At the same time, the rest of the British Empire was disintegrating as the world settled into its Cold War, with the WWII allies and others arrayed against the Soviet Union and its satellites. In rapid succession, independence or commonwealth status came to Burma, Ceylon, and Malaysia. The British ended the Mandate in Palestine that year, and the first Arab-Israeli war marked the founding of the State of Israel. By the 1960s, almost all the British Empire had fallen away.

In Europe the lines of the Cold War hardened, and the Soviets strengthened their control over Eastern Europe. The British and the Americans began their airlift to feed Berlin, trapped as it was in the middle of Soviet-controlled East Germany. A year or so later, the Western European states started the long march towards European integration with the creation of the European Coal and Steel Community and sheltered under the alliance umbrella of the North Atlantic Treaty Organization (NATO). In Britain, the Labour Party, with a comfortable majority in Parliament as a result of their landslide victory in 1945, set out to create the modern British Welfare State and work towards dismantling the Empire. France, Italy, and other Western European states embarked on rebuilding after the devastation of the war and began to realign themselves towards what would become, eventually, the European Union. The Soviet Union consolidated its control over Eastern Europe. Around all of this, a fledgling United Nations struggled to develop as the voice of collective security in international relations.

Events in the U.S. also marked a new kind of world order: the creation of the Bretton Woods system as a basis for global economic organization with the founding of the General Agreement on Tariffs and Trade (GATT), the World Bank, and the International Monetary Fund (IMF). Truman signed the Marshall Plan into law providing massive financial support to Western Europe, the House Un-American Activities Committee began the examination of the Alger Hiss case in what was to become a prelude to red-baiting McCarthyism, and the Truman Doctrine (supporting "free peoples" against oppressors and containing communism) became the core of much American foreign policy. That year, also, the United Nations created the World Health Organization, and, at the end of the year, the UN, after much deliberation, adopted the Universal Declaration of Human Rights. There were, after all, some bright spots.

As the Cold War intensified and the former European empires, chiefly the British, collapsed, the prospects for a peaceful world rapidly evaporated. While Gregg was fully aware of and dismayed by these developments, his own life took a turn that would lead him further along the path to simple living and organic farming. In early 1948 with his wife now in the sanatorium, Gregg decided to follow a connection he made some years before, with the radical economist and activist Scott Nearing. In 1949, he joined Nearing and his wife Helen on their maple sugar farm near Jamaica, Vermont.

The Nearings had bought the land in 1932 and called it Forest Farm. As Helen described it later: "Our new place was a typical run-down farm, with a wooden house in poor repair, a good-sized barn with bad sills and a leaky roof, a Finnish bath house, and 65 acres of land from which the timber had been cut, …The place had a plenteous spring of excellent water, a meadow, a swamp or two, and some rough land facing south and stretching perhaps a third of a mile up Pinnacle Mountain, which lay east of Stratton."[273] Clearly, the farm needed a lot of work. Still, the Nearings were intent on developing it as an organic going concern and set about building stone cottages, rehabilitating old barns, and tapping water from the clear springs that flowed across the property.

Gregg helped in some of this and he stayed for seven years. With the Nearings' help, he built a small cottage that became a refuge for him. The farm, and the Nearings, played a significant role in his life from then on. Gregg and Scott shared similar values and ideas and enjoyed a collegial but not close relationship. Both men had come to similar conclusions about how to live their lives, ending up together on the farm. But Nearing, a couple of years older, could be sharp and intolerant and, while Gregg liked Nearing's intellectual conversation and commitment, Nearing's background and personality were very different. By all accounts, Nearing was not an easy man to work with: demanding, sometimes dogmatic, and frequently abrupt.[274]

Nearing was born in Pennsylvania, the child of upper-middle-class parents (his father was a stockbroker). He took up an academic career—one that would radicalize him quickly. He pursued a doctorate in economics at the University of Pennsylvania's Wharton School of Business and graduated in 1909, very much a child of the Progressive Era. He taught economics and sociology at Wharton and Swarthmore. He was influenced by the head of the economics department at Wharton, Simon Patten. Patten was one of the first economists to explore the economics of abundance and consumption. By 1915, while the war raged in Europe, Nearing became a well-known radical, speaking and publishing on progressive causes and against the war.

He was fired from his position at Wharton for his political activities in 1915, and then later from Toledo University in 1917, where he was hired after being dismissed from Wharton. In 1917, Nearing joined the Socialist Party and continued writing and teaching, traveled to the Soviet Union and China, and, after the collapse of the Socialist Party, became a member of the Communist Party of America (CPA) in 1927. The Party expelled him in

1930 for failing to allow the Party to scrutinize one of his publications on imperialism.[275] Nearing promoted radical and pacifist causes throughout his life. A prolific writer and scholar, he authored more than one hundred books and pamphlets and gave hundreds of lectures and speeches during the first half of the twentieth century.[276]

A significant figure in the American progressive movements of the 1920s, Nearing, in the early 1930s, ended most of his involvement with the organized Left to pursue homesteading at the farm in Vermont, focusing on simple living and self-sufficiency. Nearing, in 1928, met Helen Knothe, who became his second wife in 1947. Together they established the farm in Vermont and began an experiment in self-sufficient organic farming. They co-authored *Living the Good Life: How to Live Sanely and Simply in a Troubled World* (1954).[277] The work reported back on their experiments and was seen by many as the successor to the writings of Thoreau and Emerson. *Living the Good Life* did not get a lot of notice in the early 1950s. Still, when reprinted in the '70s, the ideas and story resonated strongly with the American counterculture movement. The Nearings became well-known for their efforts to live a simpler life, one in harmony with nature. Their experiment became one of the lodestones of many who turned their backs on the consumer culture and a political and social system distorted and broken by the Vietnam War and the Watergate political scandal.

Gregg and Nearing shared perspectives about pacifism, the turn towards organic farming and alternative lifestyles, and the disdain for modern capitalism. But for Nearing, these views came from a life of radical politics and engagement with social and political causes from the end of WWI through to the end of his long life (he lived to be one hundred). But Gregg's views flowed from his religious beliefs and his experience of the conflict between capital and labor in the first decades of the twentieth century and, of course, from living and working with Gandhi.

Gregg helped with the sugar harvest immediately. He was very enamored of this life and wrote excitedly to his sister Elinor about the experience, particularly the joy of harvesting seven-hundred-and-fifty gallons of syrup. He had finally found a place where he could live as he chose and experiment with organic food production, all in the sanctuary of Forest Farm.

Gregg's happiness was shadowed by the troubled world of global politics. Pacifists became increasingly concerned that the promise of peace at the end of the war was rapidly turning into an even more dangerous and lethal set of global conflicts. In mid-1949, Gregg got a letter from the American Friends Service Committee inviting him to a World Pacifist Conference in India in December. Gregg welcomed the opportunity to meet old friends and renew his role in the pacifist movement. Still, he was conflicted: Nonie was in the sanatorium, and, while he did try to visit her regularly, going to the conference would entail close to three months out of the country. On the other hand, the last time he visited Nonie she did not recognize him. Hard as it was, Gregg realized that she might not even notice his absence and he decided to accept the invitation. For the rest of the summer and fall, he worked on the farm, building his stone cabin and refining techniques for organic farming. He left for India at the end of November and journeyed to Santiniketan and Sevagram, where he joined a cast of over one hundred top pacifist leaders from nearly forty countries. Sevagram was Gandhi's second ashram. After the Salt March, Gandhi decided not to return to Sabarmati and set up a new Ashram in a village called Segaon that he later renamed Sevagram ("village of service").

The conference, organized by War Resisters International, the International Fellowship of Reconciliation, and the Women's International League for Peace and Freedom, was intended to be held in 1948 with Gandhi at its center. But, following his assassination, it had been postponed. The conference included ninety-three pacifists from thirty-three separate countries. Among those attending was Jawaharlal Nehru (India's Prime Minister), Vera Brittain (from the U.K.), A. J. Muste (from the U.S.), and significant figures in the pacifist movement from Germany, Japan, and India. The conference focused on the growing Cold War between the U.S. and the Soviet Union, the consequences of the atomic bomb, and, of course, the value of nonviolent resistance. Gregg found himself part of a committee, the International Liaison Committee for Satyagraha, that called for the deployment of Satyagraha Peace Units in the represented countries.[278]

Gregg found the conference stimulating, and he met many of the key speakers. It also gave him a chance to renew old friendships and to see a little of India. But he was exhausted by both the travel and the intensity of the experience. Even so, Gregg, then in his mid-sixties, stayed a few days in London on his way home, meeting with people he had befriended during his visit in the mid-1930s. After the stopover, he took passage for the last leg of his journey back to the U.S. aboard the *Queen Mary* and arrived in New York in the second week of February 1950. After a brief stay with his sister Faith in Boston, Gregg returned to Forest Farm in March, just in time to help with the sugar harvest. For the rest of that year, he built his small stone cabin, set in the sugar bush, not far from the Nearing homestead, and it was just about habitable by July. There was much work still to do: plumbing and roof insulation, and much of the interior finishing. This was a good time for him; the first time in more than four years he had a place for himself.

Around this time Gregg had been planning a new work on religion but had also promised colleagues in India a piece on why Gandhism was superior to communism. He struggled to finish the work throughout 1951, and it was finally published in India as *"Which Way Lies Hope? An Examination of Capitalism, Communism, Socialism and Gandhi's Program."* It was extensively revised for a new edition in 1957. The book, initially a brief work (the first edition was about eighty pages), reflected Gregg's concern with the current state of the world, especially the dangers posed by the Cold

War. In it he dissected and challenged many core ideological and theoretical claims of capitalism/liberalism and Marxism/socialism, comparing them to the Gandhian alternative. His analysis throughout returned to the question of violence, which, for him, was an intrinsic part of both capitalism and socialism. But the vision he brought in this work was holistic, and he stressed throughout the absence of social, moral, and indeed, spiritual elements in both ideologies. India very much framed the argument, but there are insights in the work that speak to present concerns with the nature of science and the goals of social transformation. As he wrote, "All social theory must be held tentatively and experimentally."[279] After completing the manuscript of *Which Way Lies Hope?* he stayed on at Forest Farm, mostly broke and surviving very much as a subsistence farmer.

Occasionally, either Elinor or Faith would send gifts and Faith, sometimes, money, to help him get by. He took less frequent trips to visit Nonie, as increasingly she failed to recognize him. But the life on the farm was about to change—the Nearings had decided to move on and, in 1952, they sold the place, re-starting their homesteading experiment near Harborside on Penobscot Bay in Maine.[280] After the Nearings left, Gregg wrote to his sister Elinor that he would miss Scott, "For all his bitterness and rudeness, Scott Nearing did provide intellectual stimulus and now he is gone. I miss it."[281] Nearing died in 1983 (a couple of weeks after he turned one hundred), but Helen lived until 1995 when she was killed in a single-car accident. She had been twenty years younger than Scott.

The spring of 1954 marked a significant moment for Gregg. On the morning of May 20, Nonie died. She was eighty years old. He told Elinor that day of her passing. Her death saddened him, but she had been gone from him for too long already. They had been married for over twenty-five years. For the last decade her illness had eroded her mental abilities, despite his many efforts to treat her. He had written years before to Gandhi about these efforts and summed them up in a six-page carefully written analysis of her condition and possible treatment.[282] He had done extensive research on the causes of Nonie's presumed illness and became convinced of the therapeutic potential of mineral supplements. Gregg based this therapy on the work of Albert Carter Savage, who had become well-known in the 1940s for his work on "mineralization" of the soil.[283] Gregg experimented on himself and Nonie with a range of minerals, vitamins, and homeopathic remedies. As early as 1947, he thought that there had been some improvement in her condition as a result. But his efforts failed.

The year was significant for Gregg: the death of his wife, the end of his time on the farm in Vermont, and the completion of his next book. This book had been stewing in him for over fifteen years, and, finally, in September 1954, he was able to send off the last chapter to the typist he employed in Boston. The work, first published in India as *A Compass for Civilization*, was also published by Gollancz in the U.S. as *Self-Transcendence*, by Lippincott as *The Self Beyond Yourself*, and by the Cambridge University Press as *Spirit Through the Body*. The book brought together much of what Gregg believed about the world, about psychology, and about the human condition. In its pages, Gregg pulled together his extensive reading and many of the citations and quotes he recorded in his notebooks over the years. He laid out an argument that addressed the central assumptions we make about ourselves, our world, our individuality, and how we form and hold onto these assumptions.

The work built around the notion of the world made up of opposites, of contradictions, and of balancing forces. Gregg believed that the appropriate response was to think about these things by meditating on how to transcend the self by invoking ideas of Christian, Hindu, and, primarily, Buddhist beliefs about self-transcendence, or "nirvana." As ever, Gregg was humble in this writing and practical: the last chapter was devoted to techniques, primarily how to meditate and why this is critical to the self-transcendence he advocated. Though the book took fifteen years to finish, it was Gregg's essential statement of inner spiritual feelings and ideas. As he wrote in the introduction, ". . . I suspect we are sustained by a certain pattern or order of thoughts and feelings and meanings. Though the pattern may be perceived only dimly or unconsciously, we must have it. Without it, life does not make sense or have any lasting value."[284] For Gregg, this was a statement about the meaning of life and the search for a set of life principles. At the end, he implored his readers to embark on this journey of transcendent self-discovery. Indeed, Gregg focused on the need for meditation, but this was a means to an end for him. He argued that the world is comprised mostly of opposites—good and evil, love and hate, etc., and that humanity needs to transcend these to achieve real progress towards a better world. For Gregg, this was all about the internal work of thinking (and, yes, of spirituality), and that everything else was external. True change, or enlightenment, could not be gained without serious contemplation and meditation on these issues. Transcendence requires deep examinations of the assumptions we make about the world, including such things as the value of freedom, but Gregg insisted that "freedom, like happiness, is a by-product of other conditions. You do not win either happiness or freedom by direct effort. They come automatically once certain other conditions are established. In the case of freedom, the other conditions are mutual respect, mutual trust, trust in the power of truth, mutual patience and kindness."[285] And, of course, Gregg maintained, this could be achieved through spirituality and religious belief whether derived from Christianity, Hinduism, Buddhism, or any of the world's religions. This work, hardly known today, is a powerful statement about the need for contemplation and self-examination that seeks, ultimately, the love of oneself and all humanity. Gerald Heard described the work, in his review, as being of "incalculable importance."

Of Biodynamics and Love

Gregg was still at the Forest Farm through the end of 1955. Over the years, he had remained in touch with Evelyn Speiden, whom he had first met and worked with during his time at Kimberton in 1942. Their collegial relationship blossomed into romance, and, in April 1956, they married. She was sixty-two, and Gregg had just turned seventy-one.

They remained together until Gregg's death in 1974. They shared common interests in biodynamic farming, peace work, and religion of all varieties. Gregg had found a partner with whom he could share the last decades of his life and who would support and work with him on all their mutual interests.[286] Evelyn Speiden was a significant force in the biodynamics movement. She was born in Washington, D.C., the eldest of four children, her father a homeopathic physician. She taught school in Washington and attended Cornell University and the University of Chicago, finally getting a degree from Columbia University Teachers College. On graduating, she moved to China, where she lived and worked for nine years, learning Chinese at the University of Nanking language school and, later, living and teaching in Huchow and Hangchow. She also lived in Shanghai and Japan for a few months before returning to the States to study landscape architecture at the University of Cincinnati. During those years, she became interested in the work of Rudolph Steiner and the movements emerging, particularly in Germany, to develop sustainable approaches to agriculture and farming. This biodynamics movement began to take hold in the U.S. in the 1920s and grew rapidly in the 1930s, in no small part due to Evelyn's involvement.

As early as 1926, some friends interested in Steiner's ideas who viewed themselves as anthroposophists created a vegetarian restaurant called *Threefold* in New York City. This group purchased a farm in Spring Valley, New York, and named it after the restaurant. From this small beginning, it expanded to become a vital center for biodynamic farming and social and progressive education built around both the ideas of Steiner and the educational focus of these ideas that became the Waldorf School movement. Threefold Farm was an early focus of the biodynamics movement in the U.S. A few of the original group traveled to Europe for various conferences and, while there, met with Ehrenfried Pfeiffer, a former student of Steiner who had created a biodynamics research farm in Germany.

In 1933 Threefold Farm held its first summer conference, and Pfeiffer was the guest speaker. Evelyn (who was at that time studying landscape architecture at the University of Cincinnati) attended the meeting and met Pfeiffer. They got along well and he invited her to visit his farm in Dornach, Germany. After that experience and visits to similar initiatives in the U.K. and the Netherlands, Evelyn returned to the States. Eventually, she joined the others to create the first biodynamics center in the U.S. As a key leader of the center, Pfeiffer later set up another farm with the members of the Threefold group at Kimberton in Pennsylvania in 1940.[287] He had fled to the U.S. from Germany with his family in the late 1930s because of the rise of Nazism and the coming war.

Kimberton Farm became the core of the biodynamics movement in the U.S. and the place where Gregg took a course in biodynamics in 1942. Kimberton Farm had a brief but significant impact on the development of biodynamics. Still, due to conflicts between Pfeiffer and his wealthy co-founder, Alarik Myrin (Pfeiffer thought that, for Myrin, the project was just a "rich man's hobby."), Pfeiffer quit. He immediately set out to create a new version of the project, and with Evelyn and others founded another two hundred and eighty-five-acre farm near Chester, N.Y., in 1944. At the time, Evelyn purchased a small cottage with an inheritance from her uncle and became part of that farm community. After she married Gregg, the couple moved to her cottage in Chester in the spring of 1956.

The year before his marriage and the move to the cottage in Chester,

Gregg met another central figure in what would become the counterculture movement: the noted designer and builder of yurts, Bill Coperthwaite. Coperthwaite had discovered the writings of Richard Gregg in the summer of 1955 and met him for the first time then, probably while Gregg was still at the Nearings' former farm. Coperthwaite had been a conscientious objector during the Korean War and did alternative service with the American Friends Service Committee (AFSE), where he became familiar with pacifism and the writings of pacifists.[288] Among those writings that had the most significant impact on him was Gregg's *The Power of Non-Violence*.

Coperthwaite had read Gandhi as an undergraduate while at Bowdoin College in Maine and, while there, the Quaker and radical educator Morris Mitchell had been his mentor. Mitchell had directed the Putney Graduate School of Teacher Education in Vermont, where Gregg taught for a while, so it is not surprising that he encountered Gregg's work. Coperthwaite was keen to meet Gregg and hitchhiked from Mexico to New York to do so.

He recalled later:

> We first met [when] I was twenty-five and he was nearly seventy. In his writings I had found a kindred spirit and so sought him out to thank him. It turned out (to be) a joyous event. Age difference seemed of no consequence. It was exciting to find this gentle white-haired man with such wide knowledge of the world had long before discovered many of the things I was finding true in my world—the joy of bread labor; the importance of hands in education; simple living; the wonders of the technology of early peoples; the importance of early education; and the relationship of these to nonviolence.[289]

Gregg and Coperthwaite developed a long-term friendship. In the '60s and '70s Coperthwaite became an internationally known designer and builder of tapered walled, wood-framed structures that borrowed from the original Mongolian yurt. Coperthwaite had studied at Harvard and earned a doctoral degree from the Harvard Graduate School of Education. His education initiated a lifelong interest in progressive and alternative education. Later,

Coperthwaite traveled widely (Scandinavia, Japan, China), building yurts, working with schools, and developing his ideas about education. Although he had read most of Nearing's work (as well as Gregg's), he did not meet Scott Nearing until the fall of 1963 when Nearing invited him to the farm in Harborside, Maine. Again, as with Gregg, he built a friendship and they made up a triumvirate of pacifist organic farmers promoting alternative lifestyles in Vermont and Maine.[290] Each of them was a builder and each belived passionately in the value of manual work.

It was Gregg who introduced Coperthwaite to the writings of both Gandhi and Nearing. Coperthwaite became committed to a philosophy of "democratic living," his beliefs combined those of Thoreau, Gregg, Gandhi, and others, into the way of life that he lived on the five-hundred-and-fifty-acre farm he created in Maine. Sadly, Bill Coperthwaite died in a car accident in November 2013.

CHAPTER TEN

Nonviolence in Practice: Gandhi and King

"Nonviolence means avoiding not only external physical violence but also internal violence of spirit. You not only refuse to shoot a man, but you refuse to hate him."
—Martin Luther King, Jr., *speech to the congregation of the Beulah Baptist Church in Montgomery, Alabama, June 18, 1956*

"If we want a better world, we must be prepared to do some careful thinking. It is time we stopped being sketchy on a matter that touches us all so closely. For in reality this matter of handling conflict constructively is of immediate concern to everyone who has ever been angry or afraid, resentful, revengeful or bitter; who has ever taken part in a fight, mob violence or war; or who has been the object of anger, hatred, exploitation or oppression."
—Richard Gregg, Preface, *The Power of Non-Violence*, 1960

JUST A YEAR AFTER BROWN V. BOARD of Education, the U.S. Supreme Court ruling that outlawed publicly segregated schools, the actions around civil rights for Black Americans in the South began to escalate. The murder of Emmett Till in 1955, and the public display of his mutilated body at his funeral, mobilized activists across the country. At the end of the year Rosa Parks' refusal to sit at the back of a city bus led to the Montgomery bus boycott and Martin Luther King, Jr.'s, deep involvement and leadership in the national civil rights movement.[291] Gregg watched these developments closely and was connected to the emerging movement through his work with the Fellowship of Reconciliation (FOR) and his friendship with Glenn Smiley, Bayard Rustin, Ralph Abernathy, and others, who had all attended Myles Horton's Highlander School where they had encountered and read Gregg's *PNV*. Indeed, Rustin and Smiley had probably read the first edition of *PNV* in the 1930s, as the civil rights movement had deep origins in the work of FOR during that period. FOR was also very involved in the resistance to the internment of Japanese Americans after 1942 and in more than one-hundred-and-fifty camps where conscientious objectors were placed during the war under the Civilian Public Service Program. These camps were financially supported by religious organizations, many with deep pacifist connections. There, internees worked on forestry, soil erosion, and forest firefighting projects. Critically, the camps also served as education centers for pacifists, where Gregg's work was widely read.[292]

Within this wider context of pacifism and justice, the Congress of Racial Equality (CORE), founded in 1942, was perhaps the most important vector for bringing Gregg's work into the civil rights movement. In the 1940s the group used anti-segregation sit-ins at restaurants and movie houses across the South—which put into action the principles of nonviolent resistance. CORE's founder, George Houser, had read Gregg, and the last chapter of his *Erasing the Color Line* was called simply, The Power of Non-Violence.[293] The key players in CORE were colleagues of Gregg's and they sought his advice. Rustin, Houser, and others became committed to nonviolent resistance as a strategy for social and political change. Their acts and ideas came to influence the perspective of key groups in the South in the mid-'50s. These influences would coalesce quickly as the nonviolent strategy of the civil rights movement, especially in the critical moment of the 1956 Montgomery bus boycott, even though the leaders in Montgomery were not themselves pacifists.[294] Bayard Rustin, on arriving in Montgomery, Alabama, promoted to King the value of nonviolent resistance, but it was Glenn Smiley, in particular, who advocated the nonviolence strategy to King. Smiley gave him a copy of Gregg's *The Power of Non-Violence* to read.[295]

The original activists of the bus boycott were fighting for racial equality but had not been, as had Rustin, Smiley, Houser, and others, conscientious objectors during the war. Indeed, many of the Southern activists were armed and ready to fight. It was the efforts of Rustin and Smiley that convinced King and the leaders that nonviolence was not only the Christian way, it was also a smart political strategy. At one point, when the boycotters had been indicted for their acts, Rustin urged them to turn themselves in voluntarily but to do so, "wearing their Sunday clothes and smiling broadly." They adopted his plan, to the amazement of the local police. A large crowd turned out to witness the scene at the jail, producing "a mood of good-natured hilarity," in the words of one early chronicler. Deputies laughed and joked with the prisoners, and an exasperated sheriff finally declared, "This is no vaudeville show."[296] Indeed it was the kind of act that Gregg had advocated: nonviolent resistance as theater. It was this vision of peaceful resistance to injustice and oppression as a performance that Gregg had developed in his work, that had struck a chord with CORE, and been used effectively by them in the 1940s. It is testament to its effectiveness that nonviolent resisters in the civil rights movement would wholeheartedly take up the approach, and that King would fully promote and adopt it.

Gregg wrote to King at the beginning of April. He noted in the letter that he knew Smiley had given him a copy of *PNV*. He told King, "For several months of the four years I lived in India I was with Gandhi on his ashram and I can tell you he would mightily rejoice to know that you have chosen this way." He went on to suggest ". . . that as a part of it you try to get going among your community some constructive work, after the fashion of Gandhi's hand spinning."[297] Gregg, always stressing the constructivist program, offered the idea of neighborhood clean-ups, exercise and dancing, etc. and that these "would add to people's self-respect...use their emotions and energy...[on] self-help as well as the effort of protest." Gregg explained, "In India it was the districts where such work went on constantly which offered the strongest...and most enduring nonviolent resistance to British rule."[298] King responded on May 1, noting he was happy to have received Gregg's letter and was in the process of reading *PNV*. He noted, "I don't know when I have read anything that has given the idea of nonviolence a more realistic and depthful [sic] interpretation. I assure you that it will be a lasting influence on my life."[299] Gregg's impact on King is well known, and King frequently mentioned the technique of moral jiu-jitsu, nonviolent resistance, and the impact of Gandhi's ideas on his thinking. King's writing during this period frequently carried very similar themes and perspectives to those laid out by Gregg. There are places in King's *Pilgrimage to Nonviolence* that almost word-for-word echo those of Gregg's in *PNV*.[300] While there is no doubt that King had already been aware of Gandhi's thinking, it was Gregg's work that placed this in a context that more closely fit what would become King's strategy for the civil rights struggle. Gregg had become one of the key actors who pushed for King to connect with and embrace Gandhian philosophy. Perhaps, finally, this was the full realization of Gregg's aim to interpret Gandhi for a Western audience.

Back to India

As the civil rights movement gained momentum during the spring and summer of 1956, Richard and Evelyn married and moved to the cottage in Chester. But they did not settle down for long. India called. In September, Gregg was invited by his old friend Sri G. Ramachandran to teach Gandhian economics to students doing social service activities in Indian villages. Excited by the prospect and the opportunity to take Evelyn with him, Gregg rented out the cottage in preparation for a visit that would last nearly two years. It was testimony to Gregg's strength that he embarked on this journey at the age of seventy-one with not a hint of concern for his health.

Once in India the couple used Ramachandran's school, the Gandhigram Rural Institute of Higher Education, as their base. Ramachandran had founded the school with his wife in 1947. Located about forty miles north of Madurai in the Indian state of Tamil Nadu, the school served rural community development, following Gandhian principles. In 1956, it formally became the Gandhigram Rural Institute of Higher Education, which still exists and is part of India's university system. Gregg was fond of Ramachandran and supported his efforts, especially since the Institute was deeply committed to continuing Gandhi's educational vision, *Nai Talim*, that connected knowledge and work, particularly manual work.[301]

While at the Institute Gregg taught the economics and system of *khaddar* and the philosophy and social theory behind it. Teaching there enabled him, despite his other obligations and the extensive travel with Evelyn, to complete drafts for his next work, *A Philosophy of Indian Economic Development*. The book is his most comprehensive account of *khaddar* and the possibilities of an Indian (and possible Western) economy built around small-scale production and agriculture. The work was critical to expressing Gregg's thinking since, while he firmly believed in nonviolent resistance, he considered this only the outward manifestation of a commitment to peace. For Gregg, a peaceful world could only be achieved through the development of a decentralized small local production system and agriculture-based economy. For this to be practicable he focused on the home-spun textile production that Gandhi and he had championed. In this he followed Gandhi's vision completely. *A Philosophy of Indian Economic Development* was built on the study he had undertaken in the *Economics of Khaddar* in 1929.

It would not be a stretch to see in his writing here a precursor to ideas that re-emerged in the counterculture movements of the '60s and '70s. They have more than an echo in the contemporary anti-globalization movement and the turn to locally produced organic food and services. In the work, Gregg, after fully recognizing the great achievements of industrial capitalism, cautioned,

> ". . . although the intellectual movement of Western technology and industrialism has been intense and vigorous, its range and imagination have been too narrow to meet the whole situation in which man is placed . . . it has attacked and despoiled the topsoil and forests on which all animal life including man depends . . . technology inevitably tends towards large-scale machinery, mills, factories and plants and also tends towards centralization of control and monopoly of power . . . ."[302]

Here, again, Gregg argued that a different path was available for India and other former colonial states that had yet to undergo an industrial revolution. He pointed out, though, that this was not only an alternative for India. For Gregg, it was very much a plea to reject contemporary industrial capitalism and to return to a simpler, more meaningful life in every country. While he sent King a copy of his new book, its ideas were not embraced by King or, for that matter, by many others. It was hard enough to imagine this path as the basis for an economy in India, nearly impossible to do so in the now highly developed and technological West.

While in India and still travelling and writing, there was more tragic news for Gregg. The long trip was interrupted by news of the death of his brother Alan in the summer of 1957. Alan had been ill and endured several strokes.

Elinor had sent Gregg a postcard in April warning him that "A. is not well—he is now in hospital—Another stroke. Speech and memory poor."[303] He succumbed to a weakened heart in July. He was sixty-seven. Alan and Richard were very close, and Richard consistently sought advice from his younger brother on medical issues and public health. He wrote to him frequently, especially during his first stay in India, inquiring about all manner of public health matters and relaying Alan's insights to Gandhi. For most of Gregg's life Alan was a sounding board for much of his writing and thinking. Losing Alan was a great blow for Gregg, a third brother gone. Even more affecting was the news, six months after Alan's death, of the passing of his dear older sister, Faith, in February 1958, at the age of eighty. Faith and her family had been an anchor in Gregg's life, offering a home in Boston, financial assistance, and sisterly love. It was to her house that Gregg, over the years, would return after his many travels. He mourned her loss. Gregg's only living siblings were his sisters, Elinor and Marjorie.

Despite their sadness at Alan's and Faith's deaths, Evelyn and Richard kept a full travel schedule. Gregg worked at Gandhigram Institute, where they stayed for about five months. Once his teaching was complete, he showed Evelyn as much of his adopted beloved country as possible. They set off for New Delhi, Agra, and Sevagram (Gandhi's ashram from 1936 until his assassination). After visiting the central mountains, they headed south and west, staying with friends and colleagues (Gregg often giving lectures and discussion sessions on the way) until they reached the state of Kerala. They travelled from the southern to northern tip of the state, then headed north again so that Gregg could return to Stokes' school at Kotgarh.[304] All the while he kept up his extensive correspondence with his remaining family and pursued his ideas for influencing the direction of health and sustainability in India.

In September he met with his old acquaintance, Nehru, with whom he had corresponded since they were introduced during Gregg's first visit to India in 1925. The following month he met with India's President Rajendra Prasad in New Delhi. In March 1958 he wrote to Nehru advocating a joint project that India, Japan, and perhaps China could collaborate on in distributing contraception, especially the contraceptive pill then just being developed in the U.S., to help deal with the problem of overpopulation.[305] Nehru replied that he agreed with the idea but not with a collective action with Japan or China, as current politics made this impossible.[306] Nehru didn't take the matter further.

As was his habit, Gregg continued an active correspondence. He sent a copy of his new book to his friend Gerald Heard in November. Heard replied the following month with great affection for his friend, describing his latest psychedelic experiments with LSD and his activities with his friend Aldous Huxley.[307] While travelling, Gregg mailed a copy of *Which Ways Lies Hope* to U.S. Supreme Court Justice William O. Douglas,[308] never being reticent in getting his work out to influential and significant figures.

After crisscrossing India, Gregg and Evelyn returned to America. They traveled via Japan, arriving on the West coast in the summer of 1958, stopping to visit Elinor in Santa Fe, and finally returning to their home in Chester, New York. Immediately upon their return, Gregg tried to get the revised edition of *PNV* published by Gollanz, eager to get the manuscript out.[309] At this time, he also reengaged with Martin Luther King, Jr., and the civil rights movement, reconnecting after his India sojourn.

King, Gregg, and Civil Rights

Martin Luther King, Jr., (MLK) wrote to Gregg in December of 1958, after King had met with Kaka Kalelkar (one of Gandhi disciples). Kalelkar was an independence activist and social reformer, whom Gregg had known since they were together at Sabarmati Ashram in 1925. Kalelkar had suggested to King that he publish in India, and King told Gregg he was thinking about a trip to India and looking to publish his first book, *Stride Toward Freedom: The Montgomery Story*. Gregg replied in October, just after he and Evelyn had settled back in Chester, rejoicing at MLK's success in Montgomery and offering his congratulations—but he also wanted King to convince Harper & Bros. to allow King's book to be republished in India. Gregg pointed out that the book would hearten Gandhi's followers, but was not affordable for the vast majority of Indians. Gregg suggested that King contact the Gandhi Memorial Trust/Navajivan Trust as a potential publisher who could make it available at low cost; they had published much of Gregg's work. In his letters Gregg also cautioned King that nonviolent struggle was a great moral strain and required an outlet, a way to relax, and suggested that MLK consider Gandhi's "constructive program" as a way to integrate the training and care of nonviolent activists. To help King conceptualize the constructive program Gregg sent him a copy of *A Philosophy of Indian Economic Development* along with detailed information on vegetable gardening. He reminded King that, after the, ". . . (a)ctive struggle was over, he [Gandhi] let its results bear fruit at whatever pace the times required but he shifted his emphasis to what he called his 'constructive program,' which included hand-spinning, sanitation, education, aid for women, village crafts."

Gregg told King that the constructive program helped the local economy, "but also built up self-respect, self-confidence, self-esteem, hope, courage, cooperation, unity, and all other important moral qualities."[310] Gregg felt that these activities were essential for the long-term health of activists in the movement. Of course, these were critical strategies and ideas for Gregg, and an integral part of the program he was advocating. To push the point home, Gregg also sent a copy of the classic *A Conquest of Violence* by Bart De Ligt and a two-volume biography of Gandhi written by Gandhi's Secretary, Pyarelal Nayyar. As Gregg told King,

If you wonder why all these books are coming to you, all I can say is that I believe Gandhi was the greatest man of the last 1900 years, and I have spent the last 33 years of my life trying to explain to people why, and I am so grateful to you and your fellow workers in Montgomery for your demonstration of the moral and spiritual power exemplified by Gandhi that I feel obligated to help further the movement.[311]

When it came to promoting his ideas and the Gandhian program, Gregg was far from shy.

In his note to King, Gregg included a list of people at the publishing house that King should meet. At the end of January 1959, Gregg sent the names and addresses of people in India whom he believed King should connect with during his visit, including Pyarelal Nayyar (Gandhi's secretary); Amrit Kaur (the Minister of Health); and G. Ramachandran (Secretary of Gandhi Memorial Trust and founder of the Gandhigram Institute). He advised King to get out in the countryside where, he pointed out, eighty-three percent of the people live in seven hundred thousand villages. He firmly informed King that he would not be able to truly understand Gandhi's program otherwise. On a more casual note, he advised King to watch for pickpockets and malaria.[312] On February 3, 1959 King and his wife left for a five-week tour in India, arriving on February 10. He was welcomed by Gregg's friend Ramachandran. King traveled across India, taking Gregg's admonition to heart, making sure he saw the countryside and the villages. During the trip King visited Patna, Shantiniketan, the Gandhigram Rural Institute and, of course, the ashram at Sabarmati.

Just before King left for India, Gregg travelled from Chester down to New York City to attend the War Resisters League (WRL) Annual Dinner and to meet King in person for the first time. The League's Annual Dinner was an important event. Since 1958, the League, which was founded in 1923, had awarded an annual Peace Award at the dinner. The first recipient was Jeanette Rankin, a feminist and first woman elected to Congress.[313]

Subsequent awardees have included: Dorothy Day, Bayard Rustin, Norman Thomas, Barbara Deming, and, more recently, Daniel Berrigan, Joan Baez, Harry Belafonte, and Daniel Ellsberg.[314] The 1959 event honored A.J. Muste, and King was the keynote speaker. King's address to the League paraphrased many of Gregg's arguments in *PNV* and signaled King's embrace of nonviolent resistance as critical to the success of the civil rights struggle.[315] King left immediately for India, with Gregg's list of people to visit.

After connecting so effectively with King, Gregg became more directly involved in the civil rights movement. That fall Gregg traveled south to Atlanta, Georgia, to lead a discussion group at King's First Southwide Institute on Nonviolent Resistance to Segregation at Spelman College. At the institute Gregg led a workshop on nonviolence with several of his friends and activists, including Dick Ramsey of the American Friends Service Committee, Gordon Carey from the Congress for Racial Equality, James Lawson (then with FOR), and William Stuart Wilson from Howard University. These events were always something of a strain for Gregg, for he was not much of a public speaker and more comfortable working with small groups; the "workshop" was an ideal format for him to present his thinking.

While Gregg was working with King and the civil rights leaders, he was much heartened to know that later that year the third edition of *PNV* (called the second revised edition) was to finally be published, now with a foreword by King:

> When the great Quaker leader, Rufus Jones, wrote an introduction to the first edition of *The Power of Non-Violence*, he observed ". . . (h)ere is a new kind of book . . . a fine blend of what is and what ought to be . . . ." There is as much realism in this book as there is idealism. That was in 1935. Since then history's most devastating war has swept the globe, and new weapons of terrifying dimensions have made it more clear than ever that war and civilization cannot both continue into man's future. New ways of solving conflicts, without violence, must be discovered and put into operation. The years since 1935 have not only demonstrated how uncontrollable war is when it breaks out;

197

they have shown also how right Richard Gregg was in preparing this perceptive study in the first place. The heroic, though unanticipated nonviolent resistance against the Nazis in Denmark and Norway, recounted in this new edition, and by smaller groups in France, the Netherlands and in Germany itself, was such a demonstration. So has been the struggle in South Africa against unjust laws, the winning of its freedom by the new nation of Ghana, and our own experience in Montgomery. I am delighted that Richard Gregg, after spending another eighteen months in India in more research into this vital new kind of action, should have put the time and effort into this new version of his classic book. I hope it gets a wide readership, particularly among those, in this country and throughout the world, who are seeking ways of achieving full social, personal and political freedom in a manner consistent with human dignity."[316]
—Martin Luther King, Jr.

The new edition of *PNV* with King's foreword garnered a lot of attention, but it was hard for Gregg to capitalize on this by making as many appearances as in the past, for he was now seventy-five years old and the demands of travel and public appearances began to pose a challenge. Despite a growing infirmity, he paid attention to what was going on in the world and, for him, one of the most satisfying and rewarding developments was the formation of the Student Nonviolent Coordinating Committee (SNCC), which had developed out of the Greensboro State Woolworth Counter Sit-In of February 1960.[317] SNCC's early newsletters listed *The Power of Non-Violence* as the most important book for participants to read, placing it above King's *Stride Toward Freedom*.[318]

In the early '60s Gregg continued to build on the impact of *PNV* on the civil rights and anti-war communities by leading and participating in several further workshops and discussions. In the summer of 1960, Gregg was asked to speak at a two-week course on nonviolent action in Groton, Connecticut, organized by The New England Committee on Nonviolent Action. The course was part of the Polaris Action in Groton, which became a significant protest of the U.S. nuclear weapons program. He taught the workshop but, that year, his health took a turn for the worse: he was troubled by an enlarged prostate and suffered a hernia, both of which made him less able to travel very far.

For most of the next two years he stayed close to Chester, working the garden with Evelyn, and laying out the arguments for his next book, *The Big Idol*. This work argues for a decentralized currency (not tied to any one country) and discusses the general role of money in capitalist economies. Gregg also deals with the problem of the waste created by hoarding money. He thought that taxing money not in circulation, which tends to be hoarded or saved in periods of economic recession, would force it back into the system, thus promoting economic development and greater equity. He also argues that communities could print their own currency or scrip during these periods. Gregg used the example of two European towns where this was done and the tax (known as a demurrage tax) was applied. Although impractical for a national economy, such a strategy was considered briefly by the Roosevelt administration during the Depression. For Gregg, money has numerous, often conflicting, functions—a store of value, a medium of exchange, a measure of value, etc.— and the complexities hide the harm it causes to morality, justice, and indeed democracy.

While still working on *The Big Idol*, Gregg remained deeply connected to the Campaign for Nonviolent Action and was involved in their dramatic Polaris Campaign. He wrote a letter to the executives of the organization in August 1962, making the case for seeing the larger context of the struggle and reiterating his now increasingly dark prognosis for the future. Gregg felt that, "we are witnessing and taking part in the ending of Western civilization as we have hitherto known it. And if such a war is avoided, we may be witnessing and taking part in the preliminary birth pangs of a new civilization, perhaps better, perhaps worse." Gregg had qualms also about the efficacy and righteousness of direct action and he cautioned that, "Like happiness, peace is not something that can be obtained by direct action. It is an overall condition that results from other conditions....(t)hat is to say peace is a by-product that comes automatically once the other conditions are established."[319] Gregg had become increasingly skeptical of the kind of militant combative direct action that was emerging in the civil rights struggle and in the anti-nuclear and anti-Vietnam War movements. Despite his lifelong commitment to active nonviolent resistance he was concerned that the frequent disruptive activities did not always help the cause. Another condition for Gregg was mutual trust, the very basis of human unity. As he had repeatedly argued throughout his life, it is perseverance, honesty, trust, and actions that create the conditions for peaceful existence. These were not always evident in the new forms of direct action then developing in the various movements.

In the spring of 1962 India called him back. His friend Sri G. Ramachandran, Secretary of the Gandhi Peace Foundation, invited him to speak at a peace conference in India, sponsored by the Peace Foundation. But Gregg was still feeling the effects of his hernia operation and told his friend that he was not able to summon up the strength to travel or to undertake more conference presentations. For the first time, Gregg acknowledged that he was now too old for such adventures. Although he could not make the trip, he sent Ramachandran a statement about the current state of affairs to present to the delegates. Another old friend, A.J. Muste, was also invited to this conference, and Gregg wrote to tell him that he could not attend and included the statement he had shared with the Peace Foundation. This statement could easily have been written about contemporary world politics even though it was written just as the conflict between East and West reached a crisis point—the Cuban Missile Crisis of October 1962. In the statement Gregg clearly outlined the world as he saw it, feeling the weight of current events, "As I see the world situation today, we are in the midst of a fairly rapid breakdown of modern civilization. Two world wars within the last fifty years, an existing cold war of mutual suspicion, threats and harassments, a threatened nuclear and/or poison gas and germicidal war, plus overt violence in all continents are evidence and symptoms of this deep-seated disease."[320] Gregg looked back on the last one hundred years enumerating what he saw as the primary false and distorted assumptions of the modern world. It was a kind of summing up for Gregg of his concerns about the assumptions he saw as defining all that was wrong with human society, many of which he had already stated in *PNV*:

1. *That the only practical human relationship is of dominance on the one side and submission on the other.*
2. *That other people are a means for the purpose of those who dominate.*
3. *That political or economic power is of supreme importance.*
4. *That the use of other men in the pursuit of power by the few is a sound basis for human society.*
5. *That the valued end justifies the use of any means.*
6. *That deceit or suppression of truth by those in power is justifiable.*
7. *That the possession or use of power does not tend to corrupt the users of power.*
8. *That the activities and processes that promote fear, anger, pride, a sense of inferiority or other divisive attitudes are also a sound basis for human society.*
9. *That the production of material goods are more important than the production of healthy and normal people.*
10. *That institutions and organizations are more important than people.*
11. *That intellect and abstract reasoning are more important than love.*
12. *That there is no supreme unifying principle more inclusive or more fundamental than the principle which scientists assume underlies and unites all natural forces and phenomena.*
13. *That if there is a supreme unifying principle, it is not really and constantly as powerful in men's affairs as, for instance, the force of gravity.*

He concludes, in his letter to Muste, "If the real disease lies deeper than the threatened war, if the wars are chiefly symptoms, then the movements of the disease are too deep, too widespread, too powerful, and with too much momentum to be affected by verbal appeals or resolutions passed by any convention. There is no use asking for peace unless we give up the assumptions and activities that make for conflict and war."[321] This is a statement by a man now confronting his age and a world gone profoundly wrong. But they are also the words of a thinker and doer, whose enormous experience and dedication to his beliefs and values sing out in this rather exasperated statement.

Singing and Dancing into Old Age

By 1962, Richard was seventy-seven and Evelyn sixty-six, and it had become harder for them to manage the cottage in Chester and its extensive garden. They were also deeply troubled by the direction of politics in the U.S. and the possible consequences of the heightened Cold War. The growth of nuclear power and nuclear weapons, and the very real possibility of nuclear Armageddon, filled them with a deep and profound apprehension. Like many others at that time, they felt a sense of foreboding and doom. Closer to home, they were also aware of plans to build a new power station not far from their community and were concerned about the consequences of increased traffic and population density this would cause. Distressed by what they believed (with good reason) as the coming nuclear apocalypse, they had been thinking about moving to Australia or New Zealand. Over the previous year or so they had inquired about the possibility of joining the Riverside Community in New Zealand, a community founded by and for Christian pacifists in 1941. After much conversation they decided to not pursue the idea, as Richard's age and health made the thought of such significant travel and relocation rather daunting.[322] As an alternative, they began to explore the possibility of moving to other parts of the United States, places that might better fit their lifestyle and values and provide less demanding maintenance.

After long consideration and discussion, they found a small town in Oregon, McMinnville, that seemed to offer real possibilities as a place to live out their last years. The town had a mild climate and was only about fifty miles from Portland. It looked like a good place to start a new life. They decided on a small trailer there and, with a residence secured, and after packing up their belongings, the couple set off for Oregon in June of 1963. They traveled across country by car to take possession of their trailer, located in a park near the town. It was a small place with a little land around it and they moved quickly to build an annex and to improve the plumbing and basic infrastructure. It helped that they were finally able to sell the cottage in Chester late in 1963 and now had funds for the move and to fix up the trailer. They still believed deeply in growing their own food and set about laying out a small vegetable garden at the site. They stayed in McMinnville, enjoying the mild Oregon climate, and tending their garden for the next four years.

Gregg continued participating in issues of peace and nonviolence as they settled into their new home. And he kept writing: he published two short pieces in a collection edited by Ramachandran and T. K. Mahadevan, *"Gandhi—His Relevance for Our Times in 1964"* and a short piece entitled *"The Best Solver of Conflicts,"* in which he enumerated, point by point, the central precepts of nonviolence and their value in the world of the H-Bomb and intercontinental ballistic missiles. Here, Gregg provided a series of bullet points, already expounded on in *PNV*, about the value and choice for nonviolent resistance. The points are worth reiterating here:

a)   *It must be nonviolent and persuasive.*

b)   *It must involve simple action more than talk. We cannot all be orators.*

c)   *Since we are all endangered, the action must be such that everyone can take part in it. That means, of course, that women as well as men can take active part in it. It is better if children also can participate.*

203

d) *It must be capable, by its very nature and processes, of inspiring interest, trust, and hope among the participants, the indifferent, the curious, the lazy and other onlookers, and even the opponents.*

e) *It must compel deeper thinking and feeling and be morally educative to everyone.*

f) *It must be capable, by its very processes, of stimulating moral and spiritual growth in the participants and all beholders, faster and more effectively and thoroughly than exhortations or present institutions.*

g) *It must be realistic, taking account of the inevitability of conflicts and of the presence of and possibilities for both evil and good in every person, including participants and opponents as well as others.*

h) *It must be based on an unshakable belief in the unity of mankind, and that this unity is deeper, stronger, more enduring and more important than the differences, whether the differences be of race, culture, nationality, economics, politics, assumptions, or any kind of ideology.*

i) *It must be a search for deeper and greater truth, both individual and social.*[323]

In *Satyagraha as a Mirror*, Gregg had argued that the first task for real peaceful change is to allow *satyagraha* to reflect the values and attitudes of both individuals and collectivities, whether group or nation. This "mirror" can then help cure civilization and individuals by making them see their true selves. Gregg reiterated the fundamental ability of *satyagraha* to provide a way to closer self-examination and self-awareness.

From his new home, Gregg corresponded with old and trusted friends. He wrote often to his old colleague William Stuart Nelson, Dean and Vice President at Howard University. Nelson was a noted scholar of nonviolence and *satyagraha*, and a pacifist. Like Gregg, he had traveled to India and been a major actor in the American civil rights era. He had also worked with Gandhi in India after WWII and during Partition. He returned there on a Fulbright Fellowship in 1958. He participated in the Selma, Alabama march and was a friend of King's. While Gregg was in Oregon, the two friends wrote to each other frequently as Nelson sought Gregg's advice on his book about Gandhi and nonviolence.[324]

By the mid to end of the '60s the United States was in turmoil. The anti-war protests, the continued escalation of the Cold War, the civil rights movement, the women's movement, and all the changes of the social and cultural pressures that framed the '60s were clear and present for Gregg. Almost all of these actions and mass demonstrations were fueled by a deep commitment to nonviolent resistance. That they did so was, in no small measure, a result of the vision that Gregg had laid out. Revolution may have been in the air, but for Gregg there was a seeming inevitability to these changes as he framed them very much in the terms he had used before in his critique of capitalism and industrialization. Indeed, the cultural revolution of those years came to validate much of what Gregg had argued throughout his long life. That he was aware of these changes is captured in letters he sent to both Rustin and Nelson. But he was not blind to the importance that new technologies would have on people's day-to-day lives and he let Rustin know that he thought that computers, automation, and technical advances had to be confronted with better education, especially for Black Americans, suggesting technical education for them as part of a movement strategy. This moment was also an opportunity for him to remind his friends of the value of Gandhi's constructivist program. He reiterated to Rustin the critical importance of the program in light of an article he had just read by the economist Robert Heilbroner that warned of the coming decline in manufacturing and the changes in employment likely to result from increasing automation of the most basic forms of work.[325]

In that same letter, Gregg echoed Emma Goldman's phrase, "I want this revolution to be known in the future as the 'singing revolution.' That persuasion has to be one of the heart, of the feelings. Song stimulates and transmits feelings better than signs or arguments." Despite being criticized by his British supporters at the PPU in the '30s for his emphasis on singing and dancing, Gregg was, once again, prescient in his insistence on the role music and dance could play in social change. His plea to Rustin came just as the folk revival was blossoming in the U.S. and Europe. Key to mobilizing radicals in the '60s, the songs of Pete Seeger, Woody Guthrie, The Weavers, Phil Ochs and, later, Bob Dylan (and many, many, others) helped mobilize and support civil rights and anti-war activists as they marched for peace and justice. Seeger's version of "We Shall Overcome" became the anthem of the early protest movements. Later, crowds around the world sang John Lennon's "Give Peace A Chance."

In October 1965, his thinking turned again to the larger issues in an unpublished manuscript about strategies for the War Resisters League. Gregg tried hard to make the WRL understand it could not only be against war—that it must develop a strategy to build small actions and institutions that bind humans together: "We have got to begin building in the midst of our warlike world a lot of little ad hoc experimental organizations and expressions of the unity of mankind. Some may begin as only neighborhood groups; others may start larger." Gregg was at pains to point out that this would mean "a lot of social and economic inventiveness. I would expect women to be better than men at this." He went on to remind Rustin that a "new society cannot grow out of a detailed blueprint à la Marx. Things are too complex, too swift, too unreliable, too unpredictable for that. The new society can come only by many small adaptions, inventions, and experiments to meet a specific local need. What is sound will grow and be imitated."[326]

All You Need is Love

By the mid-'60s Gregg realized that the time had come to take care of outstanding personal business. In October 1966 he wrote to Pearl Buck, the great writer, activist, and Nobel Prize-winning author (who was using his old cabin at Forest Farm) telling her that he was happy to surrender to her all the remaining contents of his old cabin on the Nearings' former farm and to pass on the lease to the land.[327] Gregg met Buck when she moved to Vermont, where she got to know the Nearings. Indeed, it was Buck who encouraged Helen Knothe Nearing to write *The Maple Sugar Book* about the Nearings' experience in organic farming. Buck's husband Richard Walsh was president of the John Day Company, which published the first edition of the book. In 1953, as the Nearings were selling their land in preparation for the move to Harborside in Maine, they sold two hundred-plus acres to Buck.[328] The release of Gregg's old cabin was the final chapter in his connection to the Nearing Farm.

Also, that year he wrote to E.F. Schumacher, the economist and ecologist, and sent him a copy of his *A Philosophy of Indian Economic Development*. Schumacher replied that he had just purchased a copy of *Companion Plants and How to Use Them* that Gregg had co-authored with Helen Philbrick.[329] This work (still in print) was really that of Philbrick. In fact, Gregg wrote to the publisher explaining that he had only a small part in some of the ideas for this work. But Schumacher was still enthralled by the work and wrote frequently to Gregg over the next year or two as his interest in appropriate technologies, eastern religions, and particularly the ideas of Gandhi began to have a greater and greater impact on his thinking, especially on education and teaching. In 1973 Schumacher would publish his major work *Small Is Beautiful: A Study of Economics as if People Mattered*.

In one of his last published works, Gregg took on some of the criticisms he saw in the press (and from many in the civil rights movement) of King's injunction to "love one's opponents," even the white racists who had beaten and killed Black Americans. Gregg pointed out, after a discussion of the basis of human unity (biological, physiological, psychological), that this unity could only be expressed as love because:

> Love is an important element of moral power. Like moral law, moral power grows out of the realized unity of the human species. Politics is a continuing clash of political power seekers. Though I may be mistaken, it seems to me that possession of moral power will result eventually in political power. This was demonstrated by Gandhi. But the possession of political power does not yield moral power. If, then, love generates persuasion, love becomes eventually practical politics. The love has to be expressed in detailed, everyday fashion, just as Gandhi showed his love for the Indian peasants by reviving their hand spinning which, under the conditions of the Indian climate, was a form of relief for rural unemployment. Love is not just something to talk about in Sunday School, but a sentiment expressed in what William Blake called "minute particulars." The racial problem is, I think, too deep to be settled by politics alone; it can be settled fully only by persuasion, and love is an element of persuasion. Persuasion being a living process, it takes time for growth. For these reasons, loving one's opponents is possible and sound practice.[330]

By the time Gregg wrote this he was close to eighty, and Evelyn nearly seventy. While still remarkably vibrant and closely watching what was going on in the world, they finally decided that the trailer in McMinnville, their garden, and the town's relative remoteness were now too much for them to manage. Like many others at this stage in life, and without children, they began to consider how they could look after themselves as age narrowed their options for independent living. After extensive discussion and planning they decided to seek space in a retirement home, a place that would provide some help and care for them in their last years. They found an opening at Cascade Manor in Eugene, Oregon. They moved there in August 1967 just as the Summer of Love obsessed the country. The move was, perhaps, none too soon. In early 1968 Gregg developed a slight hand tremor. It was not much at first, just something of an annoyance, especially for a man so used to working and writing with his hands. Sadly, it was the beginning of the Parkinson's Disease that eventually took his life. This growing sense of mortality was only exacerbated by the news that his younger sister Marjorie had died at the age of eighty in South Tamworth, New Hampshire. Richard and Marjorie had been close over the years, and he always wrote fond letters to her, including several during the last months of her life. He did not attend her funeral. His illness would have made that very difficult and, in any case, he said in a letter to his niece Alice that he would honor her for her life but not at a funeral—he also stated he didn't want a funeral for himself either when the time came.[331]

As Gregg began to deal with his illness, 1968 brought tumult to the American landscape: the assassinations of Marin Luther King, Jr., and Robert Kennedy, the increasing demonstrations against the war in Vietnam, and the seismic changes in the American political landscape that crystalized in the chaotic Democratic Party Convention in Chicago that summer. All of this put Gregg's final years into stark relief. On the news of King's assassination, he wrote a short note to Coretta Scott King telling her, "Your husband was the growing tip of civilization and society. Because his work was in the moral and spiritual realm, it cannot die but carries on with the march of human evolution. Be comforted, therefore, by this realization."[332] This was more than just sympathy for a widow, it was part of Gregg's growing despair for the future of humanity. But the darkness of the time did not stop his concern for the future of peace and his passion for still figuring out a way to achieve it—and how to be a better person. Parkinson's never affected his ability to think and be aware, but as the years passed at the retirement home, he wrote less and less frequently.

When he could no longer write by hand he resorted to his old typewriter, keeping up some correspondence with his friend Stuart Nelson and with E.F. Schumacher. While his mind remained bright and active, he sometimes, as the hand tremors got worse, would dictate letters for Evelyn to type. His dear sister Elinor died in March at the age of eighty-four. This left Gregg as the last member of his immediate family. He had outlived all his remarkable brothers and sisters. Elinor had been his most consistent correspondent and they shared a great number of political beliefs, values, and perspectives. He was closer to Elinor, perhaps, than to any other of his siblings.

In 1971, his grandniece, Kate Thompson, visited the couple at Cascade Manor. Gregg was a bit limited in movement but was not yet confined to a wheelchair. Richard and Evelyn showed them the garden that Evelyn had created and engaged other members of the retirement home in cultivating. Kate remembered being served a meal of millet and lentils, not so different for what she recalled eating with them at their cottage in Chester in the mid-'50s when she was very young. Kate noticed that Richard and Evelyn remained careful about their diet to the very end. By 1972, Gregg was confined to a wheelchair and had little mobility. The Parkinson's had taken away his ability to write and to garden.

In March of 2016 Evan Hardie, an independent farmer and activist in Australia, wrote about visiting Richard and Evelyn in August of 1973. He had gone to the Greggs to talk with Evelyn about her work in biodynamics but did not know Gregg's work or background. He recalled the visit vividly:

"Upon arrival at Eugene and meeting Evelyn, I was struck by her immediate wish to take me to visit her husband in hospital. Richard was lying quite still, on his back, under a white sheet. His only movement was to offer his hand in greeting and to gently look at me. He could only slightly speak in a low sort of whisper, as a result of the later stage of Parkinson's, but there were no tremors whatever. Evelyn would carefully and closely listen to what he was saying and tell us in turn. At the end of our meeting, Richard passed on to me in simple terms to follow my most inner desires in this and any other field of work. We held hands gently as though an agreement had been reached and we left that room of absolute peacefulness."

Richard Gregg died on Sunday, January 27, 1974.

CHAPTER ELEVEN

Epilogue: Living a Life of Conscience

The Quietest Radical in History

RICHARD GREGG BELIEVED IN the value of physical labor: that manual work, the work of the body, could not be distinguished from the work of the mind. He loved to garden and to dig and to harvest. Gregg was at his most content with his hands in the soil, figuring out what crops to grow and how to protect them from disease without the pesticides and the poisons of modern farming. He raised vegetables and harvested from his home in India, on the maple sugar farm in Vermont, the cottage he lived in with his second wife Evelyn, and the place they built as a retirement home in Oregon. For a good deal of his life he was a farmer. Although he learned much about the value of the land and of wholesome food from Gandhi, he began his interests in agriculture long before he felt the pull of India. The transitions from Harvard graduate to corporate lawyer, to progressive law and labor relations, and then to pacifism, Gandhism and philosophy, are the arc of a complex life. Perhaps it is only fitting that it all culminated in organic farming.

It was in the garden that Gregg integrated his life. Yes, there was the physicality of the work, but there was also the simplicity and respect for nature that he advocated and cherished. He was a scholar and writer who turned the soil. It was here that he combined theory into practice, in the garden rows and not in the streets. Gregg created some of the most important

211

ideas and strategies for active nonviolent resistance, ones that would become the hallmark of peaceful protests that range from the civil rights movement, women's liberation, the marches against the Vietnam War, and right up to Black Lives Matter. We could add to this list the campaign against apartheid in South Africa, environmental activism, the anti-nuclear weapons and anti-nuclear power actions, and the struggle for peace in Northern Ireland. Many of the social the social movements of the past fifty years were committed to nonviolent protest.

But Gregg wasn't a marcher or a street activist. Perhaps, as for many of us, this was a function of his personality. It simply wasn't who he was. As one old friend said of him in an obituary: "Richard Gregg would say the most positive things in the most diffident manner . . . (h)is literary style was far from brilliant, as he was the first to deplore, and his speaking style was slow and over-detailed, but what he said was revolutionary, and he meant revolution by it." She called him, *"the quietest radical in history."*[333] But it is worth noting that he joined theory with practice in day-to-day living and work and stood out as the man who practiced what he preached, while he never engaged in protest at the barricades.

But there was one area where he was insistent and proactive: in his complete loyalty to Gandhism and to the promotion of his own writing. He was relentless in distributing his work, sending copies of his books and articles to everyone he knew, or to whom he believed would benefit from reading his books. Indeed, throughout his notebooks, there are small memos to himself with lists of people who should receive copies. He was never shy about drawing attention to Gandhi and his interpretations of the great man's body of work. He was precise and careful about this as with everything else.

Gregg's writing reveals his commitment to detail and scholarship. And, somewhat unusual for his time, all his work is footnoted and referenced. This focus on referencing and citing his sources is an admirable academic strategy, and he drew on his notebooks where he documents and quotes everything he had read. The notebooks are indeed exactly that. Spanning twenty years and comprising over fifty volumes, they are dated and numbered, and Gregg even indexed some. Most of the notes are quotes and comments on the books and articles he was reading, interspaced with cuttings from newspapers and journals glued to the pages. These clippings are book reviews and commentary that he retained for further reference and research and are his thoughts on his reading. And there are many to-do lists and reminders. They are part a file system and a diary. Those notebooks, rescued from Coperthwaite's yurt at Dickinson's Reach, are now catalogued and digitized at the Thoreau Institute in Concord, Massachusetts, taking their place with the Scott and Helen Nearing Papers and the archive of the Ralph Waldo Emerson Society, among many others.

Forty-eight general notebooks have survived, plus several specifically dedicated to themes (for example, education), and he compiled them annually. A few are undated; some deal with key topics, such as diet, and spinning and weaving. Occasionally he made short personal comments or reflections on his life and his experiences at the time, but these are few and far between. Through this entire period, and to the end of his life, Gregg wrote hundreds of letters to his family and friends, colleagues, and acquaintances about his life, his work, his beliefs, his travels, and his gardening. He was still writing letters as the disease that finally crippled his body, but not his mind, took away his last breath.

Last, but by no means, least, Richard Gregg was a religious man, more correctly, a spiritual man. He was ambivalent about the church, however, even though he grew up the son of a minister. But God and Jesus were important to him, and Gregg took the teachings of the scriptures seriously. He was a Christian pacifist, joining a long line of others who connected their beliefs to peace. A reader, he had immersed himself in the works of the masters on almost every religion in the world, and he knew well that there were many ways to treasure the spiritual and the moral. But Gregg saw corruption and shallowness in the corporate churches of America. In the first decades of the twentieth century, he daily became aware of the hypocrisy of many church leaders, both Protestant and Catholic, as they ignored the growing social inequality in America. But he never relinquished his belief in Jesus or the Christian god. All his writings are framed in terms of his religion and, while his work was always informed by his beliefs, they are never at the forefront and he consistently gave examples and insights from all the world's major religions. He cited the Koran and the Bhagavad Gita far more often than the Bible.

With the publication of his most significant work, *The Power of Non-Violence*, Gregg found his place in the pantheon of pacifists. During the intense debates about socialism and progressive change that dominated the turbulent 1930s, the question of the pacifist response took on a new urgency. What Gregg brought to the pacifist movement in the mid-twentieth century was Gandhi's philosophy. But it was more. Gregg brought a critical honesty and a detailed specific program that turned pacifism into action, challenging the traditions of post-1918 pacifist thinking and building on them. He advocated the planning and design of nonviolent resistance strategies and built it upon a moral foundation and deep faith in humanity. His work realigned pacifist thinking in the 1930s, stressing the need for action, not words, and, indeed, calling for nonviolent resistance that required training and planning. Gregg summed this up in no uncertain terms in the introduction to *Training for Peace*:

> Honest and intelligent pacifists are troubled by a sense of ineffectiveness. Though they are sure of the soundness of their beliefs, they see on all sides the failures of those beliefs in action. Pacifism seems to consist merely of reading books and articles, going to meetings, listening to speeches, urging people who are in high places to do something. Pacifist action has been most vicarious. Education and definite public opinion are indeed necessary before society can act. Nevertheless, for successful pacifism, just as for successful militarism, there

must be ways for the individual to translate his beliefs into concrete action. Without that, pacifism, except for keeping alive the conscience and an ideal, becomes, for the most part, irresponsible, futile sentimentalism.[334]

Calling pacifism "irresponsible, futile, sentimentalism" struck a chord with many pacifists and those who were seeking guidance on how to react to the injustices and poverty of the Great Depression and the looming threat of international war. Others were upset by Gregg's dismissal of their prior work and actions. Consequently, the impact of Gregg's work, especially *PNV*, on Christian pacifists in the U.S. cannot be underestimated. By marshaling a wide range of scholarly literature and the insights of psychology and philosophy, and by documenting how all the world's dominant religions have a commitment to peace and nonviolence, he gave pacifism a practical guide that was determinedly not ethnocentric. In addition, Gregg provided explanations on why Gandhi's advocacy was unique and relevant to the West. He did not romanticize Gandhi nor shy away from the contradiction that active nonviolent resistance was itself a kind of violence, requiring training and courage. In doing so, he linked Thoreau, Emerson, Tolstoy, Ruskin, Gandhi, King, and many others, building on their legacy of civil disobedience and pacifism. And he brought to it all an analysis based on the insights of Western psychology, sociology, economics, and physics.

Gregg set out to translate Gandhi's ideas for a western audience, seeking to "restate and explain" Gandhi's nonviolence methods. In doing so, he was never simply engaged in explanation; he also tried to adapt it for a western public in ways that would resonate with their experience of life. He was particularly concerned with explaining how a philosophy developed in a colonial and largely agricultural society could resonate in an America by then at the peak of industrialization, but deeply scarred by the Great Depression. Throughout his writing, he stressed that nonviolence could only grow out of personal ethical transformation and that that could only be achieved through the grounded practice of nonviolence. He also emphasized that nonviolent resistance to power required training and the development of specific skills and attitudes. But while Gregg was seeking to bring these ideas west, he was also embarking on a complex argument about the need to transform society completely. Gregg wanted to create, as the leading Gregg scholar, Joseph Kosek, pointed out, "a counter-modernity," one which slowly reduced and then eliminated the need to rely on violence to settle disputes and to resist domination. Put simply, Gregg argued that violent resistance to domination or change through war or revolution would create more violence and more domination—that the means would define the end. A genuinely nonviolent society could only be achieved through peaceful means.

In arguing all this, Gregg set out versions of Gandhi's program that showed how nonviolence must be oriented towards cooperation, substituting for war and violence in human relations. For Gregg and Gandhi, truth and nonviolence are the basis from which all other efforts to reduce violence must be built. And this truth is also about personal self-knowledge and the conduct of one's self in all activities, and at all times. Gregg lived a life that reflected his beliefs. He was a gardener and philosopher, turning the soil was, in part, the equivalent of changing society—a slow, deliberate process that would reap rewards in the future. To get to this point, Gregg knew that understanding of the self could best be achieved through the constructivist programs that Gandhi promoted and that could be reached through collective self-government, participatory democracy, and a process of group decision-making in a nonviolent manner and form. In this, Gregg was essentially arguing for a deep commitment to what we would now call sustainable practices and ecologically sound activities as part of participatory local democracy.

Both Gregg and Gandhi were deeply aware that such personal, cultural, and political transformations could not happen overnight. Gregg argued that strongly throughout his work that this was a step-by-step process and that all such activities should be fully integrated, each with the other. Gregg very much believed that human nature was not fixed and could be improved. He would therefore advocate that learning nonviolent strategies of resistance should be accompanied by singing and dancing, by physical activities that included gardening and building, and by projects that constructed values and attitudes of peaceful cooperation. And all of these had to be built upon efforts by the individual to transcend themselves by deep self-examination and the profound embrace of love.

Gregg developed examples of constructivist programs culled from his experience in India and framed for acceptance in the West. These programs also built on the argument he developed in *The Value of Voluntary Simplicity*. He insisted that modern, technologically driven, and commodified modern life could be replaced with a simpler form (primarily agricultural), thereby eradicating the greed, waste, and alienation of contemporary capitalism. Essentially, the combination of *satyagraha* with a deep belief in collective self-governing activities (the learning by doing), creates the opportunity for individuals to experience the benefits of working cooperatively, of employing both hand and brain, creating a human-scale technology that encourages simplicity, sustainability, and an emotional connection to others and to the work. Home spinning and use of the spinning wheel (*chakra*) is the epitome of what this means. Gregg argued these points over many years and in many thousands of pages of writing and analysis. What is striking in all this is the coherency of this whole project and the careful, humble, hesitant way in which Gregg framed it.

Simplicity and love were, of course, at the very center of *satyagraha* and Gandhi's vision. In fact, a better world was impossible unless humans lived in harmony with nature, respecting and nurturing the soil. By the mid-'60s, the counterculture movements in America and Europe would model an alternative lifestyle that embraced Gregg's vision while knowing little about its author. While the origins of the counterculture are numerous and diverse, the common themes (rejection of traditional authority, the search for meaning in an alienating industrial and commercial system, the desire to create new forms of community, the journey to find an authentic self) are very much at the center of the issues Gregg struggled with in his long life. Today, there are echoes of these sentiments in the anti-globalism, localist, and organic farming movements. They are there, too, in the many efforts to build local community organizations and the numerous cooperatives that have sprung in towns and cities. Yet, up to now, few who promote and advocate alternative lifestyles, or who support and write about simple living, would know the name or the history of Richard Gregg.

Richard Gregg and Dad

It was by trying to better understand my father's dedication to his beliefs, which eventually led him to jail, that I found my way to Richard Gregg. Unlike Gregg (or me), my father never went to college. But he did educate himself, became a pacifist, and believed deeply in the cause of the struggles of working people against exploitation. For Dad, most of that translated into his support for the British Labour Party and, even more so, his commitment to the ideals of the cooperative movement. The extensive network of shops, funeral homes, educational programs, and wholesalers dated from its beginning in small retail stores to serve workers in the North of England in the 1830s. In the twentieth century it became a national movement, linked to the unions and the Labour Party, and a feature of life in the country. In the U.S., especially since the '60s, numerous forms of cooperation, although not generally embedded in trade unions or political parties, have emerged: small businesses that are worker-owned such as bakeries and cafés, food coops of many sorts, and a variety of efforts to nurture mutuality and local community.

My father's political values and pacifism were linked. He clearly felt strongly enough about these to stand trial and to refuse to argue on religious grounds for an exemption from conscription. But I didn't know about his imprisonment as a conscientious objector until after he had died, not long after I turned sixteen. In fact, I don't remember much about him, but what I do remember was that he was kind and gentle, somewhat otherworldly, and frequently vague. Quiet, too. Not one for a lot of talking. His name was Walter Gerald Wooding. Everyone called him Gerry.

My father was from a small village just outside of Northampton, England, where I grew up. It was once famous for its boots and shoes, and there are still old factory buildings around the town, and they still make Doc Martens there. Looking back on it, it always seemed to me a bit of a sad, decrepit place. Like many post-industrial cities, its core industry is long gone, replaced by shopping malls and hideous industrial estates that are devoid of soul or any redeeming architectural value. In the '60s and '70s, the town's only claim to fame was as the site of the ugliest bus station in Europe, a product of a deranged architect and some moronic city planners bent on post-war progress. But it was my town. I knew its by-ways and secret places, the back streets, and the best chip shops.

I had a paper route when I was about thirteen and got up pretty early in the morning to deliver the *Daily Mirror* to the local neighborhood and the *Times* and *Financial Times* to the posh folks a few blocks away. Dad was always up then, and before I set off, we drank tea together, always ensuring that the dog got some in a saucer with lots of sugar and milk. It was a little ritual that I look back on and treasure. Sometimes we would hear The Beatles singing on the radio. Dad said it was a bit raucous but admitted, "those lads can sing."

My dad was born in 1913, twenty-eight years after Richard Gregg, and left school at fourteen. Both men lived and worked through the twentieth century, Gregg dying in 1974 and my father in 1969. After leaving high school, Dad got a job as an errand boy in the grocery department of the local Cooperative Society, and, from that moment on, he was a Co-Op man. He got some credentials through studying at the free classes the Society held and embraced the cooperative, trade unionist, and socialist ideals that marked the cooperative movement in England in the years after WWII. One of his heroes was Robert Owen, the Welsh philanthropist, social reformer, utopian socialist, and one of the founders of the cooperative movement. As a result, my older brother is named Robert *Owen* Wooding (Bob).

My father's dad was a TallyMan who sold stuff on credit door-to-door, and he was also a lay preacher. Probably, as a result, my dad had some religious sympathies early on in life. I never knew him to speak of religion, however: none of us were baptized or ever went to church, and I always assumed we were atheists. But his religious father left Dad with a deep sense of morality and some firmly held beliefs. During the 1930s, Dad worked at a grocery store (the Co-Op, of course), and he met my mum in 1935, and they were married in 1938. As the war approached, he had utterly rejected the established church in any form (although he had a soft spot for the Quakers), and, when he refused to accept his call-up papers, he was arrested and tried as a conscientious objector. As a member of the Peace Pledge Union (PPU), Dad refused to do any work that would aid the war effort and was sent to jail. After his release, it was hard for a CO to get a job, and he ended up as a gardener/handyman at a children's home. This job was ironic, as he was a hopeless gardener and could barely hammer a nail. When the war ended, he went back to working at the Co-Op, ending up in the local Cooperative coal depot. He was there most of his life after the war, delivering coal and, later, running the depot. He was, for a while, president of the local union. One thing I remember was that he always referred to his fellow workers as "brother"—this always confused me as a kid.

Back then, we were all Labour Party. We got the *Daily Mirror* when it still played at being socialist. I remember the prime ministers, Harold Macmillan and Harold Wilson, the welfare state, and The Beatles. I also remember wanting a toy gun and a cowboy hat. *The Lone Ranger* was on TV then in glorious black and white—for me a much, much more exciting world than the drab streets of a Midlands town in the '50s and early '60s. I had to push to get the gun. Looking back, I can now see why arming a ten-year-old boy might be anathema for a man who went to jail because he didn't want to shoot people. But there's a picture of me from some time in the early '60s, looking very debonair, toting a plastic gun and a rather snazzy hat. Clearly, youngest sons had more clout than the British state.

When I remember my dad, I remember a good man. Perhaps a would-be intellectual. There were some books in the house, in a built-in cabinet in the living room behind a couple of glass doors, although I don't remember what they were other than the *Pears' Cyclopedia* which, I just found out, was started by the Pears Soap company and published annually as a one-volume encyclopedia. I think we got it from collecting soap packets. I still have a vague memory of a copy of the Webb's *History of British Trade Unionism*— no doubt a Penguin used paperback, as there were a few of those about, too. They had such lovely covers. Like Gregg, Dad was a reader but, unlike Gregg, pretty much self-taught. I only found out recently that he was Chair of the local Co-Op Education Committee and took learning seriously. I also remember that one of his friends who came to the house was an actor. I now realize he was probably gay and a victim of discrimination (homosexuality was a crime in England until the '70s). I did not know this at the time, but Dad and Mum gave him refuge. Not many ordinary folks would have done that in the grim and homophobic England of the 1950s.

I also remember Dad's astonishment that I passed the 11+, the exam every kid had to take back then at the age of eleven so that it could be decided whether they would go to the secondary school and learn how to be fodder for the factory or the warehouse, or to grammar school where they had some chance of going to college or university—maybe. "Blimey," he said, "the lad's passed the Exam." I guess he was proud of me, but I don't know. The years between then and when he died are fuzzy. A lot was going on: grammar school, puberty, great British rock n' roll, my paper route, and figuring out girls. Somewhere in there, my older brother Bob, probably about sixteen years old, joined the Youth Campaign for Nuclear Disarmament. I don't remember much about that, but I guess the apple doesn't fall . . . .

I have an older sister, Jan, who was born in 1942, barely nine months after Dad got out of prison. She was married at eighteen and had three kids by the time she was twenty-three. She brought up a great family and worked most of her life as a shop assistant in a local department store. Neither my brother nor my sister went to college, and both left school at fifteen. In the mid-fifties, they went to the same primary school (I went there, too), and my brother remembers how difficult it was to be the son of a "conchie." He told me once that when he was about ten, the school announced that *everyone* must buy and wear a poppy to celebrate the 1918 armistice and the end of WWI and of WWII. Each teacher had a supply, and kids were to line up in the classroom and buy the poppies. My brother asked Mum for the money to buy the poppy, and she resisted giving it to him, "because Mum and Dad don't celebrate war." My brother persisted, and she finally gave in. The next day he lined up to buy the poppy, and when he got to the head of the queue, the teacher said, "We don't want your money" and sent him away. This insult was given in front of the whole school. My brother still burns with the shame of being embarrassed because his father was a CO.

My father died of a heart attack in 1968. He had had problems with angina and went fast. The coal dust didn't help. I never sat down and talked to him about going to prison because he didn't believe in killing people. Never asked him what it meant to be a pacifist. I never had a conversation about what he believed in and why. I don't remember much conversation even at the very end. I only remember visiting him in hospital. The sharpest image I have of that moment is him lying there with the little sucker units on his chest that held the sensors for what I assume to be an electrocardiogram. He looked grey and old. I cried a little bit as I held his hand. He died that evening. I wasn't there.

Like Richard Gregg, my father was the son of a religious man, and religion played a large part in his early life. Like Gregg, however, he rejected the formal church and explored other ideas and belief systems. Given the difference in culture and class, it is not surprising that my father embraced socialism and the cooperative movement where Gregg eventually sought meaning in India and Gandhi. But both were genuinely horrified by the impact of capitalism on working people and both supported unions and progressive politics. They also both embraced some of the fundamental tenets of cooperation and mutual aid through education and work. Part of that link is the implicit and, frequently, explicit commitment to the Quakers' support for cooperatives and pacifism. Although neither man was a Quaker, both recognized and had sympathy with the Quaker pacifist vision and the core belief that everyone has something of god within them. What further links them is their willingness to promote, advocate, and, in no small measure, suffer for that belief. Both were guided by a moral compass, a sense of what was right, that drove them to do extraordinary things. Learning and writing about Richard Gregg made me realize that believing in what is right must be matched to doing what is right. It is the only way to build a better world.

Good Trouble

Getting into "good trouble" is what Richard Gregg and my father did. They pushed into the world, looking for ways to make it better. It is what Martin Luther King, Jr., did. It is what civil rights activist and congressman John Lewis did all his life. It is what defined Nelson Mandela. Over the last several years millions have stood up and said, "Black Lives Matter" as they confront racism, inequality, and police violence. Since the '30s innumerable acts of brave resistance to oppression and injustice saw unarmed passive resistance to brutality and violence. People made nonviolence *the* act of resistance.

Students at my university take courses on the history of peace movements and hunger to learn about how conflict can be resolved without the pain of violence. We bring in activists and scholars under the Greeley Scholar for Peace Studies program, and they bring stories and ideas from across the world: from the struggles for peace in Northern Ireland, the fight to end apartheid in South Africa, and organizing to put an end to genocide. Peace activist and Nobel Peace prize-winner Leymah Gbowee was the 2011 Greeley Scholar. She organized a peace movement that helped end the Second Liberian Civil War in 2003. As a social worker, she organized the Women of Liberia Mass Action for Peace, bringing together Christian and Muslim women to pray and sing for peace, eventually forcing national leaders to create a peace process to end a civil war. One year we were joined by Tawakkol Abdel-Salam Khalid Karman who shared the Nobel Peace Prize in 2011 in recognition of her work in the nonviolent struggle for the right of expression, the safety of women, and women's rights to full participation in peace-building work in Yemen.

In the local community hundreds have dedicated their work to improving the lives of the poor and the disenfranchised by helping them get jobs, find enough decent food to feed their families, fight racism and homophobia, celebrate their cultures, get access to affordable health care and education, and gain and protect their civil rights. Such work goes on across America and the world as people band together to demand democracy and a decent life. The vast majority of this work is based on the assertion of the right we have as human beings to live a better life in a better world. The only way that can be achieved is by the power of nonviolence.

[1] See: Spinney, Robert G. *City of Big Shoulders: A History of Chicago* (United States: Cornell University Press, 2020), 11-150; Pierce, Bessie Louise. *History of Chicago, Volume III: The Rise of a Modern City, 1871-1893* (United Kingdom: University of Chicago Press, 2007).

[2] See: Cronon, W. *Nature's Metropolis: Chicago and the Great West* (United States: W. W. Norton, 2009).

[3] Richard Bartlett Gregg (hereinafter RBG), *My Memories of Gandhi*, unpublished manuscript, n.d., 1. RBG, *Letter to Family*, October 24, 1924. Madison, Wisconsin. Walden Woods Project's Thoreau Institute Library, Special Collections, Richard Bartlett Gregg Papers.

[4] RBG, *Letter to Family*.

[5] It was probably this edition: Prasad, Rajendra Gandhi, Mahatma. *Young India 1919-1922* (India: B. W. Huebsch, 1923).

[6] RBG, *Letter to Family*.

[7] Source: Library of Congress, Huebsch Papers, biographical note, Accessed March 9, 2016.

[8] Coperthwaite, William S. *A Handmade Life: In Search of Simplicity* (United States: Chelsea Green 2002). 116.

[9] Gregg, Richard, *General Notebook 1*, May 1925, 12. Walden Woods Project's Thoreau Institute Library, Special Collections, Richard Bartlett Gregg Papers. Hereafter *RBG, Notebook*.

[10] For an extensive history, see Bonner, Hypatia Bradlaugh and John Mackinnon Robertsson, *Charles Bradlaugh: A Record of His Life and Work*. (United Kingdom: T. Fisher Unwin, 1894); Niblett, Bryan. *Dare to Stand Alone: The Story of Charles Bradlaugh*. (United Kingdom: Kramedart Press, 2010).

[11] For the background and life of Bill Coperthwaite, see: Saltmarsh, J., Peter Forbes, and William Coperthwaite, *Handmade Life: In Search of Simplicity*. (United States: Chelsea Green Publishing, 2007); Whybrow, H. and Peter Forbes, *A Man Apart: Bill Coperthwaite's Radical Experiment in Living*. (United States: Chelsea Green Publishing, 2015).

[12] Saltmarsh, John A. *Scott Nearing: An Intellectual Biography*. (United States: Temple University Press, 1991).

[13] My student assistant, Janelle Bourgeois, was more dedicated. She read through several notebooks and gave me a very useful synopsis for each at the start of this project. I am indebted to her work here.

[14] Quoted in Gregg, Richard B., Richard to Alice Thompson, July 2, 1972. Hereinafter all letters from Richard Gregg cited as "RBG."

[15] *Gregg Family Biographies*, unpublished manuscript, multiple authors. Personal collection, 1970.

[16] Tim Blevins, Dennis Daily, Chris Nicholl, Calvin P. Otto, and Katherine Scott Sturdevant, *Legends, Labors and Loves: William Jackson Palmer, 1836-1909* (United States: Pikes Peak Library District with the Colorado Springs Pioneers Museum and Colorado College, 2009).

[17] For details of Palmer's role in building Colorado Springs, see Marshall Sprague, *Newport in the Rockies: The Life and Good Times of Colorado Springs* (Greece: Swallow Press/Ohio University Press, 1987).

[18] First Congregational Church, Colorado Springs. *"Our Heritage,"* https://www.fcucc.org/who-we-are/history Accessed July 12, 2017.

[19] Oral History Research Office, Colombia University, *The Reminiscences of Dr. Alan Gregg*, unpublished manuscript, 1958, 12.

[20] Elizabeth Wallace, *Colorado Springs*, (United States: Arcadia, 2003).

[21] Margaret Humphreys, *Malaria: Poverty, Race, and Public Health in the United States* (United States: Johns Hopkins University Press, 2003). 38.

[22] *Gregg Family Biographies*, 1970.

[23] First Congregational Church, Colorado Springs *"Our Heritage,"* https://www.fcucc.org/who-we-are/history (accessed, July 15, 2017).

[24] James M. Usher, Charles Brooks and William Henry Whitmore. *History of the Town of Medford, Middlesex County, Massachusetts: From Its First Settlement in 1630 to 1855.* (United States: Rand, Avery, 1886).

[25] Medford Historical Society Papers, Volume 20, *Medford Branch Railroad,* http://www.perseus.tufts.edu/hopper/text?doc=Perseus%3Atext%3A2005.05.0020%3Achapter%3D15 (accessed June, 22 , 2019).

[26] Wilder Penfield, *The Difficult Art of Giving: The Epic of Alan Gregg.* (Boston, MA: Little, Brown, 1967), 7-13.

[27] Jacqueline S. Pflaum, *Helper Woman: A Biography of Elinor Delight Gregg.* (N.p.: University of San Diego, 1996).

[28] *The Harvard Graduates' Magazine, 1907.* (United States: Harvard Graduates' Magazine Association. 1941).

[29] Gregg, Richard, *A Biographical Sketch of Mary Needham Gregg*, unpublished manuscript, October 1970.

[30] Gregg, *Mary Needham*, 2.

[31] Gregg, *Mary Needham*, 3.

[32] Penfield, *The Difficult Art of Giving*, 24.

[33] Penfield, *The Difficult Art of Giving*, 22.

[34] Gregg, Elinor, *To Donald Gregg*, ALS, 1 May 1908, Elinor Gregg Papers, Box 1, Santa Fe, New Mexico.

[35] Cited in Penfield, *The Difficult Art of Giving*, 31.

[36] Penfield, *The Difficult Art of Giving*, 180.

[37] Penfield, 22.

[38] Penfield, 21.

[39] Oral History Research Office, *The Reminiscences of Dr. Alan Gregg*, 3.

⁴⁰ For the background on Tesla, see Marc J. Seifer, *Wizard: The Life and Times of Nikola Tesla*, (United States: Citadel Press, 2010); Inez Hunt and Wanetta W. Draper, *Lightning in His Hand: The Life Story of Nikola Tesla*, (United States: Sage Books, 1964); W. Bernard Carlson, *Tesla: Inventor of the Electrical Age* (Princeton NJ: Princeton University Press, 2003), 264; and Richard Munson, *Tesla: Inventor of the Modern* (United States: W. W. Norton, 2018).

⁴¹ For the story of Tesla's experimental station at Pikes Peak, see: Hunt and Draper, *Lightening in his Hand*; Jim Glenn and Margaret Cheney, 2000. "Tesla: Life and Legacy—Colorado Springs."*Public Broadcasting Service.* http://www.pbs.org/tesla/ll/ll_colspr.html. (December 12, 2000); Harry Goldman, 1971. "Nikola Tesla's Bold Adventure: Strange experiments conducted by an electronic wizard at the turn of the century." *The American West* (March). 4-9; Donald Mitchell, 1972. "Nikola Tesla's Investigation of High-Frequency Phenomena and Radio Communication." *Mental Landscape LLC*. 1972; and James Borràs Ros, 2013. "Colorado Springs Laboratory." *Tesla Research*. http://teslaresearch.jimdo.com/colorado-springs-lab-1899-1900/. Accessed June 14, 2016.

⁴² Cited in Carlson, *Tesla: Inventor of the Electrical Age*, 278.

⁴³ This point is made by Joseph Kip Kosek. Kosek's work was invaluable in writing this biography and I have drawn heavily on his analysis and his history throughout. See Joseph Kip Kosek, *Acts of Conscience: Christian Nonviolence and Modern American Democracy* (New York: Columbia University Press, 2011), 89.

⁴⁴ Jameson, Elizabeth. *All that Glitters: Class, Conflict, and Community in Cripple Creek* (United States: University of Illinois Press, 1998), 6. For an overview and analysis, see George G. Suggs, *Colorado's War on Militant Unionism: James H. Peabody and the Western Federation of Miners* (United States: University of Oklahoma Press, 1991) and Jameson, *All that Glitters*, 57.

⁴⁵ Philip Sheldon Foner, *The Industrial Workers of the World, 1905-1917* (United Kingdom: International Publishers, 1965), and Melvyn Dubovsky, *We Shall Be All: A History of the Industrial Workers of the World* (Chicago: Quadrangle Books, 1969).

⁴⁶ Alan Gregg, "*The Reminiscences of Dr. Alan Gregg*," The IWW (Industrial Workers of the World) were founded in 1905. They, unlike the more conservative labor unions in the United States, sought to organize across race, ethnicity, gender, nationality, and skill level. The group quickly gained a reputation as the most radical element in the labor movement. See also: Melvyn Dubofsky, *We Shall be All: A History of the Industrial Workers of the World* (United States: University of Illinois Press, 2000).

⁴⁷ See Penfield, *The Difficult Art of Giving*, 95. Rockefeller Foundation, Alan Gregg Biography, http://rockefeller100.org/biography/show/alan-gregg. Accessed April 15, 2015).

⁴⁸ Donald Gregg in *Family Biographies*, unpublished manuscript, October 1970.

⁴⁹ Source: Joshua Dorin, "Channing Sanitarium." *Wellesley History*, 30, April 2014.

⁵⁰ James Ayer, Dr. Donald Gregg, 1881-1939, Archives of neurology and psychiatry, v.42, #1, 1939, 134.

[51] Waltham Training School for Nurses, and Florence Nightingale. *The Waltham Training School for Nurses, 1885-1921* (Waltham, Mass.: Waltham Training School for Nurses, 1921); Teddy Jones and Edwina McConnell, *A Stone for Every Journey: Traveling the Life of Elinor Gregg, R.N.* (Santa Fe, NM: Sunstone Press, 2005), 101.

[52] *Elinor Delight Gregg video*, Archives and Special Collections, Consortium Library, University of Alaska, Anchorage, Biographical Note. Accessed May 22, 2016; Jones, *A Stone for Every Journey*. 104-7.

[53] Elinor D. Gregg, *The Indians and the Nurse* (United States: University of Oklahoma Press, 1965).

[54] Nancy Wirth, Interview by John Wooding, in person. Santa Fe, NM, August 10-12, 2015.

[55] Carney, Cary Michael. *Native American Higher Education in the United States* (United States: Transaction Publishers, 1999), 130. See also: Raymond Wolters, *The New Negro on Campus: Black College Rebellions of the 1920s* (Princeton University Press, 1975); Harvard College, Class of 1897. *Twenty-Fifth Anniversary Report, Class of 1897* (Methuen, MA: Riverside Press, 1922).

[56] "History" at http://www.hamptonu.edu/about/history.cfm Accessed July 5, 2020.

[57] See James Edgar Gregg, *Race Riots: Preventive Measures.* (Hampton, VA: Hampton Institute Press, 1919); James Edgar Gregg, *Lynching: A National Menace; The White South's Protest Against Lynching* (Hampton, VA: Hampton Normal and Agricultural Institute, 1919). James Edgar Gregg, *Industrial Training for the Negro* (Hampton, VA: Hampton Normal and Agricultural Institute, 1928), and James Edgar Gregg, *The Comparison of the Races* (Hampton, VA: Hampton Institute Press, 1919).

[58] Penfield, *The Difficult Art of Giving*, 23; *Family Biographies, Marjorie True Gregg*, unpublished manuscript, October 1970.

[59] Janet Johl, *The Fascinating Story of Dolls*, (Watkins Glen, New York: Century House, 1970). 198.

[60] Johl, *The Fascinating Story*: 199.

[61] Alice Thompson, Interview by John Wooding in person, July 23, 2015, South Tamworth, New Hampshire.

[62] Phone Interview with Nancy Wirth, by John Wooding, April 10-11, 2015, Personal interview, Santa Fe August 10, 2015.

[63] Pelt, Rhonda Van, *The Bemis Family: A Deep Rooted Legacy*, Colorado College Alumni Bulletin, https://sites.coloradocollege.edu/bulletin/2009/11/the-bemis-family-a-deep-rooted-legacy/ Accessed, March 16, 2017.

[64] Alan Gregg, Faith Mary Gregg, *Family Biographies*, unpublished manuscript, October 1970.

[65] RBG, *To Donald Gregg*, September 18, 1900, Colorado Springs. Walden Woods Project's Thoreau Institute Library, Special Collections, Richard Bartlett Gregg Papers, personal correspondence.

[66] RBG, *To Donald Gregg*, Sept. 18, 1900. Walden Woods Project's Thoreau Institute Library, Special Collections, Richard Bartlett Gregg Papers, personal correspondence

[67] RBG, *To Donald Gregg*, Oct 12, 1902, Colorado Springs. Walden Woods Project's Thoreau Institute Library, Special Collections, Richard Bartlett Gregg Papers, personal correspondence.

[68] Harvard College Class of 1907 *Secretary's First Report*, Harvard College (1780-). Class of 1907, 213.

[69] For an overview of this period, see Lewis L. Gould, *America in the Progressive Era, 1890-1914* (United Kingdom: Taylor & Francis, 2014).

[70] Richard Gregg, *Richard Gregg*, Fiftieth Anniversary Report of the Harvard College Class of 1907 (Cambridge, MA: Harvard University Press, 1957), 271.

[71] RBG, *Letter to Family*, October 24, 1924, Madison, Wisconsin, 2. Walden Woods Project's Thoreau Institute Library, Special Collections, Richard Bartlett Gregg Papers, personal correspondence.

[72] Funding Universe, Bemis Company, Inc. History, http://www.fundinguniverse.com/company-histories/bemis-company-inc-history/ Accessed July 22, 2018.

[73] See Bemis Company, Celebrating 150 Years, History: http://www.bemis150.com/content/timeline.asp Accessed September 24, 2017.

[74] For an excellent overview of the trade and manufacture of jute, see Anthony Cox, *Empire, Industry and Class: The Imperial Nexus of Jute, 1840-1940* (United Kingdom: Routledge, 2013).

[75] Richard Gregg, *"My Memories of Gandhi,"* unpublished manuscript, n.d., 1.

[76] Gregg, *"My Memories of Gandhi,"* 1-2.

[77] Quoted in Joseph Kip Kosek, "Richard Gregg, Mohandas Gandhi, and the Strategy of Nonviolence." *Journal of American History* 91, no. 4, 1324.

[78] Richard Gregg, *"A Monument to An Ancient Love,"* *The Bellman*, v. 19, September 11, 1915, 288-89.

[79] Gregg, *"My Memories of Gandhi,"* 2.

[80] Source: Mass Historical Society, Robert G. Valentine Family Papers, *Biographical Sketches, 1870-1930*, http://www.masshist.org/collection-guides/view/fa0383 Accessed July 19, 2016.

[81] Frederick Winslow Taylor, *The Principles of Scientific Management* (United States: Cosimo, Incorporated, 2010). See also Stephen P. Waring, *Taylorism Transformed: Scientific Management Theory Since 1945* (United Kingdom: University of North Carolina Press, 2016).

[82] *Dr. Ordway Tead, Educator, 82, Dies*, New York Times, November 17, 1973, 38.

[83] This section draws on Janelle Bourgeois, *Gregg Biography*, unpublished manuscript, 12.

[84] Richard Gregg, *Class of 1907*. Secretary's Fourth Report. Norwood, MA: Plimpton Press, 1917. 158-9.

[85] Gregg, *My Memories of Gandhi*, 3.

[86] Gregg, *My Memories of Gandhi*, 4.

[87] Richard Gregg, "The National War Labor Board," *Harvard Law Review*, 33-1, November 1919, 56. Cited in: Peter M. Pizzola, *"The significance of unionization at Bethlehem Steel in 1910 and 1918-1919"* (1996). Theses and Dissertations. Paper 425, Lehigh University.

[88] RBG, *To Alan Gregg*, November 16, 1919. Walden Woods Project's Thoreau Institute Library, Special Collections, Richard Bartlett Gregg Papers, personal correspondence.

[89] RBG, *to Alan Gregg*, November 16, 1919. Walden Woods Project's Thoreau Institute Library, Special Collections, Richard Bartlett Gregg Papers, personal correspondence.

[90] See: M. J. Wiener, *Between Two Worlds: the Political Thought of Graham Wallas (Oxford:* Clarendon Press, 1971).

[91] The best biography of Laski is: B. Sheerman and Isaac I. Kramnick, *Harold Laski: A Life on the Left*, (United Kingdom: Allen Lane, Penguin Press, 1993). See also: M. Newman, *Harold Laski: A Political Biography*, (United Kingdom: Palgrave Macmillan UK, 1993).

[92] See: Ramesh, J. *A Chequered Brilliance: The Many Lives of V.K. Krishna Menon* (India: Penguin Random House India Private Limited, 2019).

[93] RBG, *To Father*, Feb. 4, 1920. Walden Woods Project's Thoreau Institute Library, Special Collections, Richard Bartlett Gregg Papers, personal correspondence.

[94] On RED see Estelle May Stewart, *Handbook of American Trade-unions* (*United States: U.S. Government Printing Office,* 1926) 247-249.

[95] *Leland Olds*, Dictionary of American Biography, Supplement 6: 1956-1960. (American Council of Learned Societies, 1980); Robert A Caro, *Master of the Senate: The Years of Lyndon Johnson, Volume III* (United States: Knopf Doubleday Publishing Group, 2009); and Joseph P. Harris, "The Senatorial Rejection of Leland Olds: A Case Study," *The American Political Science Review*, Vol. 45, No. 3, September 1951, pp. 674-692.

[96] Caro, *Master of the Senate, v. III*, 260-267.

[97] Gregg, *My Memories of Gandhi*, p.4

[98] S. Norwood, Bogalusa Burning: The War Against Biracial Unionism in the Deep South, 1919, *The Journal of Southern History*, 63 no. 3 (1997). 591-628.

[99] RBG, *To Alan Gregg*, Nov. 22, 1921. Walden Woods Project's Thoreau Institute Library, Special Collections, Richard Bartlett Gregg Papers, personal correspondence.

[100] Colin J. Davis, "Bitter Conflict: The 1922 Railroad Shopmen's Strike," *Labor History* 33, no. 4, (1992), 433-455. Colin J. Davis, *Power at Odds: The 1922 National Railroad Shopmen's Strike* (United States: University of Illinois Press, 1997); James Rada, "Nation's 1922 railroad strike became matter of life and death." *Cumberland Times-News*, 4 June2011. http://www.times-news.com/news/local_news/nation-s-railroad-strike-became-matter-of-life-and-death/article_9ffac5a1-d168-50e1-ab88-e267ee1aee12.html

[101] Davis, *Bitter Conflict*, 433-455.

[102] RBG, *To Mother*, August 12, 1923, Chicago. Walden Woods Project's Thoreau Institute Library, Special Collections, Richard Bartlett Gregg Papers, personal correspondence.

[103] RBG, *To Mother*, September 13, October 25, all from Chicago. November 13, 1923, from Madison, Wisconsin. Walden Woods Project's Thoreau Institute Library, Special Collections, Richard Bartlett Gregg Papers, personal correspondence.

[104] RBG, *To Daddy*, August 13, 1921, Chicago. Walden Woods Project's Thoreau Institute Library, Special Collections, Richard Bartlett Gregg Papers, personal correspondence.

[105] RBG, *To Daddy*, Nov. 1, 1921, from Chicago, p.2. Walden Woods Project's Thoreau Institute Library, Special Collections, Richard Bartlett Gregg Papers, personal correspondence.

[106] RBG, *To Daddy*, p.5

[107] RBG, *To Alan Gregg*, May 21, 1924, Phillips, Wisconsin. Walden Woods Project's Thoreau Institute Library, Special Collections, Richard Bartlett Gregg Papers, personal correspondence.

[108] J. M. Gitterman and Franz Oppenheimer, *The State: Its History and Development Viewed Sociologically* (United States: Bobbs-Merrill Company, 1914).

[109] A fine study of Henry George is in Edward T. O'Donnell, *Henry George and the Crisis of Inequality: Progress and Poverty in the Gilded Age* (United States: Columbia University Press, 2015).

[110] RBG, *Letter to Family*, 2.

[111] RBG, *Letter to family*, 2.

[112] RBG, *Letter to family*, 3-4.

[113] I am grateful for much of the following to Janelle Bourgeois, *Biography*, 16-18.

[114] Shahid Amin, *Event, Metaphor, Memory: Chauri Chaura 1922-1992* (Berkeley: University of California Press, 1995), 12.

[115] Amin, *Event, Metaphor, Memory*, 13.

[116] Amin, *Event, Metaphor, Memory*, 14.

[117] Amin, *Event, Metaphor, Memory*, 48.

[118] Rajmohan Gandhi, *Gandhi: The Man, His People, and the Empire* (Berkeley: University of California Press, 2008), 252.

[119] Carl Olson, *The Many Colors of Hinduism: a Thematic-Historical Introduction* (New Brunswick, N.J.: Rutgers University Press, 2007), 30.

[120] A. Annamalai A., Gandhi's Experiments With Health. *Indian Journal of Medical Research*. 2019;149 (Suppl): S57-S61. doi:10.4103/0971-5916.251658

[121] Robert J. Burrowes, *The Strategy of Nonviolence Defense: A Gandhian Approach* (Albany, N.Y.: State University of New York, 1996).

[122] Jake C. Miller, *Prophets of a Just Society* (Huntington, NY: Nova Science Publishers, 2002), 37.

[123] RBG, *To Elinor Gregg*, January 2, 1925. Walden Woods Project's Thoreau Institute Library, Special Collections, Richard Bartlett Gregg Papers, personal correspondence.

[124] RBG, *To Alan Gregg*, January 24, 1925. Walden Woods Project's Thoreau Institute Library, Special Collections, Richard Bartlett Gregg Papers, personal correspondence.

[125] RBG, *To Mother*, January 25, 1925. Walden Woods Project's Thoreau Institute Library, Special Collections, Richard Bartlett Gregg Papers, personal correspondence.

[126] James Fitzpatrick "Fitzpatrick Pictures Presents: Gateway to India," Produced and Narrated by James Fitzpatrick, 1932, http://www.youtube.com/watch?v=ob8n_Aaog58. Accessed Nov. 7, 2013.

[127] The best overall biography is: Hugh Tinker, *The Ordeal of Love: C. F. Andrews and India* (India: Oxford University Press, 1997); See also Daniel O'Connor, *A Clear Star: C. F. Andrews and India 1904-1914* (India: Chronicle Books, 2005); Charles Freer Andrews. N.p.: Publications Division Ministry of Information & Broadcasting, 2017: http://www.bu.edu/missiology/missionary-biography/a-c/andrews-charles-freer-1871-1940/ Accessed January 17, 2017.

[128] See: Eric Sharpe, "The Legacy of C. F. Andrews," *International Bulletin of Mission Research*, 9. July 3, 1985, 117-121.

[129] Quoted in Marcus Braybrooke, "C.F. Andrews: Gandhi's Friend, *The InterFaith Observer*, January 26, 2016. http://www.theinterfaithobserver.org/journal-articles/2016/1/27/c-f-andrews-gandhis-friend.html. Accessed May 2, 2016.

[130] These sources cited in Bourgeois, *Biography*, and quoted in Sabarmati Ashram, Ahmedabad, Gujarat, Sabarmati Ashram, Ahmedabad, Gujarat

[131] Mark Thomson, *Gandhi and His Ashrams*, (Popolar Prakashan Pvt, Mumbai, India, 1993), 104-105.

[132] G.A. Patel, "The Gandhi Ashram," *Poona Agricultural College Magazine*, Volumes 36-40, University of California, 1945.

[133] Weber, Thomas, *Gandhi as Disciple and Mentor* (New York: Cambridge University Press, 2004), 95.

[134] Gregg, *My Memories of Gandhi*, 7-9.

[135] Lisa Trivedi, *Clothing Gandhi's Nation: Homespun and Modern India* (Bloomington Indiana: Indiana University Press, 2007), 9-10.

[136] Michael Nojeim, *Gandhi and King: The Power of Nonviolent Resistance* (Westport, Connecticut: Praeger, 2004), 82.

[137] Nojeim, *Gandhi and King*, 83.

[138] Trivedi, *Clothing Gandhi's Nation*, 9.

[139] RBG, *To Mother*, February 20, 1925, Sabarmati. Walden Woods Project's Thoreau Institute Library, Special Collections, Richard Bartlett Gregg Papers, personal correspondence.

[140] Weber, *Gandhi as Disciple and Mentor*, 85.

[141] Weber, *Gandhi as Disciple and Mentor*, 86.

[142] Gandhi was arrested on March 10, 1922. He had an appendectomy on January 12, 1924, and was released from Yervada Prison on February 5. Source: https://www.mkgandhi.org/arrestofmahatma.htm

[143] RBG, *My Memories of Gandhi*, 10.

[144] RBG, *My Memories of Gandhi*, 5.

[145] RBG, Notebook I, 1925, 67.

[146] RBG, Notebook I, 1925, 15.

[147] RGB, *My Memories of Gandhi*, 9.

[148] RGB, *My Memories of Gandhi*, 12

[149] Gandhi, *The Takli Teacher, Collected Works of Mahatma Gandhi*, v. 30, 286.

[150] RGB, Notebook I, 1925, 63.

[151] RGB, Notebook I, 1925, 64.

[152] RGB, Notebook VII, 32.

[153] Gandhi, M. "My Best Comrade Gone" *Young India*, 1927-1928, 26 April, 1928 (India: S. Ganesan, 1935). 713.

[154] RGB, *My Memories of Gandhi*, 18.

[155] There are many fine works on Nehru. Among the best are Shashi Tharoor, *Nehru: the Invention of India* (New York: Arcade Pub., 2003); M. J. Akbar, *Nehru: The Making of India* (United Kingdom: Viking, 1988); and Benjamin Zachariah, *Nehru* (United Kingdom: Taylor & Francis, 2004).

[156] Harold Branam, "Rabindranath Tagore." *Critical Survey of Poetry*, 1, no. 6, September 2002. Ipswich: Salem Press.

[157] Rosemary Reisman, "Rabindranath Tagore." *Magill's Survey of World Literature*, 1-5, January 2009. Ipswich: Salem Press.

[158] Andrew Robinson and Krishna Dutta, *Rabindranath Tagore: The Myriad-minded Man* (India: Bloomsbury, 1997).

[159] Sabyasachhi Bhattacharya, *Rabindranath Tagore: An Interpretation* (India: Penguin Books Limited, 2017).

[160] Asha Sharma, *An American in Gandhi's India: the Biography of Satyanand Stokes* (United States: Indiana University Press, 2008) and K. Clymer, "Samuel Evans Stokes, Mahatma Gandhi, and Indian Nationalism." *Pacific Historical Review, 59*, no.1, 1990, 51-76.

[161] Sharma, *An American in Gandhi's India*, 213.

[162] Sharma, *An American In Gandhi's India*, 208.

[163] RGB, *To Florence Stokes*, September 22, 1926, quoted in Sharma, *An American In Gandhi's India*, 231.

[164] RGB, *To Mother*, November 17, 1925. Walden Woods Project's Thoreau Institute Library, Special Collections, Richard Bartlett Gregg Papers, personal correspondence.

[165] David Fisher, *Romain Rolland and the Politics of the Intellectual Engagement* (United Kingdom: Taylor & Francis), 2017 and W. T. Starr, *Romain Rolland. One Against All: A Biography* (Germany: Mouton, 1971).

[166] RGB, *My Memories of Gandhi*, 21.

[167] Her autobiography may be found in Slade, Madeleine and Vincent Sheean, *The Spirit's Pilgrimage* (United States: Literary Licensing, LLC, 2013). See also Thomas Weber, *Going Native: Gandhi's Relationship with Western Women.* (N.p.: Roli Books Private Limited, 2011).

[168] RGB, *To Mother*, January 29, 1926, Sabarmati. Walden Woods Project's Thoreau Institute Library, Special Collections, Richard Bartlett Gregg Papers, personal correspondence.

[169] RGB, *To Alan Gregg*, Feb. 5, 1926, Sabarmati. Walden Woods Project's Thoreau Institute Library, Special Collections, Richard Bartlett Gregg Papers, personal correspondence.

[170] RGB, *Notebook 1*, 63-64.

[171] Katy Thompson, unpublished. "Notes from meeting with Uncle Richard," March 1971, Cascade Manor, Oregon.

[172] RBG to Gandhi, quoted by Gandhi in his note on "Indian Textbooks" Gandhi, *Collected Works*, v. XXI, 409. https://www.gandhiheritageportal.org/cwmg_volume_thumbview/MzE= - page/442/mode/2up.

[173] Gregg, Richard, *A Preparation for Science* (Ahmedabad: Gujarat Vidyapith, 1928).

[174] RGB, *Notebook 1*, 66.

[175] RGB, *To Faith Gregg*, September 26, 1926. Walden Woods Project's Thoreau Institute Library, Special Collections, Richard Bartlett Gregg Papers, personal correspondence.

[176] RGB, *To Alan Gregg*, October 18, 1926. Kotgarh, Walden Woods Project's Thoreau Institute Library, Special Collections, Richard Bartlett Gregg Papers, personal correspondence.

[177] Gregg, Richard, *The Economics of Khaddar* (Madras, India: S Ganesan, 1928).

[178] Gandhi, Mahatma. *The Collected Works of Mahatma Gandhi* (New Delhi: Ministry of Information and Broadcasting, 2000-2001), 176.

[179] Gregg, *The Economics of Khaddar*, 11.

[180] Gregg, *The Economics of Khaddar*, 10.

[181] Gregg, *The Economics of Khaddar*, 46.

[182] RGB, *My Memories of Gandhi*, 21-30.

[183] Gregg, Richard, "Aspects of Spiritual and Moral Beauty in Charkha," *Modern Review*, November 1925, 561.

[184] Gregg, "Aspects of Spiritual and Moral Beauty," 563.

[185] Gregg, Richard, "The Morals of Machinery," *Current Thought*, February 1926, 172-79.

[186] Gregg, *The Economics of Khaddar*, 215.

[187] RGB, *Notebook VII*, 84.

[188] RGB, *Notebook VII*, 144.

[189] Adi H. Doctor, *Sarvodaya: A Political and Economic Study* (New York: Asia Publishing House, 1967), 5. There is a significant body of research on Gandhian economics. See M. Vinaik, "The Evolution of Gandhian Economics," *Sarvodaya*, June 1962, 209-213.

[190] Gregg, Richard, *Gandhiji's Satyagraha: or, Nonviolent Resistance* (Madras: S. Ganesan, 1930).

[191] Gregg, Richard, *The Psychology and Strategy of Gandhi's Nonviolent Resistance* (Madras: S. Ganesan. 1929).

[192] Gregg, Richard, *Gandhiism Vs. Socialism* (New York: The John Day Company, 1932).

[193] Gregg, Richard, *The Power of Non-Violence*, 44.

[194] The work of James Tully was extremely helpful with this section. An excellent and full discussion of these issues can be found in Tully's Introduction in James Tully, (ed.) *The Power of Non-Violence*, Cambridge University Press, 2018. Another invaluable source used throughout this work is Kopek, *Acts of Conscience*.

[195] Gregg, *Gandhism and Socialism*, 7-8.

[196] Gregg, *Gandhism and Socialism*, 21.

[197] The explanations on this quiescence came to be framed as ideological or cultural hegemony. These views are mostly closely associated with the Italian Marxist Antonio Gramsci—see his: Gramsci, Antonio. *Selections from the Prison Notebooks of Antonio Gramsci* (United Kingdom: International Publishers, 1971) and *Rethinking Gramsci* (United Kingdom: Taylor & Francis, 2011). Later European Marxists explored these ideas in greater detail.

[198] There is much written by and about Du Bois. See W. E. B. Du Bois *The Souls of Black Folk* (United States: Dover Publications, 2012). One of the best recent biographies is Lewis, David L. *W. E. B. Du Bois: A Biography 1868-1963* (United States: Henry Holt and Company, 2009).

[199] RBG, *To W. E. B. Du Bois*, Nov. 19, 1926. Walden Woods Project's Thoreau Institute Library, Special Collections, Richard Bartlett Gregg Papers, personal correspondence.

[200] Gregg, *Economics of Khaddar*, 10.

[201] RBG, *Notebook IV*, 265.

[202] RBG, *To Farwell Bemis*, May 15, 1927. Walden Woods Project's Thoreau Institute Library, Special Collections, Richard Bartlett Gregg Papers, personal correspondence.

[203] RBG, *To Alan Gregg*, August 15, 1927. Walden Woods Project's Thoreau Institute Library, Special Collections, Richard Bartlett Gregg Papers, personal correspondence.

[204] For example, Gandhi, M., *To Richard Gregg*, May 13, 1927 and Gandhi, M., *To Richard Gregg*, April 26, 1927 in Reddy, E.S. (ed), *Mahatma Gandhi: Letters to Americans* (New York, Bharatiya Vidya Bhavan, 1998).

[205] Gandhi, M. *To Richard Gregg*, April 26, 1927.

[206] Gandhi, *To Richard Gregg*, January 1928, Collected Works of Mahatma Gandhi, v. XXV, 502.

[207] RGB, *To Gandhi*, http://www.gandhiserve.org/correspondence/1928.html.

[208] Gandhi, *To Richard Gregg*, Collected Works of Mahatma Gandhi, v. XXVI, 414.

[209] RBG, *Notebook VII*, 1927, 105.

[210] Zimmerman, S., "The Evolution of the Lyman Estate," The Vale, *Historic New England*, vol. 12, no. 2, Fall 2011, 28.

[211] RBG, *To Donald Gregg*, June 19,1929. Walden Woods Project's Thoreau Institute Library, Special Collections, Richard Bartlett Gregg Papers, personal correspondence.

[212] RBG, *To Alan and Elinor Gregg*. Simla, April 3, 1930. Walden Woods Project's Thoreau Institute Library, Special Collections, Richard Bartlett Gregg Papers, personal correspondence.

[213] See Gandhi, Rajmohan. *Gandhi: The Man, His People, and the Empire* (United States: University of California Press, 2008). 302-345.

[214] Richard Gregg, "India Confronts Britain," *The Nation*, 130, no. 3389, June 18, 1930, 696-699.

[215] RBG, *To Alan and Elinor Gregg*, April 3, 1930. Walden Woods Project's Thoreau Institute Library, Special Collections, Richard Bartlett Gregg Papers, personal correspondence.

[216] RBG, *General Notebook 10*, 1930.

[217] Cited in Carey John (ed.), *Eyewitness to History* (New York: Avon, 1987), 501-504.

[218] Gregg, "India Confronts Britain," 698.

[219] Gregg, "India Confronts Britain," and Richard Gregg, "Will Gandhi Win?" *The Nation*, 130, No. 3387, June 4, 1930, 661-663.

[220] This was the Laski that Gregg met for the first time in New York in 1919. See: Mahatma Gandhi, *To Richard Gregg (Govind)*, April 29, 1931, *Collected Works of Mahatma Gandhi*, *vol. 52*, April 29-July 1, 1931. https://www.gandhiashramsevagram.org/gandhi-literature/mahatma-gandhi-collected-works-volume-52.pdf. RBG, *To Gandhi*, July 27, 1931.

[221] RBG, *To Gandhi*, October 16, 1931. *Collected Works of Mahatma Gandhi, vol. 52*, April 29-July 1, 1931. https://www.gandhiashramsevagram.org/gandhi-literature/mahatma-gandhi-collected-works-volume-52.pdf.

[222] Gregg, *Gandhiji's Satyagraha, x-xi*.

[223] Richard Gregg, *The Value of Voluntary Simplicity* (Wallingford, PA: Pendle Hill Publications, 1936).

[224] Gregg, *Gandhiism Vs. Socialism*, 8.

[225] Gregg, *Gandhiism Vs. Socialism*, 2.

[226] Gregg, *Gandhiism Vs. Socialism*, 11.

227 *New York Times Book Review*, December 2, 1934, 13. Author unknown.

228 Quoted in Kosek, *Acts of Conscience*, 110. See also: Leilah Danielson, *American Gandhi: A. J. Muste and the History of Radicalism in the Twentieth Century* (United States: University of Pennsylvania Press, Incorporated, 2014), 202-213.

229 The phrase is Gregg's.

230 See Gregg, *PNV*; Kosek, *Acts of Conscience*, 95-103; and Tully, Introduction, *The Power of Non-Violence*.

231 Kosek, *"Richard Gregg, Mohandas Gandhi, and the Strategy of Nonviolence,"* 1325.

232 RBG, *Notebook XXII*, 1925, 14.

233 For further discussion of Gregg's *The Power of Non-Violence*, see especially Tully, *The Power of Non Violence*; Kosek, *Acts of Conscience*, 98-111; Patricia Appelbaum, *Kingdom to Commune: Protestant Pacifist Culture between World War I and the Vietnam Era* (Chapel Hill: University of North Carolina Press, 2009), 128-42.

234 RBG, *Notebook 1*, 77.

235 For a full treatment of these debates and their origins, see Leilah C. Danielson. (2003). "In My Extremity I Turned to Gandhi: American Pacifists, Christianity, and Gandhian Non-Violence,1915-1941." *Church History, 72*(2), 361-388.

236 Niebuhr, *Moral Man, and Immoral Society*. See also Fox, *Reinhold Niebuhr: A Biography*.

237 A discussion of Gregg's impact on this moment can be found in Danielson, *American Gandhi*, 375-377.

238 The impact of Gregg's work is carefully established in Kosek, *"Richard Gregg, Mohandas Gandhi, and the Strategy of Nonviolence,"* 1336-1339.

239 RBG, *Notebook 21*, 1934, 166-167.

240 RBG, *Notebook 21*, 11.

241 RBG, *Notebook, 21*, 1934, 16.

242 Kosek, *Acts of Conscience*, 95.

243 Douglas Gwyn, *Personality and Place: The Life and Times of Pendle Hill* (United States: CreateSpace Independent Publishing Platform), 2014. 68-81.

244 Roger S. Powers, *Protest, Power, and Change: An Encyclopedia of Nonviolent Action from ACT-UP to Women's Suffrage* (New York: Routledge, 2012), 406.; John Simkin, "Peace Pledge Union," Spartacus Educational. https://spartacus-educational.com/2WW peaceunion.htm. Accessed June 18, 2017.

245 Simkin, *Peace Pledge Union*.

246 Powers, *Protest, Power and Change*, 406. For a complete discussion of the PPU, see Ceadel's magisterial history of pacifism: Ceadel, Martin. *Pacifism in Britain, 1914-45: The Defining of a Faith* (United Kingdom: Oxford University Press, 1980).

247 Nonie Gregg, *To Marge*, July 5, 1936.

[248] RBG, *To Nonie Gregg*, July 8, 1936

[249] On the life and impact of Gerald Heard, see: Alison Falby, *Between the Pigeonholes : Gerald Heard, 1889-1971* (United Kingdom: Cambridge Scholars Pub., 2008).

[250] RBG, *To Nonie*, July 13, 1936, Bloomsbury, London. Walden Woods Project's Thoreau Institute Library, Special Collections, Richard Bartlett Gregg Papers, personal correspondence.

[251] RBG, *To Nonie*, July 14, 1936, Bloomsbury, London. Walden Woods Project's Thoreau Institute Library, Special Collections, Richard Bartlett Gregg Papers, personal correspondence.

[252] Richard Bartlett Gregg, *Training for Peace: A Programme for Peace Workers* (United Kingdom: Peace Pledge Union, n.d.).

[253] Powers, *Protest, Power and Change*, 406.

[254] Gregg, *Training for Peace*, 1.

[255] Gregg, *Training for Peace*, 9, and 20-21.

[256] Nicholas Murray, *Aldous Huxley: A Biography* (United States: St. Martin's Publishing Group, 2003) and Sybille Bedford, *Aldous Huxley* (United States: Ivan R. Dee, 2002).

[257] Cited in George Woodcock, *Dawn and the Darkest Hour: A Study of Aldous Huxley* (New York: Viking Press, 1971), 271. I am grateful to Janelle Bourgeois for information in this section—see, Bourgeois, Janelle, *Biography*. See also: Janelle Bourgeois and John Wooding, "Peace Profile: Richard Gregg," *Peace Review*, 2016, 28, no. 2, 238-245.

[258] Huxley, Aldous. *What Are You Going to Do about It?: The Case for Constructive Peace* (N.p.: Franklin Classics Trade Press, 2018).

[259] Bernfried Nugel, *Now More Than Ever: Proceedings of the Aldous Huxley Centenary Symposium Munster, 1994* (New York: Peter Lang, 1996), 131.

[260] Richard Gregg, *Pacifist Program in a Time of War, Threatened War, or Fascism* (Wallingford PA: Pendle Hill Publications, 1939), 13.

[261] Published in S. Rada Krishnan (ed). *M. Gandhi*, London 1939. Collection presented to him on his 70th birthday.

[262] Richard Gregg, *A Discipline for Nonviolence*, Pendle Hill Pamphlet #11, 1941, 2.

[263] "Ehrenfried Pfeiffer, The Threefold Community, and the Birth of Biodynamic in America," *Biodynamic*, Fall 2008. Adapted version available at: http://www.pfeiffercenter.org/about_us/ehrenfried_pfeiffer.

[264] Henry Barnes, *Into the Heart's Land: A Century of Rudolf Steiner's Work in North America* (Great Barrington, MA: Steiner Books, 2005), 286.

[265] Stephanie Mills, *On Gandhi's Path: Bob Swann's Work for Peace and Community Economics* (United States: New Society Publishers, 2010), 27.

[266] See: Claus Bernet, *Rufus Jones (1863-1948): Life and Bibliography of an American Scholar, Writer, and Social Activist* (Austria: Peter Lang, 2009).

[267] RBG, *To Elinor Gregg*, August 8, 1945, Putney, Vermont. Walden Woods Project's Thoreau

Institute Library, Special Collections, Richard Bartlett Gregg Papers, personal correspondence.

[268] Interview with Kate Thompson, July 23, 2015, South Tamworth, NH.

[269] See: "Putney at a glance" *Website*. Putney School. Retrieved July 6, 2016. https://www.putneyschool.org/at-a-glance/

[270] RBG, *To Elinor Gregg*, September 7, 1945, Putney, Vermont. Walden Woods Project's Thoreau Institute Library, Special Collections, Richard Bartlett Gregg Papers, personal correspondence.

[271] Richard Gregg, *Letter to the editor*, unpublished manuscript, n.d. Division of Special Collections and University Archives, University of Oregon Libraries.

[272] RBG, *My Memories of Gandhi*, 12.

[273] Scott and Helen Nearing, *Living the Good Life: How to Live Sanely and Simply in a Troubled World* (New York: Schocken Books, 1970), 9.

[274] RBG, *To Elinor Gregg*, June 29, 1953. Walden Woods Project's Thoreau Institute Library, Special Collections, Richard Bartlett Gregg Papers, personal correspondence. See also Margaret O. Killinger, *The Good Life of Helen K. Nearing* (Lebanon: University of Vermont Press, 2007), 69-70.

[275] John Saltmarsh, *Scott Nearing: An Intellectual Biography.* (Philadelphia: Temple University Press, 1991), 2.

[276] See Saltmarsh, *Scott Nearing*; and Scott Nearing, *The Making of a Radical: A Political Autobiography* (United States: Chelsea Green Publishing Company, 2000).

[277] Helen and Scott Nearing, *Living the Good Life*.

[278] Lawrence S. Wittner, *The Struggle Against the Bomb, Volume 2* (Connecticut, Stanford University Press, 1993). 156-7. See also: Jake Hodder, "Conferencing the International at the World Pacifist Meeting in India, 1949," *Political Geography*, 49, April 15, 2015, 40-50.

[279] See the discussion in Paul Schwartzentruber, "Which Way Lies Hope?" Opening a Dialogue with Richard Gregg. A Retrospective on the Nationhood of India, in *Ahisma Nonviolence*, XII, no. 1, Jan-April 2016.

[280] The homestead they built became the Good Life Center, a still functioning farm with buildings that enshrines their legacy.

[281] RBG, *To Elinor Gregg*, June 29, 1953. Walden Woods Project's Thoreau Institute Library, Special Collections, Richard Bartlett Gregg Papers, personal correspondence.

[282] His summary of her condition and his treatments was included in a letter he wrote to his sister, see: RBG, *To Elinor Gregg*, October 11, 1947. Walden Woods Project's Thoreau Institute Library, Special Collections, Richard Bartlett Gregg Papers, personal correspondence.

[283] F.A. Behymer, "Mineralized Garden Brings Health, Acclaim to Kentucky Soil Doctor." https://www.seleneriverpress.com/historical/mineralized-garden-brings-health-acclaim-to-kentucky-soil-doctor/ accessed July 19, 2018.

[284] Gregg, Introduction to *Self-Transcendence*.

[285] Gregg, *Self-Transcendence*, 191.

[286] RBG, *Letter to Friends*, April 1956. Walden Woods Project's Thoreau Institute Library, Special Collections, Richard Bartlett Gregg Papers, personal correspondence.

[287] Barnes, *Into the Heart's Land*. 286-290.

[288] Saltmarsh, *A Handmade Life: In Search of Simplicity*; Whybrow, *A Man Apart* and Rebecca Kneale Gould, *At Home in Nature: Modern Homesteading and Spiritual Practice in America* (United States: University of California Press, 2005), 13-20.

[289] Saltmarsh, *A Handmade Life*, xvii.

[290] For Coperthwaite's full story, see: Whybrow, *A Man Apart*.

[291] The literature on Martin Luther King, Jr., and the civil rights movement is of course vast. See: Michael Nojeim, *Gandhi and King: The Power of Nonviolent Resistance* (Westport, Connecticut: Praeger, 2004); Lewis Perry, *Civil Disobedience: An American Tradition* (New Haven: Yale University Press, 2013); Aldon D. Morris, *Origins of the Civil Rights Movement* (United Kingdom: Free Press, 1986); David Lewis, *M. L. King: a Biography* (United Kingdom: University of Illinois Press, 1978); John D'emilio, *Lost Prophet: The Life and Times of Bayard Rustin* (United Kingdom: Free Press, 2010); Raymond Arsenault, *Freedom Riders: 1961 and the Struggle for Racial Justice* (New York: Oxford University Press, 2006).

[292] Paul R. Dekar, *Creating the Beloved Community: A Journey with the Fellowship of Reconciliation* (United States: Cascadia Publishing House, 2005). Derek Charles Catsam, *Freedom's Main Line: The Journey of Reconciliation and the Freedom Rides* (Kentucky: University of Kentucky Press, 2009). See also Applebaum, *Kingdom to Commune* and Kosek, *Acts of Conscience*.

[293] George M. Houser, *Erasing the Color Line; Foreword by A. Philip Randolph, illustrations by William Huntington* (New York, N. Y., Fellowship publications, 1945).

[294] See Kosek, *Richard Gregg, Mohandas Gandhi and the Strategy of Non-Violence*, 1342-43.

[295] See Kosek, *Acts of Conscience*, 215-17.

[296] Kosek, *Richard Gregg, Mohandas Gandhi and the Strategy of Non-Violence*, 1344.

[297] RBG *To Martin Luther King, Jr.* April 2, 1956, in *Papers of Martin Luther King, Jr.*, ed. Carson, III, 211-12.

[298] RBG, *To Martin Luther King, Jr.*, Jamaica, VT; April 2, 1956, 2.

[299] Martin Luther King, Jr., *To Richard Gregg*, May 1, 1956, in Susan Carson, Pete Holloran, Tenisha Armstrong, et al., eds. *The Papers of Martin Luther King, Jr., Volume III: Birth of a New Age, December 1955-December 1956.* (United Kingdom: University of California Press, 1992).

[300] Martin Luther King, Jr., *Stride Toward Freedom: The Montgomery Story* (New York: Harper & Row, 1958).

301 Nai Talim is a "craft-based" education centered on the development of practical skills as a core set of abilities serving to enhance cultural and social development and knowledge. Traditional subjects are integrated in an interdisciplinary fashion with practical skills and manual work. The history and background of the Institute is available at, http://ruraluniv. ac.in/aboutgri?content=GenesisofGRI. Accessed, April 4, 2017.

302 Gregg, *A Philosophy of Indian Economic Development*, 138.

303 Gregg, Elinor, *postcard to Richard Gregg*, April 16, 1957. Walden Woods Project's Thoreau Institute Library, Special Collections, Richard Bartlett Gregg Papers, personal correspondence.

304 Details in: RBG, *To Elinor Gregg*, December 25, 1957. Walden Woods Project's Thoreau Institute Library, Special Collections, Richard Bartlett Gregg Papers, personal correspondence.

305 RBG, *To Jawaharlal Nehru*, March 12, 1958. Walden Woods Project's Thoreau Institute Library, Special Collections, Richard Bartlett Gregg Papers, personal correspondence.

306 Nehru, Jawaharlal, *To Richard Gregg*, March 14, 1958. Walden Woods Project's Thoreau Institute Library, Special Collections, Richard Bartlett Gregg Papers, personal correspondence.

307 RBG, *To David Heard*, December 7, 1957. Walden Woods Project's Thoreau Institute Library, Special Collections, Richard Bartlett Gregg Papers, personal correspondence.

308 RBG, *To William O. Douglas*, October 23, 1957. Walden Woods Project's Thoreau Institute Library, Special Collections, Richard Bartlett Gregg Papers, personal correspondence.

309 RBG, *To Victor Gollanz*, July 28, 1958. Walden Woods Project's Thoreau Institute Library, Special Collections, Richard Bartlett Gregg Papers, personal correspondence.

310 RBG, *To Martin Luther King, Jr.*, Chester, NY, Oct. 27,1958, Walden Woods Project's Thoreau Institute Library, Special Collections, Richard Bartlett Gregg Papers, personal correspondence.

311 RBG, *To Martin Luther King, Jr.*, Chester NY; Dec. 20, 1958. Walden Woods Project's Thoreau Institute Library, Special Collections, Richard Bartlett Gregg Papers, personal correspondence.

312 RBG, *To Martin Luther King, Jr.*, Chester NY; Dec. 20, 1958. Walden Woods Project's Thoreau Institute Library, Special Collections, Richard Bartlett Gregg Papers, personal correspondence.

313 From Matt Meyer and Judith Mahoney Pasternak, *90 Years of Resisting War: WRL's Journey from "Wars Will Cease When Men Refuse to Fight" to "Revolutionary Nonviolence," WIN Magazine*, Summer/Fall 2013.

314 Scott Bennett, *Radical Pacifism: The War Resisters League and Gandhian Nonviolence in America, 1915*-1963 (United Kingdom: Syracuse University Press, 2003).

315 Martin Luther King, Jr., *Address at the Thirty-Sixth Annual Dinner of the War resisters League*, The Martin Luther King, Jr., Papers Project, February 2, 1959.

316 Martin Luther King, Jr., *Foreword* to *The Power of Non Violence*.

[317] See: Wesley C. Hogan, *Many Minds, One Heart: SNCC's Dream for a New America* (United States: University of North Carolina Press, 2013); William H. Chafe, *Civilities and Civil Rights: Greensboro, North Carolina, and the Black Struggle for Freedom* (United Kingdom: Oxford University Press, 1981); and, Clayborne Carson, *In Struggle: SNCC and the Black Awakening of the 1960s* (United Kingdom: Harvard University Press, 1995).

[318] Kosek, *Richard Gregg, Mohandas Gandhi and the Strategy of Non-Violence*, 1346.

[319] RBG, *To Executive Committee, Campaign for Nonviolent Action*, August 30, 1962. Walden Woods Project's Thoreau Institute Library, Special Collections, Richard Bartlett Gregg Papers, personal correspondence.

[320] RBG, *To A.J. Muste*, June 8, 1962. Walden Woods Project's Thoreau Institute Library, Special Collections, Richard Bartlett Gregg Papers, personal correspondence.

[321] RBG, *To AJ Muste*, June 8, 1962. Walden Woods Project's Thoreau Institute Library, Special Collections, Richard Bartlett Gregg Papers, personal correspondence.

[322] Barrington, A.G., Riverside Community, *To Richard Gregg*, Lower Moutere, New Zealand, September 24, 1963. Walden Woods Project's Thoreau Institute Library, Special Collections, Richard Bartlett Gregg Papers, personal correspondence.

[323] Gregg, *The Best Solver of Conflicts*, 3-4.

[324] RBG, *To William Nelson*, February 7, 1964. Nelson, William, *To Richard Gregg*, March 17, 1964. Walden Woods Project's Thoreau Institute Library, Special Collections, Richard Bartlett Gregg Papers, personal correspondence.

[325] RBG, *To Bayard Rustin*, November. 23, 1964. Walden Woods Project's Thoreau Institute Library, Special Collections, Richard Bartlett Gregg Papers, personal correspondence.

[326] Gregg, Richard, *Considerations for W.R.I. and for Pacifists*, unpublished manuscript, October 23, 1965. Division of Special Collections and University Archives, University of Oregon Libraries.

[327] RBG, *To Pearl Buck-Walsh*, October 29, 1967. Walden Woods Project's Thoreau Institute Library, Special Collections, Richard Bartlett Gregg Papers, personal correspondence.

[328] Killinger, *The Good Life of Helen K. Nearing*, 58-61.

[329] Ernst F. Schumacher, *To Richard Gregg*, Caterham, Surry, U.K., December 6, 1967. Walden Woods Project's Thoreau Institute Library, Special Collections, Richard Bartlett Gregg Papers, personal correspondence.

[330] Gregg, "On Loving Ones Opponents," *Fellowship*, November 1966, 22-23.

[331] RBG, *To Alice Thompson*, Sept. 7, 1968. Walden Woods Project's Thoreau Institute Library, Special Collections, Richard Bartlett Gregg Papers, personal correspondence.

[332] RBG, *To Mrs. Martin Luther King*, April 6. 1968. Walden Woods Project's Thoreau Institute Library, Special Collections, Richard Bartlett Gregg Papers, personal correspondence.

[333] Mildred B. Young, "Richard Gregg: In Memoriam," *Friends Journal*, May 15, 1974, 303.

[334] Gregg, *Training for Peace*, 1.

Acknowledgements

No work of this kind is the effort of one person. This is certainly true of this biography. I have many people to thank for helping me write this book about Richard Gregg, and I owe all of them a great debt.First and foremost, my deep gratitude and thanks to John Saltmarsh. John sent me on this adventure, helped me find sources, and was extremely thoughtful in editing and commenting on early drafts. He gave me encouragement and direction. He is my dear friend and colleague. I could not have done this without him. I will buy him many cups of coffee.

As I began the project, I had research assistance from Timothy Brunson, Titiksha Fernandes, Nicole McHarrie, and Sean Perry, all undergraduates at the time at the University of Massachusetts, Lowell (UML). Timothy, Titiksha and Nicole found sources and references. Sean did a great job of providing a brief synopsis of the lives of some of Gregg's colleagues. Janelle Bourgeois, also an undergraduate at UML, worked extraordinarily hard at tracking down sources, helped frame early questions, and wrote an excellent research paper on Gregg's early life that provided rich material and sources for this book. She co-authored an article about Gregg with me. Her help was invaluable and exceptional. An emerging scholar at UML, Janelle received financial support from UML's Center for Women and Work. I also thank Kyrie Kowalik for making careful digital copies of many of Gregg's personal letters.

AJ Angulo and Jim Nehring commented on early draft chapters

and helped me think more carefully about my writing. John Kaag gave me invaluable advice and support, read a first draft, and changed how I thought about writing. Greg Delaurier has been my friend for longer than either of us care to remember. He gave great advice and suggestions on some chapter drafts, as well as support and friendship throughout the project. Jeff Gerson and Bob Forrant were on my team and I thank them for all their advice, encouragement, and insightful comments. Les Leopold read the Prologue and advised on publication strategies, as did Jeff Cramer. I thank them both.

Joan Ross and Jim Higgins worked tirelessly to design and format this book. I owe them my gratitude and much thanks.

There is no way this book could have been written without the help and kindness of Richard Gregg's family. They have been enormously supportive and generous with their time. I thank Robert Gregg for providing copies of many of Richard's early letters to his family, for meeting with me, and helping with the family's early history and complex family tree. Ann Day put me in touch with other family members and provided access to material on Richard. Nancy Wirth was kind enough to meet with me in her lovely home and share stories about Richard. She sent me many of Richard's personal letters with key details about his movements over time. Alice Wiggin gave me access to materials she had on Richard. She arranged discussions with other family members that were very useful and a pleasure to be a part of. Sadly, Alice passed away in October 2019. I must also make special mention of Kate Thompson, who allowed me access to her extensive collection of family photos and memorabilia. Very supportive through the entire project, she shared anecdotes and stories that brought Richard Gregg to life. Kate has really helped this project.

John Suiter in Chicago located McClurg's Bookstore where Gregg found Gandhi.

Rosemary Noon read the whole manuscript and found errors and omissions. I thank her for all of that and for her friendship these many years.

Paul Marion is my friend. We have worked and conspired together for over fifteen years. He provided extensive comments and editing on the manuscript finding my many errors and faults and offering correction and support. This book is immeasurably better because of Paul's work. He took on the project for his Loom Press and encouraged me to complete this and many other things. He is a poet and writer. I hope some of his expertise has fallen on me. I owe him a deep debt of gratitude for his wise advice and constant companionship.

Finally, nothing in my life would have been possible without my wife, Joan Parker. She has put up with me for more than thirty-five years and with my obsession with Gregg for the last six. She edited the entire manuscript. The book is all the better for her work, and I am a better man because she has shared her life with me. Her love and support are everything to me. I dedicate this book and my love to her.

Bibliography

Books

Akbar, M. J. *Nehru: The Making of India.* United Kingdom: Viking, 1988.

Amin, Shahid. *Event, Metaphor, Memory: Chauri Chaura 1922-1992.* Berkeley: University of California Press, 1995.

Ansbro, John J. *Martin Luther King, Jr., Nonviolent Strategies and Tactics for Social Change.* United Kingdom: Madison Books, 2000.

Appelbaum, Patricia. *Kingdom to Commune: Protestant Pacifist Culture Between World War I and the Vietnam Era.* Chapel Hill: University of North Carolina Press, 2009.

Arsenault, Raymond. *Freedom Riders: 1961 and the Struggle for Racial Justice.* New York: Oxford University Press, 2006.

Azaransky, Sarah. *This Worldwide Struggle: Religion and the International Roots of the Civil Rights Movement.* United States: Oxford University Press, 2017.

Bairoch, Paul. *Economics and World History: Myths and Paradoxes.* Chicago: University of Chicago Press, 1993.

Barnes, Henry. *Into the Heart's Land: A Century of Rudolf Steiner's Work in North America.* Great Barrington, MA: Steiner Books, 2005.

Bedford, Sybille. *Aldous Huxley,* United States: Ivan R. Dee, 2002.

Bennett, Scott H. *Radical Pacifism: The War Resisters League and Gandhian Nonviolence in America, 1915-1963.* United Kingdom: Syracuse University Press, 2003.

Bernet, Claus. *Rufus Jones (1863-1948): Life and Bibliography of an American Scholar, Writer, and Social Activist.* Austria: Peter Lang, 2009.

Bhattacharya, Sabyasachhi. *Rabindranath Tagore: An Interpretation.* India: Penguin Books Limited, 2017.

Bleiker, Roland. *Popular Dissent, Human Agency, and Global Politics.* United Kingdom: Cambridge University Press, 2000.

Blevins Tim, Dennis Daily, Chris Nicholl, Calvin P. Otto, and Katherine Scott Sturdevant. *Legends, Labors and Loves: William Jackson Palmer, 1836-1909.* United States: Pikes Peak Library District with the Colorado Springs Pioneers Museum and Colorado College, 2009.

Bondurant, Joan. *The Conquest of Violence: The Gandhian Philosophy of Conflict.* Princeton: Princeton University Press, 1958.

Bonner, Hypatia, and John Mackinnon Robertson. *Charles Bradlaugh: A Record of His Life and Work.* United Kingdom: T. Fisher Unwin, 1894.

Burrowes, Robert J. *The Strategy of Nonviolence Defense: A Gandhian Approach.* Albany, N.Y: State University of New York, 1996.

Burrow, Rufus. *Extremist for Love: Martin Luther King, Jr., Man of Ideas and Nonviolent Social Action.* United Kingdom: Fortress Press, 2014.

Carey John, ed. *Eyewitness to History.* New York: Avon, 1987.

Carlson, W. Bernar. *Tesla: Inventor of the Electrical Age.* Princeton NJ: Princeton University Press, 2003.

Carney, Cary Michael. *Native American Higher Education in the United States.* United States: Transaction Publishers, 1999.

Caro, Robert A. *Master of the Senate: The Years of Lyndon Johnson III.* United States: Knopf Doubleday Publishing Group, 2009.

Carson, Clayborne. *In Struggle: SNCC and the Black Awakening of the 1960s.* United Kingdom: Harvard University Press, 1995.

Catsam, Derek C. *Freedom's Main Line: The Journey of Reconciliation and the Freedom Rides.* Kentucky: University of Kentucky Press, 2009.

Ceadel, Martin. *Pacifism in Britain, 1914-1945: The Defining of a Faith.* United Kingdom: Clarendon Press, 1980.

Chabot, Sean. *Transnational Roots of the Civil Rights Movement: African American Explorations of the Gandhian Repertoire*. New York: Lexington Books, 2012.

Chafe, William H. *Civilities and Civil Rights: Greensboro, North Carolina, and the Black Struggle for Freedom*. United Kingdom: Oxford University Press, 1981.

Chatfield, Charles. *For Peace and Justice: Pacifism in America, 1914-1941*. Knoxville, TN: University of Tennessee Press, 1971.

Chenoweth, Erica and Maria Stephan. *Why Civil Resistance Works*. New York: Columbia University Press, 2012.

Coperthwaite, William S. *A Handmade Life: In Search of Simplicity*. United States: Chelsea Green Publisher, 2002.

Cox, Anthony. *Empire, Industry and Class: The Imperial Nexus of Jute, 1840-1940*. United Kingdom: Routledge, 2013.

Cronon, W. *Nature's Metropolis: Chicago and the Great West*. United States: W.W. Norton, 2009.

Dalton, Dennis. *Mahatma Gandhi: Nonviolent Power in Action*. New York: Columbia University Press, 2012.

Danielson, Leilah. *American Gandhi: A. J. Muste and the History of Radicalism in the Twentieth Century*. United States: University of Pennsylvania Press, 2014.

D'Emilio, John. *Lost Prophet: The Life and Times of Bayard Rustin*. United States: University of Chicago Press, 2003.

Davis, Colin J. *Power at Odds: The 1922 National Railroad Shopmen's Strike*. United States: University of Illinois Press, 1997.

Dekar, Paul R. *Creating the Beloved Community: A Journey with the Fellowship of Reconciliation*. United States: Cascadia Publishing House, 2005.

Doctor, Adi H. *Sarvodaya: A Political and Economic Study*. New York: Asia Publishing House, 1967.

Dubois, W. E. B. *The Souls of Black Folk*. United States: Dover Publications, 2012.

Dubovsky, Melvin. *We Shall Be All: A History of the Industrial Workers of the World*. New York: Quadrangle Books, 1969.

Dupée, Jeffrey N. *Traveling India in the Age of Gandhi*. United States: University Press of America, 2008.

Elgin, Duane. *Voluntary Simplicity: Toward a Way of Life that is Outwardly Simple, Inwardly Rich*. New York: Morrow Press, 1981.

Falby, Alison. *Between the Pigeonholes: Gerald Heard, 1889-1971*. United Kingdom: Cambridge Scholars Publisher, 2008.

Farmer, James. *Lay Bare the Heart: An Autobiography of the Civil Rights Movement*. United States: Texas Christian University Press, 1998.

Fink, Leo. *Progressive Intellectuals and the Dilemmas of Democratic Commitment*. United Kingdom: Harvard University Press, 1997.

Fischer, Louis. *The Life of Mahatma Gandhi*. United Kingdom: Penguin Random House, 2015.

Fisher, David James. *Romain Rolland and the Politics of Intellectual Engagement*. United Kingdom: Transaction Publishers, 2004.

Fisher, James Terence. *The Catholic Counterculture in America, 1933-1962*. United States: University of North Carolina Press, 1989.

Foner, Philip Sheldon. *The Industrial Workers of the World, 1905-1917*. United Kingdom: International Publishers, 1965.

Fox, Richard Gabriel and Orin Starn, eds. *Between Resistance and Revolution: Cultural Politics and Social Protest*. United Kingdom: Rutgers University Press, 1997.

Fox, Richard Wightman, *Reinhold Niebuhr: A Biography*. United Kingdom: Harper & Row, 1987.

Gandhi, M. K. *An Autobiography; or, The Story of My Experiments with Truth*, trans. Mahadev Desai Ahmedabad, 1927.

Gandhi, Mahatma. Satyagraha in South Africa. India: Navajivan, 1972.

Gandhi, M. K. *The Collected Works of Mahatma Gandhi*. India: Publications Division, Ministry of Information and Broadcasting, Government of India, 2000.

Gandhi, Rajmohan, *Gandhi: The Man, His People, and the Empire*. Berkeley: University of California Press, 2008.

Gramsci, Antonio. *Selections from the Prison Notebooks of Antonio Gramsci*. United Kingdom: International Publishers, 1971.

Green, M.E. *Rethinking Gramsci*. United Kingdom: Taylor & Francis, 2011.

Gregg, Elinor D. *The Indians and the Nurse: By Elinor D. Gregg*. United States: University of Oklahoma Press, 1965.

Gregg, James Edgar. *The Comparison of the Races*. Hampton, VA: Hampton Institute Press, 1919.

Gregg, James Edgar. *Race Riots: Preventive Measures*. Hampton, VA: Hampton Institute Press, 1919.

Gregg, James Edgar. *Lynching: A National Menace; The White South's Protest Against Lynching*. Hampton, VA: Hampton Normal and Agricultural Institute, 1919.

Gregg, James Edgar. *Industrial Training for the Negro*. Hampton, VA: Hampton Normal and Agricultural Institute, 1928.

Gregg, Richard:

------ (with Maganlal K. Gandhi). *The Takli Teacher*. Ahmedabad: All India Spinner's Association, 1926.

------ *A Preparation for Science*. Ahmedabad: Gujarat Vidyapith, 1928.

------ *The Economics of Khaddar*. Madras, India: S. Ganesan, 1928.

------ *The Psychology and Strategy of Gandhi's Nonviolent Resistance*. Madras: S. Ganesan. 1929.

------ *Gandhiji's Satyagraha: or, Nonviolent Resistance*. Madras: S. Ganesan, 1930.

------ *Gandhiism Vs. Socialism*. New York: The John Day Company, 1932.

------ *The Power of Non-Violence*. Philadelphia and London: Lippincott, 1934

------ *The Value of Voluntary Simplicity*. Wallingford, PA: Pendle Hill Publications, 1936.

------ *Training for Peace: A Program for Peace Workers*, Introduction by Aldous Huxley. London: Routledge and Sons, 1937.

------ "Gandhiji as a Social Scientist and Social Inventor" in *Mahatma Gandhi: Essays and Reflections on his life and work presented to him on his seventieth birthday*, ed. Radhakrishnan Sarvepalli, London: George Allen and Unwin Ltd. 1939.

------ *Pacifist Program in a Time of War, Threatened War, or Fascism.* Wallingford PA: Pendle Hill Publications, 1939.

------ *The Power of Nonviolence*, (revised) Second Edition, Introduction by Rufus M. Jones. New York: Fellowship Publications, 1944.

------ *The Power of Nonviolence*, Second Edition, new Introduction by Richard Gregg. Ahmedabad: Navajivan Press, 1951.

------ *Which Way Lies Hope? An Examination of Capitalism, Communism, Socialism and Gandhiji's Programme.* Ahmedabad: Navajivan Publishing, 1956.

------ *A Compass for Civilization.* Ahmedabad: Navajivan Publishing House, 1956.

Also published as:

The Self Beyond Yourself. London: J.B. Lippincott, 1956. *Spirit through Body.* Boston: University Press of Cambridge, 1956. *Self-Transcendence.* New York: Gollancz, 1956.

------ *A Philosophy of Indian Economic Development.* Ahmedabad: Navajivan Publishing House, 1958.

------ *The Power of Nonviolence* Third Edition, Introduction by Martin Luther King, Jr. New York: Fellowship Publications, 1959.

------ *The Power of Nonviolence.* New York: Schocken Books, 1966.

------ *What's It All About and What Am I?* New York: Grossman Publishers, 1968.

Gitterman, J. M. and Franz Oppenheimer. *The State: Its History and Development Viewed Sociologically.* United States: Bobbs-Merrill Company, 1914.

Gould, Rebecca Kneale. *At Home in Nature: Modern Homesteading and Spiritual Practice in America.* United States: University of California Press, 2005.

Guha, Ramachandra. *Gandhi Before India*. United Kingdom: Knopf Doubleday Publishing Group, 2014.

Gwyn, Douglas. *Personality and Place: The Life and Times of Pendle Hill*. United States: CreateSpace Independent Publishing Platform, 2014.

Hawken, Paul. *Blessed Unrest*. United Kingdom: Viking, 2007.

Hentoff, Nat. *Peace Agitator: The Story of A. J. Muste*. New York, MacMillan, 1963.

Hogan, Wesley. C. *Many Minds, One Heart: SNCC's Dream for a New America*. United States: University of North Carolina Press, 2013

Holmes, John Haynes. *My Gandhi*. New York: Harper & Brothers, 1953.

Houser, George M. *Erasing the Color Line*. United States: Fellowship Publications, 1945.

Howell, John Harris. *Bloodless Victories: The Rise and Fall of the Open Shop in the Philadelphia Metal Trades, 1890-1940*. New York: Cambridge University Press, 2000.

Humphreys, Margaret. *Malaria: Poverty, Race, and Public Health in the United States*. United States: Johns Hopkins University Press, 2003.

Hunt, Inez and Wanetta Draper. *Lightning in His Hand: The Life Story of Nikola Tesla*. United States: Sage Books, 1964.

Huxley, Aldous. *What Are You Going to Do About It?: The Case for Constructive Peace*. London: Chatto and Windus, 1936.

Huxley, Aldous. *Ends and Means: An Enquiry into the Nature of Ideals and the Methods Employed for Their Realization*. London: Chatto & Windus, 1937.

Huxley, Aldous. "Introduction," Richard Gregg, *Training for Peace: A Program for Peace Workers*. London: Routledge and Sons, 1937.

Huxley, Aldous. *The Perennial Philosophy*. London: Triad Grafton, 1945.

Irschick, Eugene F. *Politics and Social Conflict in South India: the Non-Brahman Movement and Tamil Separatism 1916-1929*. Berkeley: University of California Press, 1969.

Jameson, Elizabeth. *All that Glitters: Class, Conflict, and Community in Cripple Creek*. United States: University of Illinois Press, 1998.

Johl, Janet, *The Fascinating Story of Dolls*. Watkins Glen, New York: Century House, 1970.

Johnson, Richard. *Gandhi's Experiments with Truth: Essential Writings By and About Mahatma Gandhi*. Lanham, MD: Lexington Books, 2006.

Jones, Teddy and Edwina McConnell. *A Stone for Every Journey: Traveling the Life of Elinor Gregg. R.N.* Santa Fe, NM: Sunstone Press, 2005.

King, Martin Luther, Jr. *Stride Toward Freedom: The Montgomery Story.* New York: Harper & Row, 1958.

Kosek, Joseph Kip. *Acts of Conscience: Christian Nonviolence and Modern American Democracy.* New York: Columbia University Press, 2009.

Kulkarni, Sudheendra. *Music of the Spinning Wheel: Mahatma Gandhi's Manifesto for the Internet Age.* New Delhi: Amaryllis, 2012.

Levine, Daniel. *Bayard Rustin and the Civil Rights Movement.* United Kingdom: Rutgers University Press, 2000.

Lewis, David. *M. L. King: A Biography*. United Kingdom: University of Illinois Press, 1978.

Lewis, David. *W. E. B. Du Bois: A Biography, 1868-1963*. United States: Henry Holt and Company, 2009.

Ligt, Barthélemy de. *The Conquest of Violence: An Essay on War and Revolution*, By Bart. de Light; with an Introduction by Aldous Huxley. N.p., 1938.

Lindsey, Donald. *Indians at Hampton Institute*. 1877-1923. Urbana, IL: University of Illinois Press, 1995.

Long, Michael G., ed. *I Must Resist: Bayard Rustin's Life in Letters*, San Francisco: City Lights Books, 2012.

Lloyd, Nick. *The Amritsar Massacre: The Untold Story of One Fateful Day*, United Kingdom: Bloomsbury Publishing, 2011.

Maurini, Alessandro. *Aldous Huxley: The Political Thought of a Man of Letters.* United States: Lexington Books, 2017.

Meier, August and Elliott Rudwick. *Core: A Study in the Civil Rights Movement, 1942-1968.* United States: University of Illinois Press, 1973.

Meyer, Donald. *The Protestant Search for Political Realism, 1919—1941.* United States: Wesleyan University Press, Middletown, 1988.

Miller, Jake C. *Prophets of a Just Society.* Huntington, N.Y.: Nova Science Publishers, 2002.

Mills, Stephanie. *On Gandhi's Path: Bob Swann's Work for Peace and Community Economics.* United States: New Society Publishers, 2010.

Molin, Marian. *Radical Pacifism in Modern America: Egalitarianism and Protest.* Philadelphia: University of Pennsylvania Press, 2006.

Montgomery, David. *The Fall of the House of Labor: The Workplace, the State, and American Labor Activism, 1865-1925.* United Kingdom: Cambridge University Press, 1989.

Morris, Aldon D. *Origins of the Civil Rights Movements.* United Kingdom: Free Press, 1986.

Moses, Greg. *Revolution of Conscience: Martin Luther King, Jr., and the Philosophy of Nonviolence.* New York: Guilford Press, 1997.

Munson, Richard. *Tesla: Inventor of the Modern.* United States: W. W. Norton, 2018.

Murray, Nicholas. *Aldous Huxley: A Biography.* United States: St. Martin's Publishing Group, 2002.

Nearing, Helen and Scott Nearing. *Living the Good Life: How to Live Sanely and Simply in a Troubled World.* New York: Schocken Books, 1970.

Newman, M. *Harold Laski: A Political Biography.* United Kingdom: Palgrave Macmillan, 1993.

Niblett, Bryan. *Dare to Stand Alone: The Story of Charles Bradlaugh.* United Kingdom: Kramedart Press, 2010.

Niebuhr, Reinhold. *Moral Man and Immoral Society: A Study in Ethics and Politics.* N.p.: Papamoa Press, 2017.

Nojeim, Michael. *Gandhi and King: The Power of Nonviolent Resistance.* Westport, CT: Praeger, 2004.

Nugel, Bernfried. *Now More Than Ever: Proceedings of the Aldous Huxley Centenary Symposium. 1994.* New York: Peter Lang, 1996.

O'Connor, Daniel. *A Clear Star: C. F. Andrews and India, 1904-1914*. India: Chronicle Books, 2005.

O'Donnell, Edward T. *Henry George and the Crisis of Inequality: Progress and Poverty in the Gilded Age*. United States: Columbia University Press, 2015.

Olson, Carl. *The Many Colors of Hinduism: A Thematic-Historical Introduction*. New Brunswick: Rutgers University Press, 2007.

Penfield, Wilder, *The Difficult Art of Giving: The Epic of Alan Gregg*. Boston: Little, Brown and Company, 1967.

Perry, Lewis. *Civil Disobedience: An American Tradition*. New Haven: Yale University Press, 2013.

Pflaum, Jacqueline S. *Helper Woman: A Biography of Elinor Delight Gregg*. N.p.: University of San Diego, 1996.

Piehl, Mel. *Breaking Bread: The Catholic Worker and the Origin of Catholic Radicalism in America*. Philadelphia, 1982.

Pierce, Bessie Louise. *History of Chicago, Volume III: The Rise of a Modern City, 1871-1893*. United Kingdom: University of Chicago Press, 2007.

Pletcher, Kenneth. *The History of India*. New York: Britannica Educational Publications, 2011.

Podair, Jerald. *Bayard Rustin: American Dreamer*. United States: Rowman & Littlefield, 2009.

Powers, Roger S. *Protest, Power, and Change: An Encyclopedia of Nonviolent Action from ACT-UP to Women's Suffrage*. New York: Routledge, 2012.

Ramachandran, G. and T.K. Mahadevan, eds. *Gandhi—His Relevance for Our Times.*New Delhi: Gandhi Peace Foundation, 1964.

Rajendra, Prasad and Mahatma Gandhi. *Young India, 1919-1922*. India: B. W. Huebsch, 1923.

Ramesh, J. A, *Chequered Brilliance: The Many Lives of V.K. Krishna Menon*. India: Penguin Random House India, Private Limited, 2019.

Reddy, E. S., ed. *Mahatma Gandhi, Letters to Americans*: United States: Bharatiya Vidya Bhavan, 1998.

Roberts, Nancy L. *Dorothy Day and the Catholic Worker*. United States: State University of New York Press, 1984.

Robinson, Andrew and Krishna Dutta. *Rabindranath Tagore: The Myriad-minded Man*. India: Bloomsbury, 1997.

Rustin, Bayard. *I Must Resist: Bayard Rustin's Life in Letters*. United States: City Lights Books, 2012.

Saltmarsh, John. *Scott Nearing: An Intellectual Biography*. Philadelphia: Temple University Press, 1991.

Saltmarsh, J., Peter Forbes, and William Coperthwaite. *Handmade Life: In Search of Simplicity*. United States: Chelsea Green Publishing, 2007.

Scalmer, Sean. *Gandhi in the West: The Mahatma and the Rise of Radical Protest*. United Kingdom: Cambridge University Press, 2011.

Schneider, William, ed. *Rockefeller Philanthropy and Modern Biomedicine: International Initiatives from World War I to the Cold War*. Bloomington: Indiana University Press, 2002.

Schumacher, E.F. *Small Is Beautiful: A Study of Economics as if People Mattered*. London: Blond & Briggs. 1973.

Seeley, Robert A. *The Handbook of Non-violence*. United States: Westport, Connecticut: Lawrence Hill and Company, 1986.

Seifer, M. *Wizard: The Life and Times of Nikola Tesla*. United States: Citadel Press, 2010.

Sharma, Asha. *An American in Gandhi's India: The Biography of Satyanand Stokes*. Bloomington and Indianapolis: Indiana University Press, 2008.

Sharp, Gene. *Gandhi as a Political Strategist*. Boston: Porter Sargent, 1979.

Sharp, Gene. *The Politics of Nonviolent Action,* Boston: Porter Sargent, 1973.

Sheerman, B. and Isaac Kramnick. *Harold Laski: A Life on the Left,* United Kingdom: Allen Lane, Penguin Press, 1993.

Sheppard, Hugh, R. L. *We Say No! The Plain Man's Guide to Pacifism*. United States: Cascade Books, 2013.

Slade, Madeleine and Vincent Sheean, *The Spirit's Pilgrimage*. United States: Literary Licensing, LLC, 2013.

Slate, Nicolo. *Colored Cosmopolitanism: The Shared Struggle of the United States and India*. Cambridge: Harvard University Press, 2012.

Sprague, Marshall. *Newport in the Rockies: The Life and Good Times of Colorado Springs*. Greece: Swallow Press/Ohio University Press, 1987.

Spinney, Robert G. *City of Big Shoulders: A History of Chicago*. United States: Cornell University Press, 2020.

Starr, W. T. *Romain Rolland. One Against All: A Biography*. Germany: Mouton, 1971.

Stewart, Estelle May. *Handbook of American Trade-unions*. United States: U.S. Government Printing Office, 1926.

Tagore, Rabindranath. *Rabindranath Tagore: An Anthology*. United States: St. Martin's Press, 1999.

Taylor, Frederick Winslow. *The Principles of Scientific Management*. United States: Cosimo, Incorporated, 2010.

Tharoor, Shashi. *Nehru: The Invention of India*. New York: Arcade Pub., 2003.

Thomson, Mark. *Gandhi and His Ashrams*. Mumbai, India: Popolar Prakashan Pvt., 1993.

Tinker, Hugh. *The Ordeal of Love: C. F. Andrews and India*. India: Oxford University Press, 1997.

Tracy, James. *Direct Action: Radical Pacifism from the Union Eight to the Chicago Seven*.Chicago: University of Chicago Press, 1996.

Trivedi, Lisa. *Clothing Gandhi's Nation: Homespun and Modern India*. Bloomington: Indiana University Press, 2007.

Tully, James. ed. *The Power of Nonviolence*, United Kingdom: Cambridge University Press, 2018.

Usher, James M., Charles Brooks, and William Henry Whitmore. *History of the Town of Medford, Middlesex County, Massachusetts: From Its First Settlement in 1630 to 1855*. United States: Rand, Avery, 1886.

Wallace, Elizabeth. *Colorado Springs*. United States: Arcadia, 2003.

Waltham Training School for Nurses, and Florence Nightingale. *The Waltham Training School for Nurses, 1885-1921.* Waltham, MA: Waltham Training School for Nurses, 1921.

Waring, Stephen P. *Taylorism Transformed: Scientific Management Theory Since 1945.* United Kingdom: University of North Carolina Press, 2016.

Weber, Thomas. *Gandhi as Disciple and Mentor.* New York: Cambridge University Press, 2004.

Weber, Thomas. *Gandhi's Peace Army: The Shanti Sena and Unarmed Peacekeeping.* United States: Syracuse University Press, 1996.

Whitfield, Stephen. *Scott Nearing: Apostle of American Radicalism.* New York: Columbia University Press, 1974.

Whybrow, H. and Peter Forbes. *A Man Apart: Bill Coperthwaite's Radical Experiment in Living.* United States: Chelsea Green Publishing, 2015.

Wiener, M. J. *Between Two Worlds: The Political Thought of Graham Wallas.* Oxford: Clarendon Press, 1971.

Wilkinson, Ala., *Dissent or Conform? War, Peace, and the English Churches, 1900-1945.* London: SCM Press, 1996.

Wittner, Lawrence S. *Rebels Against War: The American Peace Movement, 1933—1983,* Philadelphia, 1984.

Wittner, Lawrence S. *The Struggle Against the Bomb, Volume 2.* Connecticut, Stanford University Press, 1993.

Woodcock, George. *Dawn and the Darkest Hour: A Study of Aldous Huxley.* New York: Viking Press, 1971.

Wolters, Raymond. *The New Negro on Campus: Black College Rebellions of the 1920s.* Princeton University Press, 1975.

Zachariah, Benjamin. *Nehru.* United Kingdom: Taylor & Francis, 2004.

Zaki, Hoda. *Civil Rights and Politics at Hampton Institute: The Legacy of Alonzo G. Moron.* Urbana, IL: University of Illinois Press, 2007.

Articles

Ayer, James. "Dr. Donald Gregg, 1881-1939." *Archives of Neurology and Psychiatry*, 42, no. 1 (1939): 134.

Bourgeois, Janelle and John Wooding, "Peace Profile: Richard Gregg." *Peace Review*, 28, no. 2 (2016): 238-245, DOI: 10.1080/10402659.2016.1166794.

Clymer, K. "Samuel Evans Stokes, Mahatma Gandhi, and Indian Nationalism." *Pacific Historical Review*, 59, no. 1 (1990): 51-76.

Danielson, Leilah, C. "In My Extremity I Turned to Gandhi: American Pacifists, Christianity, and Gandhian Non-violence, 1915-1941." *Church History*, 72, no. 2 (2003): 361-388.

Davis, Colin, J. "Bitter Conflict: The 1922 Railroad Shopmen's Strike." *Labor History*, 33, no. 4, (1992): 433-455.

Day, Bill. "Ehrenfried Pfeiffer, the Threefold Community, and the Birth of Biodynamics in America," *Biodynamics*. Fall 2008. https://www.biodynamics.com/threefold-day.

Gandhi, M. "My Best Comrade Gone." *Young India*. 1927-1928, (April 1928): 713.

Goldman, Harry L. "Nikola Tesla's Bold Adventure: Strange Experiments Conducted by an Electronic Wizard at the Turn of the Century." *American West*. 8, no. 2 (1971): 4-9.

Gregg, Richard:

------ "A Monument to an Ancient Love." *The Bellman*, v. 19, (September 11, 1915).

------ "The National War Labour Board." *Harvard Law Review* 33, no.1 (November 1919): 39-63. https://archive.org/details/jstor-1328084

------ "Aspects of Spiritual and Moral Beauty in Charkha and Khaddar." *Modern Review*, (November 1925): 560-566. http://www.southasiaarchive.com/Content/sarf.120016/204563/018.

------ "The Morals of Machinery." *Current Thought*, (February 1926): 172-179.

------ "An American on Spiritual Fasts." *Harijan*, (December 8. 1933).

------ "Will Gandhi Win?" *Nation*, (June 4, 1930): 661-663.

------ "India Confronts Britain." *Nation,* (June 18, 1930): 696-99.

------ "Letter to W. E. B. Du Bois." In The Browsing Reader Section, *Crisis,* (1930): 341.

------ "Experiments in Ahimsa." *Harijan,* (April 2, 1938).

------ "Creative Group Fellowship." *Fellowship,* 4, no. 8 (October 1938): 9-10.

------ "Non-Violence the only way." *Harijan,* 6, no. 46 (December 24, 1938)): 389-91.

------ "The Next Two Years." *Fellowship,* 5, no. 5 (1939): 4-5.

------ "Non-Violence and Khadi." *Harijan,* 22, no. 3 (1940): 308-310.

------ "The Validity of Indian Handicrafts in this Industrial Era." In K. Bharatha Iyer, ed., *Art and Thought: Issued in Honor of Dr. Ananada K. Coomaraswamy on the Occasion of His 70th birthday,* London: Luzac & Company, 1947: 95-100.

------ (ed.) Charuchandra Guha, *Seven Months with Mahatma Gandhi, Being an Inside View of the Indian Non-cooperation Movement 1921-1922.* Ahmedabad: Navajivan Publishing, 1951.

------ "The Structure of a Nonviolent Society." *Fellowship of Reconciliation,* (1953): 9-11.

------ "A Possible Help for the Indian Scavenger." *Gandhi Marg,* 2, no. 1,(1957): 38-42.

------ "A Peasants' Five Year Plan." *Gandhi Marg,* no. 2 (April 1958): 1-6.

------ "Gandhi and the World Crisis." *Gandhi Marg,* 6, no.1 (1962): 1-3.

------ "An Idea Whose Time Has Come." *Peace News,* (April 13, 1963): 14.

------ "The Best Solver of Conflicts," in G. Ramachandran & T.K. Mahadevan, eds., *Gandhi—His Relevance for Our Times,* (New Delhi: Gandhi Peace Foundation, 1967), 127-134.

------ "On Loving Ones Opponents." *Fellowship,* (November 1966): 22-23.

------ "A Possible Aid to Satyagrahis." in Sarvepalli Radhakrishnan, ed., *Mahatma Gandhi 100 Years,* (New Delhi: Gandhi Peace Foundation, 1968), 102-106.

Gross, Minerva and Susan Solomon, "Building Bridges: Alan Gregg and Soviet Russia 1925-1928." *A Review of Science, Learning and Policy* 61, no. 2 (June 2003): 167-176.

Harris, Joseph P. "The Senatorial Rejection of Leland Olds: A Case Study." *The American Political Science Review*, 45, no. 3 (September 1951): 674-692.

Hodder, Jake. "Conferencing the International at the World Pacifist Meeting in India, 1949," *Political Geography*, 49 (April 15, 2015): 40-50. https://babel.hathitrust.org/cgi/pt?id=uc1.$b156699;view=1up;seq=6

King, Martin Luther, Jr. "Address at the Thirty-Sixth Annual Dinner of the War Resisters League." *The Martin Luther King, Jr., Papers Project*, (February 2, 1959).

Kosek, Joseph Kip. "Richard Gregg, Mohandas Gandhi, and the Strategy of Nonviolence." *Journal of American History* 91, no. 4 (2005): 1318-1348.

Leland Olds. "Dictionary of American Biography, Supplement 6: 1956-1960." American Council of Learned Societies (1980).

Meyer, Matt and Judith Mahoney Pasternak. "90 Years of Resisting War: WRL's Journey from 'Wars Will Cease When Men Refuse to Fight' to 'Revolutionary Nonviolence.'" *WIN Magazine*, 30, nos. 2/3 (2013). https://www.warresisters.org/win/win-summerfall-2013/90-years-resisting-war.

Mitchell, Donald. "Nikola Tesla's Investigation of High-Frequency Phenomena and Radio Communication." *Mental Landscape LLC.* (1972). http://mentallandscape.com/Tesla1.htm.

Muste, A. J. "Review of *My India, My America* by Krishnalal Shridarani." *Fellowship*, 7 (1941): 194.

New York Times Book Review, (December 2, 1934): 13. Author unknown.

New York Times: Dr. Ordway Tead, Educator, 82, Dies, November 17, 1973, 38. Author unknown.

Norwood, S. "Bogalusa Burning: The War Against Biracial Unionism in the Deep South, 1919." *The Journal of Southern History*, 63, no. 3 (1997): 591-628.

Patel, G.A. "The Gandhi Ashram." *Poona Agricultural College Magazine*, (1945): 36-40.

Prashad John Vijay, "The Influence of Gandhi on the American Non-Violence Movement." *Little India*, (2002). https://littleindia.com/India/marcho2/ahisma.htm.

Rada, James. "Nation's 1922 Railroad Strike Became Matter of Life and Death." *Cumberland Times-News*, (June 4, 2011). https://www.times-news.com/news/local_news/nation-s-railroad- strike-became-matter-of-life-and-death/article_9ffac5a1-d168-50e1-ab88-e267ee1aee12.html.

Schneider, William. "The Model American Foundation Officer: Alan Gregg and the Rockefeller Foundation Medical Divisions." *A Review of Science, Learning, and Policy* 41, no. 2 (June 2003): 155-169.

Schwartzentruber, Paul. "Which Way Lies Hope? Opening a Dialogue with Richard Gregg. A Retrospective on the Nationhood of India." *Ahisma Nonviolence*, 12, no. 1 (Jan-April 2016): 4-78.

Sharpe, Eric. "The Legacy of C. F. Andrews." *International Bulletin of Mission Research*, 9 (July 3, 1985): 117-121.

Shridharani, Krishnalal. "Has Not Renounced Satyagraha." *Fellowship*, 8, no. 1 (January 1942): 15.

Swomley, John M. Jr. "Richard Gregg," *Fellowship*, 40, no. 4 (April 1974): 23.

Vinaik, M. "The Evolution of Gandhian Economics." *Sarvodaya*, (June 1962): 209-213 www.mkgandhi.org/articles/Satya%20as%20a%20mirror.htm.

Young, Mildred B., "Richard B. Gregg, In Memoriam." *Friends Journal,* (May 15, 1974): 303.

Zimmerman, S. "The Evolution of the Lyman Estate, The Vale." *Historic New England,* 12, no. 2 (Fall 2011): 28.

Pamphlets, Newsletters

The Harvard Graduates' Magazine. (1907). United States: Harvard Graduates' Magazine Association. 1941.

Reports

Gregg, James Bartlett. *Harvard University, The Twentieth Secretary's Report of the Class of 1866.* Cambridge, MA: Harvard University Press, 1922

Gregg, Richard. Class of 1907. Secretary's Fourth Report. Norwood, Mass.: Plimpton Press, 1917.

Gregg, Richard, *Fiftieth Anniversary Report of the Harvard Class of 1907*. Cambridge, MA: Harvard University Press, 1957.

Harvard College, Class of 1897. *Twenty-Fifth Anniversary Report, Class of 1897*. Methuen, MA: Riverside Press, 1922.

Harvard College Class of 1907 Secretary's First Report By Harvard College (1780-). Class of 1907

Unpublished Papers, Speeches, Journals, Memoranda

Alan Gregg Papers. National Library of Medicine, Bethesda, Maryland.

Bourgeois, Janelle, "Gregg Biography," unpublished manuscript, 2014.

Cooney, David Scott, "A Consistent Witness of Conscience. Methodist Nonviolent Activists, 1940-1970," Ph.D. dissertation. Iliff School of Theology and the University of Denver.

Gregg, Richard, "Considerations for W.R.I. and for Pacifists," unpublished manuscript, October 23, 1965. Division of Special Collections and University Archives, University of Oregon Libraries.

Gregg, Richard, *Family Biographies*, unpublished manuscript, 1970.

Gregg, Richard, *Letter to the Editor*, unpublished manuscript, n.d., Division of Special Collections and University Archives, University of Oregon Libraries.

Gregg, Richard, *Notebooks,* Walden Woods Project's Thoreau Institute Library, Special Collections, Richard Bartlett Gregg Papers.

Gregg, Richard. *"My Memories of Gandhi,"* Unpublished manuscript, 1948. Walden Woods Project's Thoreau Institute Library, Special Collections, Richard Bartlett Gregg Papers.

Oral History Research Office, Columbia University, "The Reminiscences of Dr. Alan Gregg," unpublished manuscript, 1958.

Pizzola, Peter M., "The Significance of Unionization at Bethlehem Steel in 1910 and 1918-1919." (1996). Theses and Dissertations. Paper 425, LeHigh University.

Gregg, Alan, "The Reminiscences of Dr. Alan Gregg, E. D. Alan Gregg: Oral History." (1956). Columbia University In the City of New York, 1965.

Videos, Films

Eleanor Delight Gregg video, Archives and Special Collections, Consortium Library, University of Alaska, Anchorage, Biographical Note. Accessed May 22, 2016.

James Fitzpatrick "Fitzpatrick Pictures Presents: Gateway to India," Produced and Narrated by James Fitzpatrick, 1932. http://www.youtube.com/watch?v=ob8n_Aaog58. Accessed Nov. 7, 2013,

Websites

"Putney at a Glance." *Website.* Putney School. Accessed July 6, 2016.

"Ehrenfried Pfeiffer, the Threefold Community, and the Birth of Biodynamic in America," *Biodynamic,* Fall 2008. Adapted version available at: http://www.pfeiffercenter.org/about_us/ehrenfried_pfeiffer.

"Letters to Richard B. Gregg and Nella Cram Cook." Comprehensive Site, Gandhian Institute. http://mkgandhi.org/letters/richardcook/main.htm. Accessed December 17, 2013.

Alan Gregg Biography. http://rockefeller100.org/biography/show/alan-gregg. Accessed April 15, 2015.

Behymer, F.A. "Mineralized Garden Brings Health, Acclaim to Kentucky Soil Doctor." https://www.seleneriverpress.com/historical/mineralized-garden-brings-health-acclaim-to-kentucky-soil-doctor/. Accessed July 19, 2018.

Bemis Company, Celebrating 150 Years, History: http://www.bemis150.com/content/timeline.asp. Accessed September 24, 2017.

Borràs Ros, James. "Colorado Springs Laboratory." *Tesla Research*, 2013. http://teslaresearch.jimdo.com/colorado-springs-lab-1899-1900/. Accessed June 14, 2016.

Braybrooke, Marcus. "C.F. Andrews: Gandhi's Friend." *The InterFaith Observer*, January 26, 2016. http://www.theinterfaithobserver.org/journal-articles/2016/1/27/c-f-andrews-gandhis-friend.html. Accessed May 2, 2016.

Charles Freer Andrews. N.P.: Publications Division Ministry of Information & Broadcasting, 2017. http://www.bu.edu/missiology/missionary-biography/a-c/andrews-charles-freer-1871-1940/. Accessed January 27, 2017.

Dorin, Joshua. "Channing Sanitarium." *Wellesley History*, 30, (2014). https://wellesleyhistory.wordpress.com/2014/04/30/channing-sanitarium/

First Congregational Church, Colorado Springs, *"Our Heritage."* https://www.fcucc.org/who-we-are/history. Accessed July 12, 2017.

Funding Universe, Bemis Company, Inc. History, http://www.fundinguniverse.com/company-histories/bemis-company-inc-history/_ Accessed July 22, 2018.

Jim Glenn and Margaret Cheney. "Tesla: Life and Legacy—Colorado Springs." *Public Broadcasting Service*. http://www.pbs.org/tesla/ll/ll_colspr.html. Accessed December 12, 2000.

John Sinkin. "Peace Pledge Union," Spartacus Educational. http://www.spartacus.schoolnet.co.uk/2WWpeaceunion.htm.

"Letters to Richard B. Gregg and Nella Cram Cook." Comprehensive Site, Gandhian Institute. http://mkgandhi.org/letters/richardcook/main.htm. Accessed December 17, 2013.

Massachusetts Historical Society, Robert G. Valentine Family Papers, Biographical Sketches, 1870-1930. http://www.masshist.org/collection-guides/view/fa0383. Accessed July 19, 2016.

Medford Historical Society Papers, Volume 20, *Medford Branch Railroad,* http://www.perseus.tufts.edu/hopper/text?doc=Perseus%3Atext%3A2005.05.0020%3Achapter%3D15. Accessed June 22, 2019.

Pelt, Rhonda Van. "The Bemis Family: A Deep Rooted Legacy, *Colorado College Alumni Bulletin*. https://sites.coloradocollege.edu/bulletin/2009/11/the-bemis-family-a-deep-rooted-legacy/. Accessed, March 16, 2017.

Sabarmati Ashram, Ahmedabad, Gujarat. https://gandhiashramsabarmati.org/en/

Interviews

Thompson, Kate. Interview by Wooding, John. In person. South Tamworth, NH, July 23, 2015.

Day, Ann. Interview by Wooding, John. In person. Concord, MA. March 16, 2015.

Wirth, Nancy. Interview by Wooding, John. In person. Santa Fe, NM, August 11-12, 2015.

Gregg, Robert. Interview by Wooding, John. In person., Medfield, MA, April 14, 2015.

Photo Credits

PAGE 147: Courtesy of Nancy Wirth

PAGE 148: (*top*) Courtesy of Kate Thompson, (*bottom photos*) Courtesy of Nancy Wirth

PAGE 149: Courtesy of Kate Thompson

PAGE 150: (*top*) Courtesy of Kate Thompson, (*bottom*) Courtesy of the Thoreau Institute

PAGE 151: (*top*) Courtesy of the Thoreau Institute, (*bottom photos*) Courtesy of Nancy Wirth

PAGE 152: Courtesy of Nancy Wirth

PAGE 153: Courtesy of Nancy Wirth

PAGE 154: (*MLK, Jr. photos*) National Archives, public domain, (*Gandhi photo*) Public domain

About the Author

John Wooding is professor emeritus in the Department of Political Science at the University of Massachusetts, Lowell, where he served as Provost for four years. On campus, he advanced interdisciplinary study and research on regional economic and social development. With Kristin G. Esterberg, he co-authored *Divided Conversations: Identities, Leadership, and Change in Public Universities* (Vanderbilt University Press, 2012), and with Charles Levenstein co-authored *The Point of Production: Work Environment in Advanced Industrial Societies* (The Guilford Press, 1999). A graduate of the London School of Economics and Brandeis University, John was born in Northampton, England, and now lives in New England.